ADVANCE PRAISE FOR THE BOOK

'*How the Light Gets In* is a wonderfully readable account of the first years of the life of an NGO. This is a story all of us should read. The Antara Foundation's bid to tackle infant mortality and malnourishment in India is a gripping tale about idealism and good intentions meeting patriarchy and the status quo, and holding their own. Moving, farcical and heartbreaking in turn, Ashok Alexander's book will endure as a practitioner's account of doing good at scale, in a diverse and challenging country'—Mukul Kesavan, historian and author

'There is an important public health message embedded in Ashok Alexander's narrative—that [when] adequately supported, government's women frontline workers, together with village mothers, can find solutions to seemingly recalcitrant health problems. A story told with honesty, compassion and a sense of humour, this is a riveting book with a profound message'—Dr Soumya Swaminathan, paediatrician and clinical scientist

'Once again Ashok Alexander transports the reader into another India— this time deep within rural Rajasthan and Madhya Pradesh. A journey at once disturbing, exhilarating and hilarious'—Karan Thapar, journalist and news presenter

PRAISE FOR *A STRANGER TRUTH*

chly detailed ethnography of sex work in India, filled with tales that ometimes desperately sad and sometimes heart-warming, always ng, thoroughly readable. It is a portrait of contemporary India like r: in its pages some of the richest and most powerful people in the ross paths with some of the poorest and most desperate . . . An y gifted writer'—Amitav Ghosh, www.amitavghosh.com/blog

cle both moving and memorable that captures the daunting f combating HIV, while letting us see the human faces embodied tics'—Abraham Verghese

nder was a tireless champion for marginalized groups during g the Gates Foundation's work in India and tells a powerful hat deserves to be widely read'—Bill Gates

HOW
THE
LIGHT
GETS
IN

'A r
are s
engag
no oth
world
unusual

'A chron
obstacles o
in dry statis

'Ashok Alexa
his time leadi
story of hope t

Celeb
Penguir

HOW THE LIGHT GETS IN

A JOURNEY THROUGH THE STRUGGLES AND HOPES OF INDIA'S POOREST MOTHERS

ASHOK ALEXANDER

VINTAGE

An imprint of Penguin Random House

VINTAGE

USA | Canada | UK | Ireland | Australia
New Zealand | India | South Africa | China | Singapore

Vintage is part of the Penguin Random House group of companies
whose addresses can be found at global.penguinrandomhouse.com

Published by Penguin Random House India Pvt. Ltd
4th Floor, Capital Tower 1, MG Road,
Gurugram 122 002, Haryana, India

First published in Vintage by Penguin Random House India 2023

10 9 8 7 6 5 4 3 2 1

ISBN 9780670094219

Typeset in Adobe Garamond Pro by Manipal Technologies Limited, Manipal
Printed at Replika Press Pvt. Ltd, India

www.penguin.co.in

To our children, and theirs

Ring the bells that still can ring
Forget your perfect offering
There is a crack, a crack, in everything
That's how the light gets in

—Leonard Cohen, 'Anthem'

Contents

Introduction

This is the story of a journey, still ongoing, to some of the most far-flung habitations of Rajasthan and Madhya Pradesh. I set out on this voyage with some haphazard notions about village life. I soon discovered a very different reality. And as I looked more closely, I experienced that feeling you sometimes get, that you have been this way before.

Ten years have passed since that first village visit and sometimes, I reflect with wonder and gratitude, that over the past twenty years, I have worked with two communities of extraordinary women. First, with sex workers in towns large and small. Today, with young mothers and women health workers, in remote villages.[1] Their worlds are different, yet essentially the same.

Sex workers and village mothers—what could they possibly have in common? The crux is that their needs and their sufferings are similar. Both sets of women are utterly marginalized in family and social contexts. Both have little control over their own lives since others make vital decisions for them. Both live in tough environments—physically and emotionally—working without a break.

xii   Introduction

Often, the driving force in a sex worker's life is her burning desire to protect her child from a harsh environment and secure her future. The situation of a young mother in a distant hamlet—faceless, voiceless, powerless to save her dying baby—is as tragic. She also wants security and a future for her child. In suffering and in need, that sex worker and this mother are virtual sisters. And if their problems are the same, their solutions will be similar.

I learnt from sex workers that poor women who live with the problem best understand the solution. Adequately supported, they will help design and drive programmes with scale and quality. That is the core principle behind The Antara Foundation, or TAF as we call her. Today, with TAF I see that change beginning with young mothers in rural India, working together, focused on their health needs. I see that attitude in the commitment and sacrifice of the women community health workers.

~

How the Light Gets In is a sequel to my previous book, *A Stranger Truth,* but it stands on its own. It is not intended to be a continuation of the previous story, as the contexts are different. Hence, they need not be read in sequence.

The book has three parts. These are:

Part 1: 'Conception' is about the origins of the idea of TAF and the travails of getting it off the ground. It is set mainly in the hushed corridors of power in corporate India and the government.

Part 2: 'Child' describes our start in Rajasthan. It chronicles how we developed a model and a set of tools to assure the wellness of village mothers and children. This part is about working with the government and surviving sudden crises. It is set largely in the villages of Jhalawar district.

Part 3: 'Adult' is about expansion and finding new horizons. It is located mainly in the beautiful tribal areas of Madhya Pradesh. It is told in the here and now, depicting our work as it happens in the field.

The book is also a portrayal of India's public health system at the grassroots—a critique as well as an appreciation. To a large extent, the officers of the Indian Administrative Service (IAS) keep that system going. In these pages, I sometimes express my anguish at the unfeeling attitude of some individual officers. But having worked with the government over the past twenty years and across multiple states, I have met many more bureaucrats who are exemplary.

~

I have disguised the names of many people and places. Otherwise, this is an entirely accurate account drawn from my diary notes. The description of the places, incidents and data is accurate— except on one occasion, where I have switched the sequence of events to maintain the flow of the narrative.

Readers tend to overlook the 'back pages' of a book, but here, they provide essential context. I urge them at this point to go to the appendices, read them and come back quickly.

The opinions I have expressed in this narrative are mine alone.

Part 1
Conception

1

Faded Blossoms

In a tiny hamlet deep within a tribal district called Barwani in Madhya Pradesh, a young woman squats on a mud floor, her dying baby asleep, hidden within the folds of a threadbare sari. The baby can be saved, but the mother is helpless, for she is surrounded by indifference. There is her alcoholic father-in-law, who will not let her leave home. There is her husband, who will not take a stand because he is paralysed by fear of his father. There is her mother-in-law, who says that in any case, every girl child is a curse.

The young woman plays many roles. She earns for the family as a daily wage field worker. She fetches water and she hauls firewood over long distances. She cooks, she cleans, she cares for the cow, the goats and the hens. She is hemmed in on all sides, but even so, she tries to be a good mother. Through the course of a long afternoon, the young woman is silent and her dying baby sleeps. I stand rooted, witness to an act of violence that is beyond my comprehension.

~

For a few months in late 2013, I travel across India, visiting grassroots NGO programmes. It is important for me to learn from others before embarking on the new venture that I have been dreaming about for almost a decade.

I take the ninety-minute flight from Delhi to Indore, a charming city of clean boulevards and green parks. I leave at six the next morning for the town of Barwani, administrative headquarters of the district with the same name.

We motor down AH47, a modern four-lane expressway that runs south-west from Indore to Barwani. Laxman the driver gratuitously tells me the story of his life. When the narrative reaches his teenage years, I manage to convey, without giving offence, that I want him to stop.

We pass through little towns with curious names like 'Galonda' and 'Berna Khurdi'. In several places I see new homes, mostly garish, standing alongside thatched mud huts. I wonder what this means. It is the first of several puzzles I will encounter on this trip.

We stop a few times along the way. Laxman insists we halt at a roadside Ganesh temple. He prostrates himself before the deity, offers flowers and some money, and reverentially accepts *prasad* from the *pujari*. I wait outside, and when he emerges from the temple, Laxman offers me some of the prasad, which I accept, one palm folded under the other. We pause again for a cup of the impossibly sweet, milky tea that seems to be the norm in these parts. Laxman sips it with deep slurping sounds to express his satisfaction. With these stops, we cover the 156 kilometres to Barwani in three hours.

Barwani is a bustling town, brisk with small shops, vendors, uniformed school children and a busy bus terminus. I meet my host, David Fisher,[1] at the town's central roundabout. David is another puzzle—a Jewish-American in tribal India, tanned so deeply that he could pass for a native, he works with an international NGO called 'True Medicine'[2] that has been in Barwani for many years. David has offered to be my guide today, taking me to one of the more remote tribal villages of Barwani. Before setting out, we decide to lunch at a dhaba just outside the town.

This part of Madhya Pradesh is famous for its black Kadaknath chicken,[*] which is carefully reared in government poultry farms. The chicken is almost pure protein and therefore much in demand with athletes. David says they are considered sacred and I ask him why, if that is the case, people eat the chickens? Seeing no contradiction, he says it is because they are delicious and points to a poster on the dhaba's grimy wall, of groups of ominously black chickens.

I decide to be adventurous and order a plateful. It costs Rs 1200 almost four times the price of regular chicken. The meat is tough and when I see that the bones are also black, I feel queasy and abandon the bird.

~

We are heading to the area where True Medicine focuses their work. It is a small set of villages in a block called Pati two hours away, by a road that gets narrower and rougher as we proceed. The landscape is a surreal mix of moonscape—rolling, bald hills with large crater-like depressions—and green hills dense with trees. On both sides, lush green fields of maize stretch as far as to the horizon. The road undulates gently. When it is slightly higher than the fields, we see the top of the maize and the fields look olive green. When the road descends, we see the maize shoots

---

[*] Indian breed of chicken originated from Dhar and Jhabua in Madhya Pradesh, mostly bred by tribal and rural people.

from the side and the fields give the illusion of being dark green. I am lulled by the slow rhythm of the changing shades of green just outside my window. Once, in the middle of the fields, we see a lone farmer wearing a bright orange kurta and white turban, knee-deep in the maize.

In the fields there are scattered trees native to central India that I have never seen before. Laxman points to the renowned mahua trees with their stubby trunks and thick foliage. The berries of the mahua, fermented and distilled, yield the heady liquor abundantly consumed by men and women alike in many tribal areas of central India.

I am surprised to see the occasional solitary palm tree. In some places, there are groves of ripening cotton closer to the road. The buds are a rusty red and fluffy creamy white cotton erupts from the top of each bud. The red and white cotton closer to us and the green fields of maize beyond, take my breath away.

We have been on the pukka road for almost an hour and now Laxman veers a sharp right onto a dirt road. It is October and there has been unseasonal rain in the previous week, and for most of the way we are driving through mud and slush.

The dirt road peters out and before us, about 200 metres away, we see the hamlet—twenty thatched mud houses, scattered across two scruffy hills. I put on my backpack and we trudge towards the nearest houses. Luckily, the rain has not reached this area yet and the ground is dry, but the walk is tiring since we are climbing a gradient.

We pass a rivulet where an old man is examining two *matkas** of fermenting mahua fruit that he has buried neck-deep in the mud. He checks with a seasoned eye if they are ready for distilling. We pause to watch and to catch our breath. The old man smiles

---

* Pots.

sheepishly, but also with a tinge of pride. Before we reach the hamlet, there is a shrine to the cobra, which consists of a small rock with an image of the snake painted on it. There is a pole about 8 feet high just behind the shrine and fluttering along its length, many small, triangular flags in varied colours, signifying that this is a holy spot. I am deathly scared of snakes and perhaps to keep on their right side, I reach down and touch the stone, then my forehead, and leave a few coins.

The air suddenly turns chilly as the sun disappears behind the clouds. I shiver and wish I had picked up my jacket when I left the car.

∼

We are a team of three—David, me and Jyoti,[3] the young Accredited Social Health Activist (ASHA) worker* who joins us when we arrive in the hamlet. She is a government health worker from the local area—her job is to go from house to house and check on the well-being of family members. She is supposed to educate them about good health and see that people who are in need meet the nurse who visits the village every month. In more urgent cases, it is her job to make sure they are taken to health facilities well beyond the village. Jyoti tells us she is visiting this hamlet after several weeks. She is pleasant and well-meaning, but it is obvious that she knows very few families here.

We pass a few homes that are almost empty—at mid-day, most people are out working in the fields. The houses speak of extreme poverty. They are small, with thatched roofs held up by baked mud and thin pieces of wood tied closely together. Loose

---

* The ASHA's role is described in more detail later, in Chapter 8.

patches of dark blue plastic sheet have been used to reinforce the roof and sides where the structure has given way. We arrive at a house where an elderly woman sits on the porch sorting through a small heap of grain. She looks up, showing no surprise at the sight of three strangers including, without any doubt, the first white person she has ever seen.

Jyoti says in Bhil, the local tribal dialect, 'Mother, can we ask you a few questions? These people have come from far to learn about your village.' That introduction seems sufficient, for the woman picks up a well-worn straw hand fan and sets the grain aside. We sit cross-legged on the ground at a respectful distance. Jyoti proves to be an able interpreter as David and I ask questions.

Phulwa was born in Dahod, an hour away across the border in Gujarat. She came to Barwani when she was sixteen and got married to Mangilal, a small farmer. They soon started having children, four girls, one after the other, in less than ten years. With the premium on a son, each successive birth was a bitter disappointment. 'Girls are a curse,' Phulwa asserts. Mangilal has only two *bighas** of land, insufficient for a family of six, and they barely get by on what he earns as a daily wage labourer, tilling other people's fields. They eat one meal a day—vegetable, onions and two rotis.

I venture, 'How did you manage eating just one meal and working the whole day?' I immediately regret asking the question in such an insensitive manner— the words had just come out of my mouth without much thought. Phulwa seems to take no offence but looks at me with a bemused smile and says, 'That is how everyone lives in these parts, one meal.'

---

* A measure of land area varying from state to state. In Madhya Pradesh 1 bigha is roughly equal to 0.12 acre.

Five years after their last girl, Phulwa had a boy child, Sohan. Mangilal went on a pilgrimage to Shirdi to offer thanks, taking the bus from Barwani. Things started looking up after that as Mangilal managed to marry off the girls and the burden on the family diminished. Sohan started working in the fields with his father from the age of ten, becoming a full-wage worker by the time he was fourteen. 'He is a good boy,' Phulwa says lovingly.

~

Almost on cue, a spindly young man of about twenty rounds the corner of the hut. He has clearly been eavesdropping and has sensed that this is the right moment to make his entrance and impress the visitors. He dips his head towards us in respectful greeting, holding one hand to his heart.

Phulwa is angry. 'O useless one!' she shouts at him, 'why are you loitering here when you should be out working in the field?' Sohan is taken aback by this frontal assault before strangers and responds peevishly, 'There is no work today; the child is sick and father is missing since morning.'

Sohan's life is uneventful and he describes it in a few sentences. He is a timid young man, raised in Mangilal's shadow, mortally afraid of his father's anger. He never went to school and has no specific skills. He is a daily-wage labourer, sometimes migrating for work across the border to Gujarat and Rajasthan.

Sohan married Champa two years ago. She is from a nearby hamlet and was barely sixteen when she had their baby, Priya. 'What is wrong with the baby?' Jyoti asks. 'You said she was sick. Can we see her and meet your wife Champa?'

'She is with the cow,' says Sohan sullenly. 'She will come after that.'

Phulwa barks, 'Bring her now,' and Sohan leaves. 'She will come now,' he says, returning in a few minutes.

~

But time drags on. It is almost half an hour and Phulwa has resumed her sifting of chaff and tiny pebbles from the wheat. We walk around the tiny property. It is the typical mud hut with thatched roof, two small rooms, one for each couple, a corner with a *chulha** and a storage area for grain. The whole hut is about 300 square feet in size. There is no bed or chair and the mud floor is dry and clean. Outside the hut is an open courtyard and beyond that a shed where the cow and a few goats are housed.

In the distance, we see Champa approaching, face covered, and I find myself thinking how tiny she is. She is holding some papers that Jyoti gently takes from her. They are a record of some brush Champa had at some point with India's health system, amounting to no more than a crumpled prescription for cough mixture and paracetamol tablets.

Champa seats herself cross-legged on the ground, adjusting her *ghunghat*† in such a way that the end of her sari falls well below her chin, and her face is entirely covered. She sits perfectly still after that, staring straight ahead of her, completely silent. Phulwa, who had paused briefly, resumes her sorting of the grain. Sohan leans against the wall of the hut, chewing a twig, preoccupied.

---

* Traditional U-shaped Indian floor-level cooking stove made from local clay. Wood and animal dung patties are used as fuel.
† A veil worn by most rural women, sometimes covering their face as well.

Jyoti asks Champa, 'Is the child sick?' There is no answer. 'Are you well?' No answer. 'Where did you come from?' No answer. The minutes go by in this way—Jyoti asking questions and getting no response.

It is then that I notice a movement deep within the folds of Champa's sari and a tiny face peering out at the world, and then directly at me. There is an emotion I can feel mounting slowly inside me, difficult to define, and I turn away from the child's gaze, discomfited.

Jyoti says, 'Look, we have come far to meet you, to find out what is wrong with your baby, to help you. Speak to us . . .' Champa does not move. After a few minutes, Jyoti tries again, whispering to Champa, 'Look, you are a woman. I am also a woman. If you don't speak to another woman, who will you speak to?' Again, silence. Jyoti takes the baby gently from within the folds of Champa's sari.

The child is tiny, with a thin frame and a large belly. She begins to whimper, but the sound she produces is barely audible. I cannot look at the baby and I cannot look away. David examines the baby together with Jyoti. They give her back to Champa, who puts Priya back inside her *pallu** and rocks her gently.

David is agitated. He says, 'The baby is what we call severely and acutely malnourished (SAM). She will die within a month if left like this.' He is red-faced with anger and turns on Jyoti, 'What were you doing? You are responsible for these people's health. I have been watching, you don't even know the families in these households.'

Jyoti is crying. She says, 'Sir, I never even knew there was a child in this house, I came here a few weeks ago and no one even

---

* The loose end of a sari, worn over the shoulder or head.

told me . . . look,' she says, pulling out a thick register in which she keeps a list.

It is becoming difficult to keep hold of the feeling mounting within me, but I manage to control myself. I turn to Phulwa and Sohan, 'What did you do to this child, that she is like this . . . did you even feed her?' Phulwa looks up at me and shakes her head, conveying that I don't understand what is going on. 'We give her whatever we get; what more can we give?' she says. Sohan looks down. Champa still has not moved. Priya has fallen asleep in the warmth of her mother's sari.

David says, 'It is not hopeless. If the baby is taken to the malnutrition treatment centre in the district hospital, she will be saved. But she will have to stay two weeks there with her mother. She will bloom like a flower in just a few weeks if she goes there.' He turns to Sohan.

'I cannot give her leave to go,' Champa's husband says, eyes downcast. 'Father has to say.'

'Then go and get him . . . quickly!' David shouts.

~

Another long wait. As time passes, I look more closely at Champa, wrapped in a threadbare sari, and I wonder about the person hidden behind it.

On the border of the sari, I see a bit of red. It is the faint, barely discernible, remnants of finely embroidered flowers. And then, farther down the sari's edging, another, and then a third. When was it, I wonder, that the grey sari was white, and bordered with blossoms? When did she wear it, on which festive occasions? Or was it her mother's sari, gifted on her wedding day, when she left her home and family? What happened that those roses disappeared so soon? Who is the girl who hides behind the sari once gay with crimson flowers?

After an hour, we see Sohan in the distance, holding his father by his forearm. Mangilal is tottering. I ask David, 'May I talk to him first?' David nods and steps away, after cautioning me not to shout at Mangilal, because it will not help.

When they come up to us, Champa pulls her ghunghat lower. Sohan takes me aside and whispers, 'Finally I found him, *behosh** in the field. Try and speak to him; it won't be easy, sir.' Mangilal is six feet tall, lanky, bearded, with a huge, bushy rust and grey moustache that slumps over his lips. His turban, which is a fetching orange with a red and green weave, is coming loose, and he tries to set it right for the visitors. He has bushy eyebrows and an inoffensive mole on his right cheek. He smiles affably.

'You cannot come to our humble house without partaking of something,' he mumbles in a friendly way. Sohan brings out a bottle of mahua. David knows the right etiquette of accepting mahua, and links his open palms together, fingers intertwined, and extends his arms, much as if he were accepting prasad. Mangilal pours the beverage into David's palms, which my friend downs in one gulp. Mangilal turns to me and I demur, saying that alcohol makes me sick. Mangilal frowns but takes a long swig directly from the bottle and turns to us.

I get straight to the point, 'The baby is dying.'

'We will give her cow's milk and ghee-*shakkar*† from now on,' he promises grandly.

'That will kill her quickly,' I say. 'She is *ati kuposhit*, severely malnourished.'

'How can milk and ghee kill anyone?' he says.

'Her body is now too weak to take any food. She must get a special nutrient, it is like medicine. She will get it in the

---

* Unconscious.
† Sugar.

government hospital, but she must go there immediately. She has to stay for two weeks, with Champa.' My voice is rising, and I realize that I am pleading.

Mangilal senses that he has the upper hand and says assertively, 'It is impossible. It will never happen.'

That feeling inside me bursts its banks and floods through me. It is a mix of many things—anger at the old fool, frustration that I cannot get through to him, helplessness that I cannot use physical force to take the baby away, anger at the baby's grandmother, still nonchalantly sorting grit from grain, anger at the father, who dare not speak, shame for Champa, who is listening to all this with a dying baby, her first, in her arms, and a deep sorrow and pain for the little tyke, at the life being snuffed out even before it has started. What was the baby trying to tell me when she looked at me, I wonder, and my eyes sting. I feel ashamed of myself, my damned fact-finding mission, eating novelty chicken, marvelling at the landscape, at my education and my cockiness, at who I am. I feel angry with myself. David has walked far away. I take a deep breath to steady my shaking breath and say, '*Main haath jodta hoon aapke saamne*'—'I'm asking you with folded hands—let this child live.'

Mangilal declares, his brow darkening, 'No daughter from my house will go to the city and stay there on her own. It is not proper. It is not safe. And what of us? She must work in the field, she must cook for all of us, she must care for the cow and the goats; who will do this?' Then, striking a philosophical note, he smiles broadly and says, 'It is all in God's hands. God is great. If he takes one child, he will always give another.'

Before I can say anything, David is at my side. 'Let me take it from here,' he says quietly.

~

The sun is low and it is getting cold. We have been in the courtyard of this tiny house for over three hours. It is time for us to leave and we climb into our Jeep. My mind is in turmoil. I am determined to do something by tomorrow, but what?

A scene comes to my mind from many years ago, when I had walked away from a dying boy, far way in an HIV home in Imphal. Then, an old-timer in public health had seen my distress and given me an axiom: 'If you must serve the public, you must understand you cannot save one life at a time. At times, you have no option but to step away.'

That night, the image of Priya ensconced in Champa's soft pallu haunts me, and I cannot sleep. David calls in the morning. 'Priya and Champa are in the malnutrition treatment centre in Barwani. My NGO took her there with her family's permission. The baby will be blooming in three weeks.' My heart sings and I gasp in disbelief. David chuckles, anticipating my question. 'Two bottles of the cheapest "English" brandy. Four hundred rupees saved Priya's life.'

I think about the thousands of remote villages that dot the tribal belt that runs east to west along the southern border of Madhya Pradesh. Priya and Champa are no different from the hundreds of thousands of babies and mothers who live there. Surely something must be done for all of them. Now I understand what Champa was trying to tell me with her silence, and Priya when she looked straight into my eyes. *It takes only one thing—you must not step away.*

That tragic encounter with Champa and baby Priya reaffirmed the need for a solution: an idea born almost a decade ago.

2

Antara Foundation

In early 2003, I accepted an invitation from the Bill and Melinda Gates Foundation (BMGF) to create Avahan, a programme to stem the growth of HIV in India. It was only afterwards that I realized that there was no precedent for HIV prevention on such a massive scale. The problems we were seeing in the field seemed impossible to resolve.[1]

And yet, three years later, Avahan had become the world's largest HIV prevention initiative, operating in more than 600 towns in the six states most affected by HIV. We were delivering HIV prevention services to almost 1,50,000 sex workers, including 4 million condoms a month, a figure that was to triple in the next two years.[2] Avahan created a model for HIV prevention—one that emphasized scale—based on partnership with communities.

I virtually lived in the field in those early years of Avahan, visiting distant towns, meeting sex workers, talking to government officials and doing advocacy. I was consumed, with no time for anything else. But even as we expanded—indeed because we were scaling up so quickly, an idea germinated in my mind.

~

There are people who know a lot of things about public health. They thrive on complex questions and complicated answers. I just about knew the difference between HIV and AIDS when I accepted the Gates Foundation's offer. My team, drawn mainly from the private sector, knew about as much as I did. Knowing little, perforce asking basic questions, we developed a way of working that was built around simple precepts.

We were bubbling over with the kind of questions a child might ask. Are some sex workers at greater risk of getting infected? Why are they in greater danger than other sex workers? Why do they put themselves in danger in the first place? How many such women are there? Where can we meet them? How can we win their trust? These questions were simple, but the answers were not obvious. Experts would give us a few useful pointers. Others would say, 'Now, that's a great question . . .' which is often another way of saying 'I have no idea.'

And then we learnt a simple truth: the answers will come from the people who live with the problem every day. It was the sex workers who helped us appreciate why some people practised unsafe sex. They explained the complex reasons and subtle considerations that were involved. They spelt out seemingly simple solutions, helped us design programmes and drove implementation. Ultimately, they are the reason why Avahan scaled up so rapidly.

In the process, I was receiving a life education. For years, I had provided smart advice to clients who paid a lot of money for answers to their problems. Now I had to ask utterly powerless people to show me the way. I was learning the real meaning and the importance of humility.

In Avahan's early days, even as we were ramping up, a thought came to me. We were asking plain questions, looking for data to substantiate the answers, working with and through the community.

Surely this could be a universal approach, applicable in other areas of public health. Could we contribute to wellness in maternal and child health?* Could we prevent death and illness among India's poorest mothers and their children? That idea had power, and it became a dream. One day, after the work that remained with Avahan was done, I had to find out if it would work.

I first named the imagined venture Kranti.† As the years went by and we learnt new lessons from Avahan, the contours of the idea became sharper in my mind. I was fully engaged with Avahan, which was more than a full-time campaign. Still, I was talking to myself, writing notes to myself, sketching out what The Antara Foundation (TAF) would look like. The idea was clear from the start, never inchoate. Three years went by like this. Then, cautiously, I started talking about TAF to a few people outside my team. I wanted to know if the experts thought the concept was sound.

These included David Wilson, who led the work on HIV at the World Bank; Sujatha Rao, who headed the National AIDS Control Programme; Peter Piot, the global head of UNAIDS and Rajat Gupta, who was chairman of Avahan's advisory panel. Everyone agreed that TAF would meet a real need. They all agreed it was a great idea and some promised to help. But for the most part, I never sensed among them the excitement that I had hoped to find.‡

Except from a most unlikely direction.

~

---

* The public health term for deaths of mothers during pregnancy, during or after labour, and deaths and sickness, including malnutrition, of newborns (till six weeks), infants (one year) and children (two years).
† I used 'Kranti', in my early notes. I switched to 'Antara' when I felt we needed a kinder name.
‡ The great exception was my late friend and mentor John Stewart, whose common-sense guidance was invaluable.

I was keen to find how one of India's sharpest businesspersons would react to the notion of TAF. I had never met Mukesh Ambani, but wrote directly to him saying I had an idea to end the tragedy of needless maternal and child deaths and severe malnutrition in India's most distant villages, and would he be able or willing to meet me? To my surprise, I got a quick reply from Mukesh himself, saying he had heard of my work and would be delighted to meet. I noted that the message had been sent at 3.30 a.m.

'How much time does Mr Ambani have for me?' I asked his assistant as I was led into the meeting room. 'I am sorry, but only five minutes, sir. I was trying to reach you, to see if we can reschedule, because some urgent matter has come up. Perhaps we might stretch it to ten, but no more.' He was very polite.

'It's no problem. I understand,' I said. I wasn't intimidated because over the years, I had learnt that if you have very little time and must explain something in a few sentences, it often comes out clearer. I decided I would explain TAF in no more than two minutes and see what Mukesh had to say.

It was a comfortable room with a few plush chairs, a sofa, and a coffee table in the centre. One chair had a writing pad and a pen on a side table, and I seated myself on the chair on the opposite side, across from the coffee table. Mukesh came in a few minutes later wearing a grey business suit, extending a warm welcome, apologizing that he had virtually no time. 'Tell me your idea,' he said immediately.

I got straight to the point. 'Mukesh, India's health record when it comes to mothers and children is among the very worst in the world. Over 2 million children under five die each year.[3] More than a third of the ones who survive are malnourished. The solutions are as simple as managing anaemia and the pregnant woman's weight, safe delivery, newborn care and exclusive breastfeeding. The problem is, how do you deliver these solutions at scale? That requires working with and through communities. It means using data to identify risk, using business thinking to deliver solutions at scale. The idea is to set up a new organization to do this.'

Mukesh made a few notes and started asking a series of questions. What were health conditions like in villages? Why didn't governments provide the requisite services? And so on—elementary questions. I saw that he had no familiarity with public health at the grassroots but did not mind revealing that he just wanted answers.

His assistant looked in and said, 'Sir, you have a call.' Mukesh waved him away and called for tea. I remember saying at one stage, 'You are building the world's largest ever supply chain for fresh produce that will link millions of farmers to markets. There must be some way to have health services piggyback on this chain.' We explored this and other ideas. I did most of the talking, while he took occasional notes.

I was suddenly aware that our meeting had taken the best part of an hour. Another learning of all these years is that it is always better that you end the meeting first, rather than someone else doing it a few minutes later. I said, 'I want to respect your time, Mukesh, you have been most generous already.' It was only then that he spoke at some length, and I was taken aback by what he said.

'This is my idea,' he started. 'I have always wanted to deliver good health to the poorest in villages across India. This is what I want to do with my life. All this (indicating the room and the world beyond with a sweep of his hand) is only for a few years. Then I will focus on giving back to society. That will be my gift to my late father. I have been planning it.' Then he said, 'Your idea and my idea are the same. Let's do it together.' He smiled warmly.

I was startled at the speed with which he had sized up the situation and made me an offer to do something big with him. I was not sure what exactly that was, though I imagined it was some 'change the world' conception that was consistent with our discussion. I told him I was honoured and would have to reflect on what he had said. He escorted me out with a firm handshake.

That evening, I was at a dinner party at the late Parmeshwar Godrej's lovely oceanside home in Walkeshwar Road. Avahan had made a grant to Parmesh's Heroes Project, and she and the Hollywood star Richard Gere were doing some splendid work involving celebrities in HIV prevention.

I am not comfortable at social events of this kind and latched on to Rajat Gupta, whom I had spotted in the crowd. Mukesh came in and spotted us. Passing by, he said, 'Rajat, has Ashok told you? He and I are going to work together.' Rajat raised his eyebrows, and I hastened to tell him what had happened.

When I got back to Delhi, I sent Mukesh a message thanking him for hearing out my idea and for his words of encouragement. I did not mention working together, because I had no intention of doing that.

~

By 2008, Avahan was operating on a pan-India scale. The earliest results from our work were encouraging. The challenge in the next five years would be to sustain that scale and momentum and to transfer our programme to the government. Avahan would cease to exist after that.

I foresaw three problems, looking forward from that mid-point of Avahan to its end point, which was to be five years later. I worried that there might well be problems in the transfer of Avahan to the government because we would, in essence, be transferring an alien way of working in which the sex workers led the way. This would certainly be a first in the government system, if at all they accepted it.[4] Also, I had been advocating internally for the foundation to take up large-scale delivery programmes in other areas of need, besides HIV, and we were already exploring that possibility. I surmised that this would eventually come up against the foundation's principle of not having large staff numbers involved in implementation. Avahan had been an exception and I felt that way of working would never materialize again. Avahan was an asset—a high-performance team with unique skills and a storehouse of knowledge—that asset, I felt, should not be lost.

I wrote a note to the foundation's leadership, proposing an eventual spin-off from Avahan into a new entity called TAF. I was not being self-serving. I honestly felt that, from all perspectives, this was the best way for the foundation to proceed. I was hoping that I would be encouraged to flesh this idea out. Nothing like that happened.

A senior person at the foundation told me, 'You've been talking a lot about Antara lately. We can all see that it will serve a useful purpose. But the foundation is not prepared to take any radical step right now.' He then added, 'In fact there is some concern that you might leave Avahan.'

Of course, I had no intention to leave Avahan till its work was done in the next five years! But I got the message. I did not mention it again, almost till the day that I left the foundation in the summer of 2012.

~

In the next few years, the foundation's portfolio of work in India expanded and I was instrumental in setting up programmes in maternal and child health in Bihar and Uttar Pradesh, two states with a terrible public health record. I did a lot of travel in the field to scout out possibilities along with two senior colleagues who were based in Seattle—Girin Beeharry and Gary Darmstadt

In Bihar, we travelled across a swathe of eight districts, from Khagaria in the centre of the state up till West Champaran in the very north-west corner, bordering Nepal. In Champaran, we went to the peepul tree where Mahatma Gandhi had launched his first satyagraha movement in India in 1917 on behalf of the local indigo farmers. Under that large, shady tree, I closed my eyes for a few moments to ask for his blessings.

Bihar, and even the capital Patna, was not a safe place in those days. The hotel we always stayed at in Patna had a fierce-looking guard named Bhanu, with an improbable belly and a moustache to match. Carrying a huge double-barrelled gun, and with an ammunition belt across his chest, he would walk up and down the lobby, slowly scratching and massaging his crotch, ensuring that all was well. It was unsafe to step out after dusk, and the hotel would be locked down at night. At dawn we would leave for our field trips, passing through the lobby, being careful not to disturb Bhanu, sound asleep on a sofa, in case he woke up and started shooting.

The interiors of Bihar in those days seemed like a wasteland. Scenes disturbing, macabre and poignant unfolded in unbroken sequence. We passed through a small town where the shops sold tea and pakoras during the day and country pistols at night; public health centres with long queues outside, others with no water and some locked down completely; labour rooms where dogs roamed freely and babies were being delivered in full view and villages where the desperately poor Moosahars[*] lived, their

---

[*] One of the poorest of scheduled caste communities, concentrated in Bihar, Jharkhand and Madhya Pradesh.

lanes paved with fresh human faeces, a community that reportedly lived off rats. At the same time, I felt hope when we spoke to overworked nurses, committed doctors and the people who were running the many small programmes we came across that were doing outstanding work in tiny, remote areas.

These visits were at times tough to stomach, but they also gave us a sense of what worked and what needed to be done, and a feeling of vast horizons, filled with the possibilities of making a big difference. These trips into the hinterlands of Bihar and Uttar Pradesh drove home to me the sheer scale of the maternal and child health problem, the helplessness of communities and the failure of the government system. It was sobering, and strengthened my resolve to somehow contribute to a lasting solution.

~

By July 2012, we had finished the handover of Avahan to the government. The Gates Foundation now had a full-fledged India country office, and together with foundation colleagues from Seattle, we had launched programmes, still nascent, in UP and Bihar. I felt good to have had the opportunity to play a leading role in that transformation. In the new set-up, the entire suite of the foundation's products and services would be available to India.

But the new way of working at the India office was different from Avahan's. Decisions about implementation on the ground and grants to be made emerged after weeks of phone conferences with colleagues in Seattle. These happened almost every day through long conference calls with the many groups who owned parts of the foundation's health budget. It was as different as could be from the free-wheeling, rough-and-tumble, edge-of-the-seat excitement of Avahan.

It was time to step aside and move on. I would be free at last to devote my time to building TAF, the dream I had nurtured for the past seven years.

But there was one very important conversation I needed to have before I stepped out.

3

Nation-Building, Almost

Bill Gates visited India in June 2012, my last month with the foundation. As head of the foundation's India office, I was required in most of his meetings, ranging from the Prime Minister's Office to field locations, sometimes in a single day. I prepared hard for these visits.

This time, I was a little anxious. I wanted to tell Bill about my plans for TAF. It would be my last chance before I left. On one of his trips some years ago, I happened to ride with him alone from the Delhi airport to the Oberoi Hotel, where he was staying. On the spur of the moment, I asked if I could tell him about my idea for a new institution. I laid it all out and he listened closely, as usual. At the end, he said it was a promising idea and '. . . for the first time, I understand what you have been trying to say.' I left it at that.

On his India visits, each minute of Bill's time is booked months in advance. Before this visit, I asked Larry Cohen, Bill's chief of staff, if he could squeeze in ten minutes for me with Bill. Larry assured me that he would make that happen sometime during the visit. That meeting did not materialize during Bill's first day in Delhi or the following one, which was spent in the field in Bihar. Now we were in Bangalore and it was the last day of his visit. By lunchtime, I was getting anxious and reminded Larry. He said, 'Let's do it this way—there is a gap of twenty minutes this afternoon between two meetings at the hotel itself. I'll tell Bill that you want a few minutes.'

Bill got delayed and it looked like the meeting would not happen. I waited anxiously in the lobby and joined him and Larry as soon as they came out of the elevator. I asked Bill if I could take five minutes, and he and I ducked into an empty room nearby after security had quickly checked it out. It turned out to be a large hall where waiters were cleaning up after a lunch, placing chairs on top of tables. I suddenly realized that I had no paper in hand—damn, I thought, how could I have been so forgetful? I called a waiter to get a napkin.

I outlined the idea of TAF for Bill on the napkin using my ballpoint. I drew a framework that integrated supply and demand, building a conducive environment. In the end, Bill said there was a real need and that if we could do it, we would be creating a new institution. I was pleasantly surprised when he asked how much money it would take. I had not worked that out, but said I would guess about $20 million over five years. Bill nodded and said, 'I think that sounds about right, but you know you won't get this money from the foundation, right?' I had in fact assumed I would get the money from the foundation, and I was sorely disappointed and asked why. Bill said, 'Well, you said you wanted to create an Indian institution. If the foundation is sponsoring it, it would be anything but that.'

The logic was undeniable. He must have sensed my dismay and added, 'What we can do is that if you get Indian funders, we will put in the same amount as they do.' I clarified, 'That means if I get five people putting in two each, you will put in ten?' Bill said, 'No, it means we would also put in two.'

I was more than satisfied.

~

'What would it be like if I do this?' is the natural question people ask about any new opportunity. I have done this too at different points in my career—weighing pros against cons, seeking advice, taking stock of what I thought was a well-considered decision.

Sometimes, though, even without getting into the pros and cons, I found myself quickly asking the reverse question: 'What would it be like if I *don't* do this? Would I spend the rest of my life wondering what it would have been like?' That was how it was with Avahan and with TAF too—nothing could have stopped me. Stepping out of the foundation in the summer of 2012, I felt a tiny frisson of excitement and anticipation when I thought about what lay ahead.

I was brimming with confidence. I assumed that donors would be eager to work with me. Had I not led Avahan? If a donor wanted impact, Avahan had averted a few hundred thousand deaths[1] and created a new global model. If a donor had heart, they would see what a difference we had made working with communities of the most marginalized women. I believed the idea of TAF would be irresistible—it may sound outrageous, but that is what I thought. It did not occur to me that for the past ten years, I had gotten used to giving away money, not asking for it. I never thought of that as a gap in my education.

I assumed that my organization would be given a warm welcome by state governments. In Avahan, I had worked with government authorities for almost a decade. I had seen my father's long career in the government up close. Surely, I knew the ways of the government? I forgot that in Avahan, we had never been dependent on governments, and that special dependency is the crux. Little did I know then that the ways of the government are not that simple to fathom.

I can see now that there was considerable hubris, and a good dose of naiveté, in my thinking. But even if some wise person had cautioned me then, I would have listened, and yet done exactly what I did—move ahead as quickly as I could. My conviction was rock solid, and that was all that mattered.

~

My wife Anjali and I designed a logo for TAF with an earthy, brick red theme. The logo incorporates a bindi with a border that depicts six people holding hands, symbolizing the importance of community. I was pleased with the result and began printing visiting cards, A4 stationery and matching envelopes, all with the logo.

Anjali laughed: 'Choki, are you crazy? You don't have a registered organization or a team or any work, and you've printed cards that you are handing out to complete strangers as though there's no tomorrow.'

I said with a sniff, 'It's just a question of time. Besides, it's good to create a buzz.'

Anjali laughed again: 'No one is excited right now but you.' She seemed to have forgotten that for me, TAF had been real for close on ten years.

At that time, I was invited to spend a semester as a Senior Fellow at the Harvard School of Public Health.* The university had given me the freedom to design and teach a course any way I wanted as long as there was an emphasis on leadership. I was

---

* Now known as the Harvard T.H. Chan School of Public Health.

keener on analysing what I'd learnt from Avahan, and created a course of sixteen classes called 'Public Health Delivery at Scale using a Business Model: Lessons in Leadership'.

We spent a wonderful three months that spring at Harvard. The school had provided us a lovely flat in Cambridge, and we walked about the town every Sunday. We would spread the *New York Times'* voluminous weekend edition out on a table upstairs at the large Starbucks in Harvard Square, taking all the time in the world to go through it. It was soothing to be among students working away for hours on their laptops, lost in their intense worlds.

Planning my course, I had the chance to step back and think about what exactly we had done with Avahan to achieve massive scale so rapidly. In effect, I was trying to refine the thinking about my new vision that I had sketched on a napkin six months earlier for Bill. I was compelled to push my thinking by an extremely bright set of students.

I must have generated some excitement because several students wanted to apply to TAF immediately. I had to explain that we were still a few months away from opening, but asked them to stay in touch. A student from another school, who had heard of my course, came up to me and breathlessly told me her name was Antara. I took a selfie with her for good luck.

In Boston, I also met an Indian–American entrepreneur and philanthropist. He and his wife espoused scale and sustainability in their social giving. They were major supporters of a celebrated pan-India programme that fed almost 2 million children every day. They graciously invited Anjali and me to their suburban home for a lovely vegetarian meal.

After dinner, I posed a question: 'More than a third of India's children are malnourished by age two. It is amazing that the programme you support is feeding millions of children of school-going age. The tragedy is that the physical health and cognitive development of those kids have already been permanently compromised by early malnutrition. Would it not make sense for this programme to backward integrate, partner with the government and other agencies that work at scale on early childhood care and development?' I perceived a stiffening as our host said quietly, 'We need to stay focused.'

I got the sense that a forthright way of speaking, which I had used at McKinsey and in Avahan, may not work with donors. This was my first inkling that there was an invisible line, and I was now on the other side.

~

Returning home, I was keen to start work on TAF. I envisaged two types of donors. There would be 'sponsors' and 'programme funders'. Sponsors would invest in building a strong institution, while programme funders would support implementation. I assumed that finding both types of givers would be straightforward. I naively assumed that my track record and reputation would convince everyone.

I went to Seattle that summer and asked Bill if I could get a starter consultancy contract from the foundation. His staff suggested that if TAF did an independent assessment of the foundation's Bihar programme,[2] that would be of value. The foundation sanctioned a small contract for us to do this project for two years. This was more like consulting work rather than the 'programme delivery at scale' that I had envisaged for TAF. On the other hand, it was nice to have some early funding with which I could start building a team and an office. More than the seed funding, it was Bill's personal encouragement and support that gave me a boost. I flew back to Delhi even keener.

I travelled extensively through the second half of 2013, visiting all kinds of grassroots NGO programmes. There were some outstanding ones with clear game plans and strong organizational backing. It quickly became evident, however, that such programmes were in a minority. Many funders gave much less money than they claimed.[3] What was visible—care and treatment, building hospitals, digital technology—took precedence over what was hidden, mainly prevention services. Programmes were often based on the predilections of the founder. Scale and sustainability were not feasible in many cases.

Now it was time to get down to fundraising. I made a list of about eighty Indian philanthropists I would approach. I knew many through my McKinsey connections, Avahan links and personal networks. I was sure I would find a few donors from such a long list. I started contacting them one by one. Most people said TAF sounded like an excellent idea and that they would be happy to meet me. However, they underestimated the speed with which I would show up at their offices, and I completed over thirty conversations between August and November.

In the south, I met one of India's best-known philanthropists. His foundation supported an eclectic mix of social ventures. I thought that TAF would fit perfectly under this broad umbrella. This gentleman knew me from McKinsey and through Avahan. He listened carefully, then told me of all that he and his family were doing by way of charity. He said, politely, that they were fully committed. 'I have no doubt that you will make a huge success of this—what you are setting out to do is nothing short of nation-building.' As I left his office, I was not sure whether to feel flattered or disappointed.

I reached out to one of India's biggest financial investors. He was an avid supporter of a small NGO that my college classmates had set up, working on educating adolescent girls in rural areas. I sent the investor a note that laid out TAF's core proposition—public health delivery at scale. He wrote back saying he would very much like to support it. However, his funds were fully committed for the next two years. After that, the world would see what he called a 'tsunami of giving' as he started giving back all the wealth he had accumulated to society. We should reconnect after two years, he said.

I called upon the aged patriarch of a family, a medical doctor who had established one of India's well-known pharma companies. He had also been my late father's friend. He listened for a few minutes, then said my idea was very exciting. However, he said he no longer made decisions on philanthropy. I should talk to his two daughters, who decided on their family's social giving—those were short conversations.

Over the next few months, I found no takers. I was receiving an education in the many polite ways to say 'no'. I was not disheartened or worried. The experience taught me that the TAF proposition was not one that would appeal to every giver. It was difficult for many to relate to a problem that seemed as remote as infant mortality and severe malnutrition. I would need to come up with more effective ways to communicate that distant reality.

In late 2013, I met a generous, India-born philanthropist based in the United States. He had amassed a large fortune in innovative information technology services. He now wanted to give back some of that wealth by setting up his own foundation in India. His mission was to provide quality health services for the poor. He had not yet developed specific plans and was focused on creating a team first.

The philanthropist is soft-spoken and a good listener. I told him all about TAF and asked if he would consider funding us, either investing in the corpus or by sponsoring programmes. I suggested there might be synergies between his foundation and TAF as both organizations got going.

He said TAF was a visionary idea. I was imagining the 'no thanks' lurking just around the corner, but he surprised me by saying, 'I have another idea. Why don't you head my foundation? You could do everything you want to do in TAF and more—you would be fully funded. I will not interfere in any way. I will focus instead on bringing in other overseas donors.' He mentioned a figure in the region of $30 million.

I had taken a liking to the philanthropist, with his soft-spoken manner and his altruism. I said I was deeply honoured, but that I would have to decline. This was not to be the last time I turned down massive funding at a time when TAF had no money. I wanted complete freedom to build and shape TAF exactly the way I wanted. I didn't believe any donor would stay hands-off.

~

Normal activities resumed—more donor discussions, more 'no thank you'. Then—hallelujah!—TAF found its first investor: Arjun Malhotra, a co-founder of HCL* and an entrepreneur who divided his time between California and New Delhi.

Arjun is a giant of a man, heavily built, well over 6 feet tall. He was unpretentious and easy to talk to. I told him about Avahan and asked if he would consider becoming a sponsor, supporting TAF over a five-year period. Without much pause, he said, 'OK, I'm on.' He was not very interested in seeing my newly drawn up business plan.

The conversation lasted less than ten minutes. Later, he explained that his mother had been a doctor working in public health and he had grown up hearing stories about the health

---

* Hindustan Computers Limited (now known as HCL), a barsati start-up in 1975, is one of India's blue chip technology companies today, with a presence in fifty-two countries and a revenue of $11 billion.

challenges faced by India's poorest mothers and children. He said, 'Besides, you had a track record from Avahan. The idea was big and you had an operating model. It was easy to support it.' The conversation brought home to me that a person will most readily support a cause that they can relate to personally.

A few weeks later, Arjun called, saying he had signed up Shiv Nadar as a sponsor. He said, 'It was no big deal, just over a scotch at his place.' Shiv is the co-founder, with Arjun, of HCL. He is one of India's biggest philanthropists, mainly supporting the cause of education.

When it rains, it pours. In the next few weeks, another prominent business leader, Cyrus Poonawalla, signed on as a sponsor. He too had taken only minutes to decide. Not one of these three givers had spent much time trying to understand what exactly TAF would do.

Now that we had funds, I needed help setting up the organization and approached Reenu Uppal, who had led administration when I was with BMGF. Reenu readily agreed to join the new venture. In January, we found a small, shoebox-shaped office in a business centre in Saket, and it was a great feeling to have a brass plate with 'The Antara Foundation' and its logo on the door.

Our chartered accountants had assured us that the Foreign Contribution (Regulation) Act (FCRA)* permission to receive foreign funds would come through within six months. We were in July now, nine months since we had applied, and nothing had progressed. There were murmurs that the new NDA government was getting tough on FCRA approvals. I had been so certain we

---

* The FCRA, whose scope is to regulate the acceptance and utilization of foreign contribution by Indian entities, especially NGOs. Any organization carrying on social welfare activities desirous of receiving foreign funds requires FCRA registration.

would get the permission within six months that I had already recruited several people. They seemed relaxed and were kind enough to say they had joined mainly to work with me—their attitude was that if I wasn't worried, they were not either. That got me seriously worried. I kept everyone busy with preparatory work, which they took up with gusto.

Most people would say it is a mistake to recruit a team before you have work. I have done it a few times. I wanted to have a team in place to hit the ground running as soon as the FCRA permission came through. If you start recruiting only after you have the funds, it is a waste. You will likely spend three months after that recruiting, and perhaps settle on a person who is not ideal because you are under pressure to get to work. I have run faster than the money whenever I felt sure the money would catch up with me.

The thought sometimes crossed my mind—what if the FCRA permission got held up indefinitely? I would not be able to take up the only project that we had, the Gates Foundation's grant for Bihar, that could not start till we got the FCRA permission. I would have seven people without any work to do. Then I would tell myself not to be so negative. It would be a matter of only weeks before the approval came in and we could get to work on the Gates grant, I would assure myself. I had the safety net of some funds already in the bank from the first instalments received from Indian donors—Arjun, Shiv and Cyrus. It was a fact, however, that at this point, TAF had only corpus funds in hand, nothing for a programme.

That is why I set so much hope on the discussions I had begun with Ratan Tata (RNT).

4

Shoebox Solace

On the last day of 2012, RNT retired as chairman of the Tata Group of companies and immediately assumed chairmanship of the Tata Trusts. More than a century ago, Jamshedji Tata had decreed that the wealth the Tatas accumulated from business must go back to society.[1] The Trusts were set up to fulfil the founder's astonishing moral vison. They do this by serving as custodians of the group's collective profits, disbursing it to deserving social causes. The Tata Trusts are one of the world's oldest, richest, and most respected philanthropies.

The question being asked by mid-2012 was whether RNT would give new impetus and direction to the Trusts after he took charge. In an interview[2] at that time, he said, 'My most visible goal is to do something in nutrition to [sic] children in India, and pregnant mothers, because that would change the mental and physical health of our population in years to come . . .' That certainly drew my interest.

I set out to learn how the Trusts gave away their money. I wanted to know if anything substantial went to maternal and child health. The Trusts' website listed ten areas for their philanthropy—natural resources, education, health, livestock, civil society, media, arts and crafts, relief, and rehabilitation, innovations, and institutions. I could not see any common theme or areas of focus. The Trusts' board met once each quarter to review individual project proposals, even some as small as for a few lakh rupees. Across India, there were more than 500 projects funded by the Trusts.

Most of the grants to the health sector were 'bricks and mortar' funding that went towards creating and sustaining physical institutions, such as hospitals and research centres. It looked like the Trusts had little experience with programmes that delivered health services directly to communities. I surmised that RNT might be considering how best to proceed.

I decided that the best way to find out was to talk to him directly. I had met him when he served on the advisory board of Avahan for a year, almost ten years previously. He had attended only two board meetings and I had barely interacted with him on those occasions. I waited till the last week of December 2012, just before he retired, and wrote a short letter, reintroducing myself. I described the problems of India's maternal and child health and my aspirations for The Antara Foundation. He was one of the first persons I approached for funding for my start-up.

To my surprise, I heard back immediately from the new chairman of the Tata Trusts. He wrote: 'Thank you for your letter. I would like to understand your vision better and see how we might support you.' He added that he would be travelling abroad for several months, and that we should plan to meet when he returned in the summer. It was a promising start.

~

That meeting happened seven months later, in July 2013. It was the monsoon season in Mumbai, a time when downtown traffic is at its most treacherous. I did not want to risk being late and left my hotel so early that I reached the Tata Trusts office in the Fort area a half hour before my appointment. I spotted a shoeshine boy squatting below a shady tree across the street and walked over to kill some time.

The shoeshine boy tapped the side of his shoebox with the edge of his brush to grab my attention as he saw me approaching. On the ground in front of him was the typical coarse plywood box that shoeshine boys sling across their shoulders. It had a raised block where the customer could place his foot, and space for brushes, small bottles of polish and laces that were for sale. The bristle on the brushes was almost all gone, except for a few small clumps, mostly at the edges. I pretended not to notice and asked for his best 'cream polish'. He warned that it would cost Rs 40, twice the standard without-cream polish rate. I said I was fine with that if he did a super job. After wiping the dust off my shoes with a damp cloth, he carefully used the tip of his forefinger to take out a tiny dab, first from the bottle with black polish, and then from the one with the white cream. He commenced to brush vigorously, ensuring that only the bristle, and not the wood, touched my shoe.

The shoeshine boy's name was Manoj, and he told me his story as he worked. He was sixteen, and from a small village in Ahmednagar district, 250 kilometres away. He had come to Mumbai a few months ago looking for a job, having left his parents and two younger sisters behind on their tiny plot of land. After doing odd jobs for a few months—washing dishes, carrying loads—he had settled for shining shoes. This part of the Fort area is always busy, and on a good day he did at least fifteen pairs of shoes. He could do more, he said— the problem was that some customers walked away when they saw his bald brushes. Manoj was a cheerful soul, and said he had no complaints. It was a steady job, and the money he earned was adequate for his needs. After spending on food, shelter and polish, he was able to send Rs 4000 home every month.

I wondered how Manoj had so completely worn out his brushes in just a few months. I guessed that he must have bought the entire set, shoe box and all, from some other shoeshine boy who had risen in life or fallen on hard times. I asked how much a new box, four bottles of polish and cream and four new brushes would cost. He squinted up at the sky and said that he could get all that for a thousand rupees.

The shoeshine job was over within five minutes and my shoes were like a mirror. I reached into my wallet and offered a hundred rupee note, saying the extra was for the special shine. I told him it was one of the best I ever had. Manoj shook his head and, reaching into his pocket, counted out three grubby Rs 20 notes. He said, 'Yeh mehnat ki kamai hai [This is honest money from the sweat of my brow]', and thank you, he did not need to be paid extra. Gently, I told Manoj that he needed to be more *chalu* (street-smart) if he was to survive on the streets of Mumbai, but he shook his head. I felt a little ashamed.

I took the change and told him I wanted him to get a full polish set, box and all, at my expense, '*aap bura na mane to* [if you don't take offence]'. I said I might come back to this spot often. Next time, I would check that he had bought a complete set, and I would claim a free shine from him every time I came by, '*hamesha ke liye* [for always]'. He thought for a moment and said, '*yeh sahi hai* [it's a deal]', taking the two Rs 500 notes and touching them to his forehead.

I left Manoj and proceeded in a good mood to meet RNT.[3]

~

Crossing the road, I stepped into the hush of the Tata Trusts building and took the elevator up to the reception on the fourth floor. Along the walls were several life-size portraits, oil paintings in the old masters' style. These were men of noble purpose who had nurtured the house of Tatas for 150 years, from Jamshedji up till J.R.D. Tata. The portraits evoked a sense of awe.

I sat down on the sofa and took a deep breath. In the next hour, I would know if there was any likelihood of TAF being supported by the Tata Trusts. Many had said 'no' to me in the past nine months, but somehow, I was optimistic.

I was soon ushered into a small conference room. RNT's assistant asked if they should set up a projector. I declined, having decided to use no slides or paper. I simply wanted to understand RNT as a person, and for him to see me as an equal *and* someone who could present him with a solution. I did not want to come across as a seeker of charity. I wanted to engender a feeling of mutual respect.

RNT arrived exactly on time, wearing a grey suit, white shirt and an immaculate tie. Mr Tata is a handsome man, distinctly hunched by age, with a thick shock of greying hair and a deep, mellow voice. He inspired awe, just like the men in the paintings.

Without wasting any time, I thanked him and explained that India's maternal and child health record was one of the worst in the world. I spent some time clarifying the term 'maternal and child health' as well as the terminology that went with it, such as neonatal mortality and infant mortality.[4] I touched upon the thousand days concept* and the difference between prevention

---

* A baby's first 1000 days of life, from conception to age two. This is the period when the brain, body and immune system grow and develop rapidly, and adoption of good health practices and nutrition during this period has lifelong impact.

and treatment. I explained scale and what got in the way of scaling up. RNT looked shocked when I mentioned that almost a third of India's children are malnourished—either wasted or stunted* or both. We covered a lot of ground in an hour. He asked many questions and I answered them deftly.

At one stage, a white-gloved attendant came in with tea and biscuits. RNT stopped mid-conversation and waited till the greying old retainer had served us. He smiled and thanked the man when he had finished.

I talked about why I had set up The Antara Foundation. I explained our model and why it was unique. I described how we were setting out to create a new institution. At this, RNT said, 'We don't do institution-building any more. We want to fund programmes.' He asked what level of funding we were looking for, and I told him. He said, 'We don't do that level of funding. We aren't the Gates Foundation.'

He went on to say, 'Look, I think yours is potentially a good idea that we would want to support. But I do not want this to be like my Avahan experience. Those board meetings were a very valuable education for me, for example, when you brought sex workers in to address us. But I didn't contribute anything.[5] I need you to define a clear and compelling role for me personally in this project before I get involved.' I said that I understood his position. I would go away, think and come back to him with a more considered answer.

On the flight back to Delhi, I wrote up my impressions. I liked RNT's direct style. It was evident that he genuinely wanted to make a big difference to maternal and child health. He was keen to learn. Overall, I was satisfied that I had created

---

* Different forms of malnourishment—a child is stunted if he/she has a low height-for-age and wasted if he/she has low weight-for-height.

interest and earned RNT's respect— he had said he wanted to
meet again.

~

'Tata' is one of the most respected brands in India. The Tata
Group's website says that they stand for 'Integrity, Responsibility
and Excellence'. RNT is seen as the embodiment of these values.
He enjoys a unique national status and carries a special aura. He
is a reticent person who makes few public statements and avoids
controversy. I had set out on the improbable task of winning this
legend's personal support for my unknown foundation, starting
from scratch.

That was only half the challenge. It is not enough to have a
donor—you need a programme for that donor to fund. TAF's
mission was to have impact at the state level, and that meant that
some state should welcome us in to have that impact. It would
have to be one of a handful of states in the north that had the
worst records in maternal and child health. It could not be Bihar
or Uttar Pradesh, states that the Gates Foundation had fully
covered. It had to be one with a political leadership committed
to the cause of mother and child. A few people suggested that I
should approach Vasundhara Raje, the chief minister of Rajasthan
at that time.

It all had to be timed perfectly. If RNT said yes, and the CM
was not ready, I would lose credibility. On the other hand, if
she welcomed TAF into Rajasthan and I had no funder, I would
look foolish. I had to persuade RNT and Vasundhara Raje, two
prominent, almost inaccessible personalities, that they should
jointly put their trust in TAF at the same time.

I thought it prudent not to tell people that I was trying
to arrange such an outrageous trapeze act, all the while with

a team waiting in the wings, ready to perform, but for the moment with nothing much to do. Those people might have burst out laughing.

~

The last time I'd met Vasundhara Raje was eight years before, when I headed the Gates Foundation in India. I had asked for an appointment with the chief minister. I did this occasionally with prominent political leaders to keep them briefed about the status of HIV in India. Her office had readily agreed, and we landed in Jaipur on a hot summer evening. I was wearing a suit for the meeting and I could feel the sweat roll down my back.

We were heading straight to the home office of the chief minister. It is not every day we meet a head of a state, so my colleague and I focused on running through our script for the meeting.

Soon, we were ushered into the CM's office. And there was Vasundhara Raje in a crisp blue sari, warmly welcoming us in. On either side of her were people wearing ingratiating looks. A few others had laminated ID cards on lanyards around their necks, the card tucked into their front shirt pockets. They looked self-assured, suggesting that they were senior bureaucrats of the Indian Administrative Service.

After some small talk, the chief minister said she would welcome the Gates Foundation's involvement in Rajasthan. I told Vasundhara Raje that would be an honour, but it was too early for the foundation to plan work outside of the Avahan HIV programme. I said I would keep her closely informed as and when we ventured into other areas of public health and look for opportunities to serve the people of Rajasthan in the future. She said she understood and invited us to the next room, where a high tea had been laid out. She was charm personified.

~

I continued my dogged pursuit of RNT. It was not easy because of his travel. The pattern he was following after retirement was of long trips abroad, some lasting as long as four months, followed by short visits to India. With such long gaps between our conversations, it was challenging to maintain a rhythm. I had to be sharp and clear every time we met, because I might not get another opportunity for a long time.

In December 2013, I secured two meetings with RNT. In the first of these, he had said that I should articulate a 'clear and compelling role' that he could play in the programme. I appreciated why RNT needed to be convinced—he likely received several requests for his personal support every day, and he would be turning down many worthy causes.

I recapped our discussion. I had laid out a vision of a programme unique in its sweep and ambition—to greatly reduce the number, currently in the tens of thousands, of children dying and falling into severe malnutrition each year in a major state. That would require a substantive three-way partnership.

There had to be an implementing organization and a leader with a proven track record in leading a programme at such a scale. Casting modesty to the winds, I said that was me. Fortunately, RNT nodded.

It needed a chief minister committed to the cause of woman and child. This would help assure everyone that innovations we developed at the district level would be rolled out state-wide. RNT nodded again.

The third partner had to be RNT himself. His support would ensure that the state government stayed committed. It would give the programme a special panache and help in advocacy.

RNT seemed to be satisfied, convinced that everyone would have a clear and compelling role. The conversation turned to nutrition, the topic that had most interested him in our first meeting. Again, he asserted that what was most needed was a new product to treat malnutrition. I gently responded that while treating malnutrition was important, preventing malnutrition was even more crucial. I had not yet succeeded in communicating that effectively to RNT. It was evident that if I was to get through, I had to run our next conversation differently.

~

The next time I brought Dr Sanjay Dang[6] with me. Sanjay is globally recognized for having developed a protocol for the care of infants in village conditions. I knew him reasonably well and I thought that as a grassroots practitioner, he would be well placed to explain how important prevention was in village conditions, including in the context of nutrition.

It would be a supporting role, but I thought he might do it in the spirit of helping move forward a public cause and, in the process, get introduced at close quarters to RNT. He readily agreed.

At a crucial point, I brought Sanjay into the conversation, thinking that he would back me up. Instead, he took the conversation immediately to his work in rural areas, how they urgently needed to build a hospital and were desperately short of funds. To my dismay, from then on, the conversation went in that direction, with Dr Dang producing his own set of slides. RNT was captivated. I realized that a hospital was easier to understand

and more appealing to a donor than the abstract notions I was suggesting, such as prevention and scale. As the precious minutes ticked by, I tried to cut in, but without success. It was as though I had introduced a friend to my date, and they were dancing the salsa together. I had been quite naive in inviting the head of another NGO to a meeting with RNT and expecting that he would not hijack the meeting.

Sanjay thanked me with a grin after the meeting.

My next meeting with RNT was two months later, in February 2014. I was determined to take yet another run at the notions of prevention, scale and mother and child health. I arrived for the meeting with just eight raw photographs I had taken on my field visits. I wanted to bring the village to him through these images. As I got up to leave, he shook my hand warmly and said, 'Thank you. That was a very productive meeting.'

~

Even as my discussions with RNT progressed, I was trying to engage with Vasundhara Raje.[7] She had lost the state election in 2008 and had made a comeback in 2013. At the start of her second term, I wanted to understand if there were any priorities that she had announced for the social sector.

I knew some of the senior bureaucrats who worked closely with the chief minister. These included Chief Secretary Rajiv Mehrishi, whom I had known since my college days. The chief minister had a lot of regard for Rajiv and took his counsel on many matters. He told me that Raje was keen to do something for mothers and children in her new term. She wanted that to be part of her legacy. He said it could be just the right time for me to explain what The Antara Foundation wanted to do for Rajasthan.

I estimated that the CM would have had a few thousand visitors since our last encounter seven years ago, when the person I had brought with me had made her feel insulted. I was, in fact, hoping that she would not remember me. In early March, I wrote her a letter asking for an appointment.

Vasundhara Raje comes from one of the wealthiest of the erstwhile royal families of the Indian state of Rajasthan. From our very first meeting, my impression was of someone exceptionally intelligent. She radiated charisma, but you also left with the feeling that you did not want to get on her wrong side. I asked someone who had worked closely with her what she was like. 'It has its ups and downs,' he said. 'You must understand that it is a triple whammy. First, she is a politician, second, of royal blood, and third, a woman.' He laughed at his attempted witticism, which I thought outrageous.

As I stepped into her elegantly furnished office, the CM welcomed me warmly, extending her hand. 'How are you, Mr Alexander? It's been a long time since we met.' I was taken aback, for that had not been a good meeting—the visitor whom I had introduced had managed to annoy her with his patronizing attitude. I responded, 'Ma'am, given how that meeting went, I was hoping you wouldn't remember.' She said with a twinkle, 'On the contrary, I remember every bit of it.' The ice was broken and I was safe, but she had indicated that she held the cards.

I told Vasundhara Raje what TAF was about and how we wanted to make a big difference to maternal and child health in Rajasthan. I mentioned that I was talking to possible donors, including RNT. She said, 'We would welcome your foundation's involvement in Rajasthan. If Mr Tata is involved, even better.' She indicated that she would be happy to meet again to take this forward.

Rajiv Mehrishi called the next day to say that the CM was enthusiastic and willing to meet me and Mr Tata. He suggested that we meet her as soon as possible in case there was any change in her plans. He added that we should have a clear action plan.

I immediately wrote to RNT, telling him I had met the CM and that she was keen for TAF to work in Rajasthan, especially if he was involved. I suggested that he write to her immediately and formally request a meeting, as was the protocol. I said that since this meeting might happen at short notice, it was important that he and I meet at the earliest. I wanted to explain to him how I was envisioning our engagement in Rajasthan and also get his views so that we could present a united front when we met the CM. Two months later, I finally got to meet RNT and laid out my thoughts on the prospective programme in Rajasthan. The idea was for us to work intensively in two districts, and for the government to roll out the innovations we developed there state-wide. That had his approval, and the same day, RNT wrote a gracious letter to the CM requesting a meeting to explore the possibility of working together to transform maternal and child health in Rajasthan. He explained that he had been in conversation with me and that I had considerable knowledge of state health transformation.

That meeting was set to happen on 9 June at the chief minister's office in Jaipur. I went in thinking that finally, after so much effort, things were falling into place.

~

The meeting with the CM was scheduled for 11 a.m. on 9 June 2014. I arrived in Jaipur the night before. It had been eighteen months since I first wrote to RNT. There had been many meetings with him in that period, both rewarding and frustrating. In the past six months, I had worked in parallel with the chief minister's staff and met Vasundhara Raje once. I was keyed up—all that work, just to arrive at this morning, when the two leaders would meet, and we would take our partnership forward.

RNT was flying in from Mumbai on the morning of the meeting on a Tata corporate jet. He would freshen up at the Rambagh Palace before we went to meet the chief minister. It is quite an experience to see RNT arrive at a Tata hotel. Word had reached the Rambagh as soon as his car left the airport. The general manager, an eager, rosy-cheeked young man, personally checked out the entire lobby, seeing that every vase of flowers was just so and no painting was even slightly askew. He received RNT with a magnificent bouquet and whisked him away, with me trotting along a few steps behind. The general manager said they had kept two of their best suites ready for him to choose from. He took us for a quick tour of the first. It was a set of several cavernous rooms, each immaculately appointed. RNT said it was fine.

He and I settled down in an elegant living room with a deeply polished, large, oval mahogany table on one side. R. Venkataraman, executive director of the Tata Trusts, and Bikram Mohandas, a former aide to RNT, were present. Bikram, who was based in New York, was a potential donor and I had asked if he could attend.

The previous day, I had sent RNT a one-page note that laid out what we could cover in the meeting with the chief minister. I thought we could get in-principle agreement on the project and move energetically towards an MoU signing. I thought I had discussed all this with RNT, but he said that he had envisaged this primarily as a meeting where we could get to know each other. He felt that we were meeting too fast.

~

The CM received us graciously in her office. 'It's good to see you again, Mr Alexander,' she said. Turning to RNT, she added, 'I know Mr Alexander is a person who gets things done, and we are always glad to see him.' She was conveying her personal support for me to him and also indicating to RNT that it wasn't just because of him that this meeting was happening. That was gracious of her.

The CM has a small conference room adjacent to her office. I knew that the senior bureaucrats were already assembled there. Vasundhara Raje takes her own time, and we settled into the plush sofas. Liveried butlers came in with an array of cakes and biscuits, and tea in Wedgwood cups. Vasundhara reminisced nostalgically about her childhood days in Bombay, how much that city had changed and her special love of that metropolis.

RNT said little. I tried to engage Vasundhara Raje on Rajasthan, its challenges and our partnership. She said, 'No other chief minister in India would allow this [partnership] because it means exposing how we have failed.' Then, just as the conversation was progressing, Bikram butted in with some prattle about what he was doing and the state of the global financial markets. What gives some people verbal diarrhoea when in the presence of power? Again, I marvelled at my habit of bringing outsiders into meetings where they did not belong. It was my naiveté that made me think that people would help out rather than help themselves.

Mercifully, we soon entered the conference room, where about fifteen people were seated around a horseshoe-shaped table.

The senior bureaucrats, the ones with dog chains tucked into their shirt pockets, were on one side of the horseshoe. Technical staff from various government departments were on the other side. RNT and I took our seats on either side of the chief minister. Before that, RNT went around the horseshoe, shaking hands with each person.

I took them through my ten slides. It had a situation assessment and the contours of a possible partnership. I had removed the last two pages, which proposed a plan of action. At one point, Mehrishi glanced sharply at me, surprised that I had not said anything about next steps. He said pointedly, 'The question is, what do we do next?'

I kept quiet. RNT said nothing. The chief minister smiled graciously. The meeting was over.

5

Akshada

I headed back to Delhi, crestfallen. There had been little of substance in the meeting. Now we would have to rewind and work towards another meeting. It occurred to me that there was no guarantee that the grant from the Trusts would come through. And then what? All my efforts so far had led to nothing but this one opening.

I took a deep breath and told myself that I had to keep TAF alive, nurture it, then see it thrive. I slept on it over the weekend. By the following week, I was optimistic again. I exchanged mails with RNT and we were back on course. I told the chief minister's office that we would develop a plan of action in the form of a partnership proposal to the state and get back to them.

~

A month later, I was back at Tata House and once again, I was early for my appointment. On a whim, I went looking for Manoj, the shoeshine boy I had met almost exactly a year ago on my first visit to the Trusts' office. To my delight, there he was, sitting at the same spot with his shoebox in front to him. I was surprised

53

that he remembered and welcomed me, tapping his box with a broad smile, and saying, '*Aiye sa'ab, aaj main bahut badhiya polish karke dikhaoonga aapko* [I'll show you a really special polish today, sir].'

He had one good brush, while the other was the same pathetic, bald thing from a year ago, just more decrepit. The box also looked the same. I said, 'I asked you to buy a full set of brushes, new box, everything.' He showed me the new brush, and said that as for the rest, he was conserving the money and buying things as they became necessary. He pointed to the veteran brush and said, 'Sir, *abhi isme to bahut jaan hai, dibbe mein bhi* [Sir, there's still lot of life in this old brush and in the shoebox].'

He said all was good with him and his family back home. He had been to see them six months ago. The monsoon had been good, everyone was well. My shoes were sparkling after Manoj was done with the polish and the cream and had executed the last snap of the soft cloth to end the job. I reached for my wallet but he stopped me immediately, reminding me of our arrangement— free shoeshines for life.

~

I had come to see RNT, to continue our discussion from the point where we had left it before the meeting in Jaipur. I thought that we had come through the storm, the matter was behind us and we could resume our agenda. But I wanted to be sure, and the best way of finding out is to ask for a small favour. Would he be magnanimous or say a curt 'no'?

The Tata empire is vast, with many huge companies, each committed to giving sizeable amounts of money to good causes by way of their Corporate Social Responsibility (CSR) obligation.[1] If any one of them was to support TAF, it would take us a long way.

I asked RNT if he would be willing to recommend TAF to any of those organizations.

RNT said he would be glad to help. He wrote separately to Cyrus Mistry,[2] whose oversight included Tata Motors, and to T.V. Narendran, the CEO of Tata Steel. He praised my experience and understanding and asked them to consider if their organizations' CSR funds could be used for TAF. It was magnanimous on RNT's part. These companies received me courteously, though nothing materialized eventually.

We had work to do: diagnose the state's health situation, develop a programme design, get that approved first by the Rajasthan government and then the Trusts' board.

I felt vulnerable, but even so, two weeks later, I turned down a massive offer of support from one of the richest men in the world.

~

It started with a phone call from a well-wisher of TAF who was based in London. The business magnate Rakesh Khandelwal[3] had told him that he wanted to give away almost all his vast fortune to good causes. Rakesh was looking for advice on how he should go about this task. The well-wisher asked if he should introduce us— I readily agreed.

I met Khandelwal at his imposing house in London's tony Mayfair district. He was portly, bald and altogether 'homely', as they say in north India. He shook my hand warmly and said he had heard great things about me and been keen to meet me. The plan was to lunch at an Italian restaurant close by. A gleaming Rolls-Royce Silver Ghost stood outside the house, but Rakesh waved the chauffeur away. 'Let us walk, it is very near,' he said.

The maître d' received Rakesh Khandelwal deferentially and took him to his favourite table. A young waiter soon appeared and asked if we were ready to order. The menu was in Italian but that did not matter because Rakesh was sure about what he wanted—a vegetarian pizza with a separate bowl of chilli flakes. The waiter jotted it down on his little pad, but I detected an invisible smirk as he asked about the chilli flakes, and whether that would be all. The novice probably did not know that this innocuous-looking person could easily buy the entire restaurant over lunch. The waiter then turned to me and I said I would have the same thing, but with no chilli flakes.

I asked Rakesh to tell me how he had built his vast empire. He asked, with a twinkle, if I wanted to know the story from the beginning, and I nodded. He had started from absolutely nothing and become one of the world's best. I took a liking to Rakesh because of his lack of pretension,

Rakesh asked me to tell him about TAF and my plans. He said, 'I heard of your excellent work with Bill Gates Foundation [sic] and now you have made Antara, working with women and children, and you may be working in Rajasthan where we have many interests. We can learn so much from you.'

I thanked him and told him about TAF's aspirations. I asked if his foundation would fund our work in Rajasthan, just to see what he had in mind. He asked how much funding I needed, and I indicated a sum for a five-year period. He smiled broadly and said, 'Why do you want only that? You should take six times that. You become the head of my foundation, which I will build, and you can do what you want to do through it.' He told me of his plans to use this foundation as the vehicle to give away his fortune.

But I had been dreaming about TAF for a decade. I had painted pictures in my mind of what it would become. I wanted to do it entirely my way. I would not have that freedom, no matter what Rakesh said, if I did TAF through his or anyone else's foundation.

I said, 'Rakesh ji, it is an immense honour for me to be offered this position, but I must decline. You are a man with big dreams, and you will naturally want to do big things with your philanthropy. I also have a dream, and I want to try and follow my own dream through my own small foundation. I won't be able to do both things at the same time.' We talked for a while. I did not change my stance, and we parted on good terms.

～

The diagnosis and design process for our programme in Rajasthan went smoothly. We visited several parts of Rajasthan and were struck by the extent of poverty, cloaked in beauty, that prevailed in many rural areas. Driving out of the lake city of Udaipur, the countryside is lovely —there are green hills, forests, even waterfalls. But in the villages, we met people who toiled hard to barely get by. The Jaisalmer that the tourists see, the fairy tale city of sand dunes and camel night safaris, was a different place by day; when the tents came down, the hotel workers went back to their villages and the starkness of life there stood exposed. Such journeys gave us a feel for the state and convinced us that opportunities to make a difference were abundant.

In December, I presented our plan before the board of the Trusts. RNT addressed the directors and the grant was approved. It took another three months to complete the formalities with the state government. Our programme was launched on 5 March 2015 in Jaipur, nine months after that last meeting in Jaipur. It eventually happened in the conference hall at the CM's office building. It boasted all the pomp befitting an event graced by RNT and Vasundhara Raje. There were more than 200 people in the auditorium, including the state's senior health officials, collectors* from every district and assorted ministers. I outlined our plans for a programme in partnership with the government and the Trusts, to transform Rajasthan's performance in maternal and child health. RNT said some gracious words and the CM said the programme would be a priority for the state and would get her full support. We named it Akshada, which means 'blessings of God'.

~

We had registered TAF in 2013. In the two years since then, I had reached out, and been politely turned down, by more than eighty potential donors. I had been offered a large amount of money on three occasions by major donors—each time, the amount was large enough to fund us in perpetuity.[4] In each case, I declined the offer without hesitation. I never imagined that I would be rejected summarily when I asked for funds or that I would be offered much larger amounts unsought at the same time which I turned down immediately. These experiences taught me something about my attitude towards TAF, and something about myself.

By 2014, I had spent ten years nurturing the idea of TAF, imagining the future. I fervently believed that the idea was pure—it could not be denied. I was prepared to keep trying, no matter how long it took. I also had a clear idea of what TAF's ambition, model and culture would be. That idea would be compromised if TAF were to come under someone else's umbrella. Laughing at myself, I realized I had become a zealot.

---

* The district collector is an officer of the Indian Administrative Service who oversees all the affairs of a district, from law and order to social and economic development. A typical district has a population of 1.5–2 million. It is an enormous responsibility the government confers on a civil servant very early in their career.

The building of the partnership with RNT had been long and arduous, with many highs and just as many lows. But I will aways be grateful to RNT for believing in us and backing us when no one else in India was even slightly inclined to do that.

But looking back now, I see it as a period of enormous stress and strain. It took something out of me, and sometimes I wonder how, but never why, I did it.

Now all that was behind us, and we could finally move forward.

Part 2
Child

6

Not a Shadow

Now everything was clear.

We had the backing of RNT and funding from the Tata Trusts. The chief minister of Rajasthan had decreed that TAF would be a state priority. We had the chance to make a big difference. Unknown pathways lay ahead, and it was a heady feeling. There was not a shadow of doubt in my mind.

But if rational people had looked at the venture, they might well have concluded that it was risky. They could have said this idea is a grand conception, but you have funding for only two years from the Trusts, and you need to run your programme for at least five to show impact. You are betting that more money will come in, but it's not as though Indian donors have been lining up so far to fund TAF and you don't have the permission to accept foreign financing. Your experience is with sex workers and HIV prevention—this is about mothers and children. You've worked with the poor, but mainly in towns—this is about rural India, a place you hardly know. You have experience of working with the government, but so far, you have built your programmes outside the government before handing it to them—now you will be dependent on the government from the very start and that is risky. You have assembled a team that has never taken on anything of the kind you envisage. You don't even have a detailed work plan. There are too many holes.

I saw it differently. Of course, there are some risks in any new venture. Some things that seemed like weaknesses were really strengths. We were stepping into an adventure for which I had been preparing for years. I was in no mood to sit and worry. Sometimes rational analysis can take you only so far.[1]

~

We had been awarded the Tata grant in January 2015. I heard it was the biggest foray the Trusts had made so far into a programme in maternal and child health. The grant and its timeframe were based on the budget that had been allocated for this project and were not about the funds required to make an impact. We were told by a long-time donee not to be concerned—'if they like the work you are doing, they will fund you for the long term.' I wasn't concerned—after all, we had changed the face of HIV prevention in India in two years!

Such was my confidence that I had been recruiting long before the grant was certain, and even as I was being politely turned away by other possible donors. By the middle of 2014, I had recruited seven people. And by March 2015, TAF had a contingent of twelve, all set to begin work.

It was a motley crew. Some had experience in public health. Others came from the world of business and had little idea what public health even meant. My senior team was made up of Reenu Uppal, who had worked with me at the Gates Foundation, Priya Roy, who was experienced in reproductive health and Neeraj Jham, who had worked in government. Piyush Mehra had left a career in top-management consulting in Malaysia and I had chosen him to lead the operating team.

I had not been looking for experience in maternal and child health or even the social sector. I always feel passion trumps everything—all the rest can be learnt. My own experience had taught me that knowing nothing when you start, coupled with the right attitude, can actually be an asset.

To recruit staff long before you have a grant may seem absurd. But I felt that we needed a team in place when that first grant came through. The team-in-waiting were doing useful preparation— travelling around Rajasthan and other states, gathering data, benchmarking other programmes. There was a keen sense of anticipation and supressed excitement.

~

The entire team had gone to Jaipur for the launch. Now, back in Delhi, we were huddled in a conference room in a business centre in Saket, where we had taken a tiny office. People in the team barely knew each other and we did a round of introductions—I urged people to ask any questions that might be on their minds.

Piyush Mehra, the team leader, had left a promising consulting career overseas to join TAF. He set the ball rolling by asking what the term 'frontline worker' meant. He followed it up by offering that he had been trained in hypnosis. After this, normal interaction resumed as other colleagues explained that they had all worked in different aspects of maternal and child health, but it was clear that their experience was limited or had been in programmes far smaller and less complex than the one on which we had embarked. After this, those who had undertaken fact-finding trips to districts in Rajasthan talked about what they had learnt. Others who had been analysing health data presented trends in the maternal and child health indicators of Rajasthan and in the districts where we would focus our work.

This went on for a week. Then Neeraj Jham, a practical man with a lot of public health experience, asked, *'Yeh sab theek hai— par hum karenge kya?* [This is all very well, but what exactly are we going to do?]' This must be put in context. Most donors told grantees exactly what they wanted done. The team leader's job was to convey those instructions precisely to the team and ensure that everything was implemented perfectly. The Tata Trusts had generously given us the freedom to design the programme as we thought best.

So all eyes were focused on me as the question hung in the air—par hum karenge kya?

The fact is that I did not have a detailed plan of action. I had an approach that was based on what I had learnt in Avahan. How was I to get that across without confusing my team or getting people worried? I can't remember exactly what I said, but it was all based on lessons I had learnt at Avahan. It went something like this:

'Guys, thousands of children die every year, many in their first few weeks. Many women are sickly when they are pregnant. The solutions are straightforward—for example, the pregnant woman must get regular check-ups. The baby must be given only breast milk.

'The first question is—how do we find those women and children most at risk? All pregnant women and newborns are not the same. Some may be more vulnerable than others.

'The second question is—why didn't that pregnant woman get those simple check-ups? Why wasn't the baby breastfed? Ignorance could not be the main reason—if so, creating awareness would fix everything. There must be other barriers that prevent the mother and child from getting these solutions, and these are not obvious. If we understand these barriers, the ways to deal with them will reveal themselves.

'The women who live with these problems daily best know how to identify who among them is most vulnerable—they understand the barriers to their good health. The smart way forward is to ask them. That requires humility. It means we don't do things *for* the women—we work in equal partnership with them.

'So, from now, we move to the field, and we stay there. Watch, listen and ask, and the work plan will come.'

7

River of Cows

We moved our headquarters to Jhalawar.[1] As we built our team, most people decided to live there, close to the villages, while the rest of us travelled regularly from Delhi.

It had become a familiar routine. We would leave from Nizamuddin at 10.30 p.m. on the Inter-City Express to Indore and hop off at 5.30 the next morning at a whistle stop called Ramganjmandi. Greeted by our popular local driver Ashok ji, we would soon be barrelling down open country road, through fields of wheat and mustard, passing small sandstone quarries, heading for Jhalawar town, which was an hour away.

And each time we came around a certain bend, the sun, as if he had been waiting, would begin his stately rise, deep red on the horizon, inducing a soothing sense of smallness.

Soon, we would check in at the Krishna Palace, a modest hotel that had fairly decent rooms on the third floor. After a shower and the Krishna breakfast, one of its kind, we would set off into the interiors of the district.

~

Jhalawar reveals herself slowly—that is her special charm. To discover her beauty, you have to return again and again and experience her many moods. We first came in the spring of 2015, when the eastern parts of the district were ablaze with palash in full bloom. The trees had slender trunks that erupted into branches laden with red-orange flowers. From a distance, the petals gave the illusion of birds with open mouths. The hills looked like they had been powdered with vermilion. Sometimes, we would stop to take pictures and soak in the experience, knowing that it would all be gone as quickly as it came, for spring in Jhalawar is fleeting.

Soon, the searing heat of Jhalawar's summer set in, with temperatures in the high forties. The palash trees stood skeletal, and now it was the turn of the rolling hills of the district. Intensely brown, smoothly rounded, they seemed like lazing behemoths. The hills were black clay, the dominant soil of the district. Some had strange crater-like depressions on their domes, and there was a surreal moonscape quality to it all.

And then the monsoon rains arrived, without warning, in great torrents. Sheets of water swaggered across the landscape and powerful winds blew. Jhalawar's three rivers raged and sometimes ran riot. On one occasion, we stood for hours by the banks of the swollen Ahu, waiting for the waters to settle, but the river kept roaring, swirling, carrying broken branches and all manner of debris with it, moving at speed. The tips of trees stuck eerily out of the water. The rain stopped as suddenly as it had come. There was a freshness and a serenity, the cautious call of birds. Monsoon in Jhalawar was my favourite season, bold and assertive, full of character.

Winter was bitterly cold, with temperatures in the single digits. In the villages, the old men huddled around wood fires as women scurried by, hands folded across their chests to keep warm. Jhalawar is crabby in winter and it was best to leave her alone. But we would say nothing negative, for we had fallen in love. You had to be patient and she would smile, and those palash trees would bloom again.

~

The locals boasted that Jhalawar produced the best coriander and garlic in India. Driving in the interiors, we would stop sometimes at the local markets. Like a connoisseur with a fine wine, I always inhaled deeply of the local produce, for it had character. In Jhalawar, there was a whiff of mystery in a sprig of coriander, and in the garlic, a trace of conceit.

Jhalawar grows huge quantities of oranges, second in India only to its famous rival Nagpur in Maharashtra. The plains around Bhawanimandi on the western border are carpeted with endless groves of oranges. The farmers offered the fruit's first pickings from September to December; the middle picking, which is the best, in December and January and the last picking, as late as June. In winter, the oranges had a uniquely sweet tang. When the crop was abundant, the farmers sometimes left large piles of the fruit on the roadside for passers-by to help themselves.

But the most exotic produce of the district was opium. Jhalawar has one of India's few licensed government opium factories because the climate is ideal for poppy cultivation. The fields on the north-east of the district, close to Kota, were red as the flower bloomed in the hottest months of May and June. The narcotics department controlled poppy cultivation carefully. We saw the blanket of red only from a distance, away from the main roads and we never saw the factory.

The poppy is a fragile flower that requires careful nurture. The licensed poppy farmers of Jhalawar are specialists, the practice often handed down through generations. They make a slit in the traditional way on the side of the unripe poppy bud. Over the next few weeks, the precious sap slowly oozes from the seeds and comes out from the slits. The sap is harvested, dried carefully and rolled into balls of pure opium.

The government required that every farmer produce a contracted amount of opium per hectare. They paid the farmers Rs 1000 for a kilo of opium. If they produced less than that, their license could be cancelled. The opium was sold by the government to pharma companies who converted it to morphine or other opiate medicines. It was also exported to countries in Europe and to the USA. In the underground market in India, the price of that kilo of opium was Rs 50,000. On the streets of New York, it could fetch a price of about Rs 50,00,000 per kilo in the form of heroin. The farmers' long-standing gripe was that the yield expected by the government was too stringent and the price too low. Many traditional poppy farmers had switched to orange cultivation.

In 2017, there was an unusual threat to opium production in Jhalawar—parrots. It must have started with a passing parrot who landed on a poppy and sucked the oozing sap. It gave the parrot a splendid feeling, and it passed the word to its mates, who landed in the poppy fields in large numbers and the party began. Soon, they were tearing open the unripe pods to find the seeds and split those open. Some even flew away with entire pods.

～

Our mandate was to create a programme that would have an impact on the health of the poorest mothers and children across the state. Our mission was to ensure that no woman would die giving birth, that every infant would survive and grow up healthy.

Yes, Jhalawar was a thing of beauty, but we could not tarry, for we had serious work ahead of us in the villages.

In the beginning, I had some notion that there was such a thing as a typical village. We soon found that it wasn't that simple. The sheer numbers were overwhelming. Jhalawar had about 1500 villages—the neighbouring district, Baran, had 1200.[2] The state had more than 45,000 villages in total. Each one of these had a unique fingerprint. The village could be a tiny hamlet or a much bigger habitation. Many castes could live in one village, or a single tribe. It might be near the highway or completely cut off. Electricity, water and the condition of the school also defined a village. But most importantly, it was whether the women of the village had a voice or no voice at all, their faces always covered. These aspects, and more, had a direct bearing on the health of the community.

These villages had evolved naturally over many years. Each one had its own unique layout. There was no man-made symmetry, no rectangles, no circles, no straight lines. There was a logic to the arrangement, but that logic was never obvious—it had to be inferred.

Many villages seemed like a maze. That was the case with Matlai, a village of about 200 households, which we visited in our first week in Jhalawar. A two-hour drive into the countryside and there it was, looking like an island in a sea of ripening green maize. We parked a short distance away and entered the village through its dusty main road, about 50 metres long, running east to west across the top half of the village. If the village was a face, this road was a crease along the forehead, and the main village lay below the crease. Above it were a few scattered huts and open fields. We strolled east to west along the road to get our bearings.

We passed four roadside shops on our right-hand side, close to each other. There was a paan kiosk, festooned with small packets of paan masala, potato chips and namkeen. There was a shop for minor cycle repairs and one for small electricals. A tea shop with three tables served pakoras and samosas. But the shop that caught my eye was the one that sold home products. It had a few items I didn't expect to see in a poor village: expensive branded products such as Colgate toothpaste, Lux soap and Stayfree sanitary napkins. We passed the village's middle school on our right. Just then, a bell signalled the mid-day interval and children poured out onto the large school yard, making a huge racket. The road ended a small distance away from the school.

Farther along, well beyond the perimeter of the village, there was a section of ramshackle thatched houses. This was the Dalit *basti*, the segregated section for the lowest caste communities. One family—a man and his wife, their two small children and aged parents—lived in a hut that had two rooms. The spaces were used for sleeping, cooking and storage. The man said he earned Rs 400 a day as a daily wage labourer in the fields nearby. His wife, face covered by her ghunghat, was busy in the background. Their children, barefoot and half-naked, played outside. There were two goats and a buffalo.

Across the road was a *kabrastaan*—a Muslim burial ground. Further down, on the left, beyond the basti, was a large plot of land with a board that said 'Shamshan Ghat', a Hindu cremation ground. We went into this open area and noticed a small building with two rooms on our left. A board announced that it was a school. This was puzzling, since we had already passed the main school.

What was such a tiny school doing inside a cremation ground? For that matter, why were there high-end consumer products like Colgate, Lux and Stayfree in a shop in a poor village? In most villages, we found these tiny pieces that didn't quite fit. We thought of them as clues that had to be deciphered to gain insights about the community.

We walked back along the main road and stepped into the main village. Here, small lanes led into each other in such a way that they encircled groups of houses in small 'mohallas' or neighbourhoods. In the bigger mohallas, most of the houses were located along the perimeter. That created a natural courtyard in the centre. If the area was big enough, there would be smaller courtyards within the large courtyard, created by clusters of a few houses bunched together. The locals called these spaces *badas*.

Many homes were made of mud with thatched roofs, sometimes patched up with tarpaulin, like the ones in the Dalit section of the village. Other houses were made of brick and had solid roofs. Some were painted blue or green, with old carved doors. They were picturesque despite the obvious poverty. Each had a space for the family livestock: cows, buffaloes, goats and chickens.

We saw three prosperous houses as we walked around the village. There was always a satellite dish on the roof, a motorcycle and in one case, even a car. The locals told us that one was the home of the politically well-connected panchayat chief. The other two houses belonged to landowners and local businessmen.

Many houses had a small, and obviously newer, structure painted indigo blue. These were toilets constructed by the central government as part of its scheme to end open defecation. Most were being used for storage. One entrepreneur had converted his would-be toilet into a *kirana** store and a few had become kiosks for beedi, paan and *gutka*.[†] It seemed that government officials had tracked how many toilets had been built, not how many were being used as toilets.

---

* A small, usually family-owned shop selling groceries and other sundries.
[†] A mixture of tobacco, crushed areca nut spices, and other ingredients. It is used like chewing tobacco.

The village was silent except for the occasional bleat of a goat or the bark of a stray dog. It was mid-day and all the able-bodied men and women had gone to the fields to work. Old men sat on charpoys, staring into the distance, smoking their hookahs, saying little to each other. They looked at us with passing curiosity. They willingly told us about the village, their families, jobs, health. They never asked us who we were or where we had come from.

We passed the drab panchayat office, with a meeting hall and two office rooms. It was the largest structure we had seen in the village, and a board in front had the name of the panchayat president and all the members. There was an ancient peepul tree outside the office, with red threads tied across the trunk and lower branches. Three old men sat on the cemented base.

Moving on, we passed two working handpumps and one that was broken. Women gathered around chatting, laughing and carrying away water in large plastic buckets.

~

I developed an ardent admiration for the cows of Jhalawar and the team found it endlessly amusing. I was used to the stray cows of Delhi who sat in the hot sun, in the middle of busy roads, oblivious to speeding traffic. Their distant cousins in Jhalawar carried themselves with a certain dignity, a decorative cord around their necks, their pointed horns painted bright red, facing skyward. We often saw cows grazing, others resting in the shade, legs folded delicately underneath them. They always watched us closely, sizing us up, for they knew we were strangers.

Once, I came across a newborn calf standing on its long spindly legs. He was tied with a long rope to a tree. His mother must have gone grazing nearby. The calf was lovely, with big dark eyes and long lashes. I went up to scratch his forehead—he shook his head in pleasure and rubbed it on my side, asking me to continue. This communion was interrupted suddenly when in the distance, I saw his mother getting purposefully to her feet, lowing loudly, clearly conveying—how dare you! I retreated quickly.

Once, we came to a corral that had several cows grazing peacefully. As we approached, they stopped and froze, watching us warily. As we got closer, a few began to kick their hind legs, lowing loudly. A few cantered away to the safety of their shed. The man in charge said laconically that the cows were afraid of us because we were wearing pants. The cows assumed therefore that we were veterinarians from town. They associated the visit of men in pants with painful injections and unpleasant treatments. No one back in Delhi believes this story, but then again, few in Delhi have met the cows of Jhalawar.

~

We found our way through the maze of lanes and mohallas and arrived near the southern end of the village, where the lanes were broader. There was a commotion and suddenly, around the bend came an endless herd of cows. They were in full flow, moving briskly, with a steady beating of the hooves. A few men with long sticks managed them with deft pokes and taps. I wondered where they were all coming from and where they were headed. I watched the bovine river for a few minutes, enchanted.

Close by, a few young men in stylishly tattered jeans and crumpled T-shirts sat on a stoop. The cows kept moving, with no indication that the flow would end anytime soon, so I walked over to the young men. They were in a great mood and I suspected there had to be a bottle somewhere close by. Sure enough, a jubilant one asked, '*Kuch piyoge*, sir? [Will you drink something, sir?]'

We spoke at length. The youngsters wore those jeans and T-shirts because they had seen it on the few TV screens that existed in the village. They didn't want to become like their fathers, eking out a living tilling someone else's land. As their façade fell away, they asked if there were jobs they could get in the city.

~

We came to a yellow box-shaped building with the words 'Anganwadi Kendra'* in Hindi above the entrance. These government centres exist in villages across India and play an important role in public health delivery at the grassroots. We took off our shoes at the entrance and were greeted by a middle-aged woman in a pink-purple sari. She was the anganwadi worker (AWW), the person responsible for the facility.

Fourteen pre-schoolers aged between two and six sat cross-legged on the floor, a slate and a piece of chalk before each one of them. Prompted by the AWW, they sang out a welcome lustily and in unison—namaste ji! We told the worker we didn't want to interrupt her class. She said it was not a problem because the children were about to get their mid-day meals in any case. As she started explaining the centre to us, the tykes realized that the teacher was not paying attention to them and became boisterous. A few chased each other across the small room. Others rough-housed. The AWW's helper, a slight young woman, shouted dire warnings without any effect—'*khamosh, khamosh, varna* . . .[silence, silence, otherwise . . .]!'

---

* Rural government child care centre mainly providing immunization, supplementary nutrition, health check-ups and early childhood development toys.

Through all this commotion, one small chap, perhaps four years old, kept staring listlessly into the distance. It seemed as though he was somewhere else. The worker explained that the boy had come to the centre a year ago, severely malnourished. He had regained some weight, but the damage to his cognitive development had been done. Severe malnutrition before the age of two has that effect, and it would likely stay with him throughout his life. The worker said that he was getting better. Seeing the little fellow in his own silent world, I felt a catch in my throat.

By this time, the helper had placed a metal thali, a spoon and a tumbler of water in front of each child. She and the worker placed two rotis, a *katori** of dal, a heaped spoonful of palak *sabji* and a banana on each thali. The helper sat down beside the silent little boy and tried to feed him by hand. She did it patiently and with care. After the mid-day meal, the children went home.

Women began trickling in, some pregnant, others with their infants. This was the monthly Village Health and Nutrition Day (VHND), when the government nurse, known as the Auxiliary Nurse Midwife (ANM),[3] would visit the village. She arrived wearing a crisp white sari, with her medical kit and cold box for vaccines. She checked the stock of medicines, placed three bulky registers on her desk and sat down to meet her first patient.

The mothers took their infants in by turn, and soon there would be the loud howling that signalled that a baby had been vaccinated. Pregnant women went in next for their check-up.

The ASHA worker arrived, a confident young woman in the prescribed blue sari. Her job was to go from house to house and check that everyone was healthy. She reminded pregnant women, and those with infants, when the nurse would be coming next.

---

* Bowl.

The nurse finished seeing her patients and the anganwadi centre (AWC) emptied out. The women in pink, white and purple sat on the ground. They pored over the 'due list' that had names of women who were pregnant and the dates when they were expected to deliver. They looked at lists of new mothers and malnourished children and started planning for the next few weeks.

It appeared everything was in order, but as we visited more and more villages, and looked more closely, we realized that things were not always what they seemed.

8

Sisters of Mercy

In the first few weeks, we paid learning visits to villages across Jhalawar to develop first impressions and get a feel for the situation on the ground. Then, we decided on a deep dive into twenty-three villages drawn from the five blocks where we would run our programme. We began to see patterns across these villages—it was a period of rich learning.

Jhikri Kalan[1] was one of those villages. It is innocuous—there are hundreds like it in Jhalawar. The village had 1315 people, 80 per cent from the Scheduled Castes. There were 241 modest houses, mostly made of mud with thatched roofs. The poorest residents lived in a cluster of twenty-five huts on the edge of the village, referred to as *khanjar basti*.

The layout of the village can be visualized as a cross with an elongated vertical beam. Two roads hang from the horizontal beam. Several small roads, both straight and curving, cut horizontally across these three verticals. Lanes—narrow, then even narrower—sprout from these roads. At the very top of the cross, more lanes sprout, just as haphazard. The houses were spaced randomly along some sections of road. In other places, they were tightly packed, one right next to the other.

~

The Indian public health system is vast. At the state level, it reaches into each district, every block and village. Ultimately, the touchstone of the strength of a health system is whether basic health services are available and delivered with quality in every village. Three female health workers play a crucial role in making this happen.[2]

The ANM operates from a basic health facility known as the sub-centre. She is responsible for four to six villages, located anywhere up to 20 kilometres from her facility. The ANM sees patients at the sub-centre and visits each village once a month, on the VHND. On that day, her main task is to vaccinate babies and do a health check on pregnant women. She refers complicated cases to government health facilities beyond the sub-centre.

The AWW oversees an anganwadi (crèche), where pre-school children in the age group of three to six years get a hot cooked meal, learn the alphabet and play. She keeps track of the growth and weight of the children. She also identifies any woman whom she sees as a 'probable pregnancy', and informs the ASHA. She begins giving the woman her rations right away.

The ASHA pays home visits to check on the health of each family member. She makes her own assessment of 'probable pregnancies', taking note of the cases that the AWW has already flagged for her attention. She marks all these cases to the ANM to confirm the pregnancy. The ASHA begins counselling and ensures that the woman takes her Take Home Ration (THR) even before her pregnancy is confirmed. She measures malnutrition in children using a Mid-Upper Arm Circumference (MUAC) tape[*] and ensures that every newborn gets Home-based Newborn Care (HBNC).[†] She, like the AWW, is also from the village.

This is a well-designed system for village-level maternal and child healthcare. The ASHA and AWW both monitor the health of women and children with copious record-keeping and report these cases to the ANM. The nurse will see those beneficiaries on the VHND at the AWC. In difficult cases, she will visit the houses personally. If the system runs perfectly, there should be few maternal and child deaths, or illnesses, within the community. We coined the term 'AAA workers', to refer to the three health workers as a unit.

~

On our first visit, we always try and do a leisurely village walk, noting interesting aspects of village life, picking up clues, talking to the locals. We did that in Jhikri Kalan, accompanied by the ASHA, who was received affectionately in several houses.

We reached the khanjar basti section of the village, which is located some distance away from the main village. The ASHA said she would not join us as she had some other work. A local who came up to us warned us that this section of the village could be dangerous ('*khatra hai yahaan*'). He said the people there made their living from theft and criminal activities. He cautioned us not to carry money or wear a watch. Once listed under the Criminal

---

[*] The MUAC measuring tape is used primarily to assess levels of malnutrition in babies and small children.
[†] HBNC is a protocol adopted by government to ensure the charter of health practices that keep a newborn safe in the first week of life.

Tribes Act,* the community is stigmatized. They are mainly nomadic people—villages do not take them in, and they make their homes outside the village's borders.

The khanjar basti in Jhikri Kalan is a scattering of thirty-three huts around two mud lanes on a vast open field. The huts are dilapidated, held up by spindly poles and patches of blue tarpaulin. When they saw us, even at a distance, people began to move away quickly. They seemed fearful. We approached some older people. They glanced at us and turned away. Finally, a wizened old woman spoke a few words to us—she shook her head when we asked if she had met the ASHA. The village school was just outside the main village.

At the AWC, we sat on the floor to talk to the AAA workers. We asked if we could look at the copious records they maintained. Comparing their bulky registers, we saw many discrepancies.

Seema,[3] the ASHA, did not know that Rukmini, who lived in house number 8, was pregnant. Otherwise, she would have counselled her on all the dos and don'ts of pregnancy. Ritu, the AWW, knew that Rukmini had missed her last two periods, and she had put her down as a 'probable pregnancy'. She told Rukmini, who probably didn't understand. She didn't start her on the THR.† She didn't inform Seema about this probable pregnancy, or Gracymol, the ANM. So, Rukmini would have missed out on the counselling and THR that was her due till she became visibly pregnant, and someone noticed.

---

* Now known as the Habitual Offenders Act.
† THR is provided under the government's Integrated Child Development Scheme (ICDS) to children aged six to thirty-six months, and to pregnant/lactating women, for consumption at home.

Rahul, age two, lived in house number 52. He looked malnourished, so Seema, the ASHA, measured his growth status using the MUAC tape. This confirmed that Rahul was mildly malnourished—however, with the right feeding, he could be pulled out of a downward spiral of malnutrition, illness, and even more malnutrition. Seema assumed that this would happen at the AWC where Rahul had started going—one of the few children from the basti who did. After all, there he would get a hot cooked meal every day, and Ritu, the AWW, could counsel Rahul's mother about his feeding. Ritu took the children's weight routinely using a weighing scale. She marked his weight as normal. Seema, however, informed the ANM about Rahul, based on her measure. The ANM examined Rahul and instructed the AWW to take heed.

We asked, gently, why there were such discrepancies. And could it be that some cases were being spotted too late, or even missed entirely?

We asked what if there was a pregnant woman who was not on the Due List? The ASHA said that did happen at times, because some women didn't know that if they missed their period, it could be that they had conceived.

We asked about children who were malnourished. That process likely started a long time earlier, when the baby was unable to get breast milk. The women nodded—yes, that happened.

The AWW said some families didn't send their children to the centre. They didn't want their child eating with low castes. Some Dalits didn't send their children because they feared they would not be treated well in the AWC. The department never replaced Ritu's faulty weighing machine, though she had reported it many times, and now she had no option but to use *andaza*.

We had just walked through the complicated maze of the village—how could anyone accurately know who out there was sick? I remembered the child staring into the distance that morning. He might have been playing and laughing like the other kids in the room if someone among the three women had spotted him early.

The ASHA spoke of her workload, of how long it took to go from house to house—she said she had a small baby at home and that he also needed attention, didn't he? She said, 'Sir, I am not a doctor, I can't always say if a woman is pregnant or a child is in danger.' The AWW's words came out in a rush, 'Sir, you have seen today how much work I have, running the centre, so many children and a hot mid-day meal for each.'

The ANM's voice trembled as she spoke. She said she oversaw five villages, scattered over a long distance. The government did not provide a vehicle, requiring them to use public transport, which was irregular. So, she depended on her husband to drop her to some villages, but he had his own work, too, and she could not visit all villages. She told us about her day: waking up at 5 a.m. to attend to the house—cleaning, cooking breakfast, getting her two children ready for school. She would end her day after 10 p.m., having finished a gruelling day's work, and come back to make dinner and snatch some time with her family.

And so it went in hundreds of villages like Jhikri Kalan— mothers and children who needed medical attention were being overlooked. One reason was that the AWW came from the Women and Child Development (WCD) ministry, the ASHA and ANM from the health ministry. So, they had different supervisors and no single line of command. The AWW passed information sideways to the ASHA, and if the ASHA didn't send it upwards to the ANM, it was lost and the pregnant woman or child would be missed out.

Another problem was that the AWW used census data, with a number allotted to every house in the village. The ASHA followed the numbering system based on her own annual survey. So, a single house would have two different numbers allotted to it by the health system. It was confusing. Most villages did not have a map. So, it was not easy to locate a house, especially when it was lost in a tangle of lanes with houses that had different numbers.

We had spoken with many such AAA teams. In Jhikri Kalan, we asked the group if there was a solution. The women just looked at each other. Over the next few weeks, we had many such conversations in different villages. We came up with a straightforward solution, working together with the AAA workers.[4]

~

The first step was to create a map of the village. The ASHA and AWW did a thorough job, walking every street and lane, noting down the different house numbers, marking every hand pump, temple, school and water body. In the first iteration, the two women left out the entire khanjar basti—it was as though the cluster was not part of the village.

In the end, Jhikri Kalan had a glorious new map—not to scale, of course, but a big step forward in terms of understanding the village. Even the khanjar basti appeared on the map eventually.

After that, the three health workers pored over the map on every VHND. The ASHA and the AWW discussed every case where their data differed—cases such as Rukmini's and Rahul's. The ASHA would ask questions—in the end, the three would come to an agreement and stick a coloured bindi on a particular house. The colour of a bindi signified whether this was a house with a pregnant woman or one who was pregnant and at-risk, and similarly for a house with a newborn or a severely malnourished child.

The system worked well from the start, the women enjoying the camaraderie and the residents receiving increased attention from the health workers. After six months, we showed the method to Chief Minister Vasundhara Raje. We could sense her mind racing. She said, 'This is very good. But it can be used for development also. You can map schools or hand pumps, whether they are working or not, right?' We nodded, of course. She continued, 'It is hardly any additional work. The ASHA does her rounds regularly. It will be no extra work for her to see if a pump is working or not. And pumps, schools and so on don't keep changing like pregnancies. Can you try that and show me?' And of course, we said yes. Why hadn't we thought of that?

~

As I write, I have before me one of the village maps we made of Jhikri Kalan. It has a unique beauty—a sprinkling of bindis on a village map that has been drawn with great care. They are red, blue, green, yellow, brown—each bindi depicting a life, of a pregnant mother, a newborn or a child—safe or at risk. There are symbols for trees, wells, temple, schools, and pumps, both working and broken. At first look, it appears a joyous picture. But as we look more closely, a tragic story emerges.

Seven pregnancies, one at high-risk —none in the khanjar basti.

Five newborns, all getting 'Home-based Newborn Care'— none in the khanjar basti.

Thirteen malnourished children, of which seven are in the khanjar basti.

Three severely malnourished children (SAM cases), of which one is in the khanjar basti.

Fourteen households that have availed of the MGNREGA benefit,* of which one is in the khanjar basti.

Eighteen individual house latrines built by government, of which one is in the khanjar basti.

Twenty-four handpumps (three not working) and standposts, of which two handpumps (one not working) are in the khanjar basti.

The map enabled a quick analysis of Jhikri Kalan's health and development situation. And it revealed how one community of people had in effect been erased from the Indian health system and overlooked by development programmes. Before the village mapping exercise, the khanjar basti had been invisible.

The AAA platform built a sense of solidarity among the three women healthcare workers. When it began, they barely knew each other, but with time, they became a team as friendships developed. Suddenly, families started coming to the AWC to see if the 'brown bindi has gone from our house':[5] they knew it stood for their malnourished child and they had been feeding her, wanting the stain removed. The people of the village treated the ASHA and AWWs with renewed respect.

A few months later, I met the chief minister (CM) and told her about the progress on the AAA platform. 'But' she said, 'your team is helping the women do this. What would happen if you were not there?' I don't know what got into me, but I said, 'Ma'am, give us till the end of the year (it was April then). We will have every single village in Jhalawar and Baran mapped perfectly. My field staff are less than twenty people. This task can be done

---

* The Mahatma Gandhi National Rural Employment Guarantee Act (2005) is a labour law and social security measure that guarantees the right to work. It assures at least 100 days of guaranteed wage employment every year in households where adult members agree to do unskilled manual work.

only if the AAA workers and the village women came together.'
She smiled and changed the topic.

When I came back, my team said, 'Ashok, we can't believe
you committed to the chief minister that 2600 villages would be
mapped in eight months, without our help!' They were laughing,
but a tad nervously. In December that year, we met the CM, at
which point, we had arranged for a bit of drama. We projected
a large map of the adjacent districts of Jhalawar and Baran. We
handed her the cursor and asked her to pick either district, then to
pick a block with her cursor—the projection would zoom in to that
block—and then we asked her to name a gram panchayat, followed
by a village. The image zoomed in further, finally pinpointing that
village. I asked her to click on the village, and when she did, a full-
blown, detailed map of the village filled the screen.[6]

The CM laughed in delight for this was proof of a simple
tool that village communities could handle on their own. It
could therefore be rolled out at scale easily. That could have huge
implications for health delivery at the village level. This meeting
must have remained in her mind and made it easy for her to
launch the AAA platform state-wide, in all the 46,000 villages in
Rajasthan, a year later.

~

We regularly monitored the impact of our work in a sample
of villages where we worked.[7] The results were exciting. Our
programme monitoring system shows that in 2018, the
percentage of pregnant women identified as highly-at-risk
increased by 60 per cent. Identification of underweight children
increased 117 per cent.

The three women community health workers who operate in
every village in India play a crucial role, for they are the first contact

between the needy and the public health system. In the recent past, however, there has been a certain amount of uninformed criticism of their skills and attitudes in official circles as well as in the media.

Our experience has been that you cannot generalize about health workers. We have certainly encountered community health workers whose attitude is reprehensible—indeed, you will meet some in these pages. But the issue is more complex than it seems. You can castigate the AAA workers of Jhikri Kalan for ignoring the people of the khanjar basti. But should they take all the blame? What about the system itself that allows such bastis to continue in isolation? What about all the powerful people of the village, who look the other way?

During our time in the field, we have met many women who, with just a little support, will become model workers. Many have inspired us with their selflessness and deep commitment. They are the unsung heroes of rural India, saving lives and averting illness every day. And very often, they have arrived at their stations having battled almost impossible odds in their personal lives.

For us, they will always be the sisters of mercy.*

---

* Homage to Leonard Cohen's song of the same name.

9

Mandarins

Every year, over a million young men and women appear for the preliminary examination for the Indian Civil Service. About a thousand of these applicants are selected for placement into the different services. From these, fewer than 200 make it into that most elite of government of India cadres, the Indian Administrative Service (IAS).

After a few months of rigorous training, the freshly minted IAS officers—bright, shining, full of idealism—are allotted to different states. Within five years they become district collectors, responsible for law and order, land revenue, health, education and much more in a single district. Each such person, barely thirty years old and with little work experience, suddenly has almost absolute power over 1.5 million people spread over more than a thousand villages of their district.

The collector soon becomes an authority on all matters to do with the district. Full of savvy, they have the power to remove barriers and get difficult work done overnight. Therefore, for our work, the most crucial person is always the collector.

I first met the collector of Jhalawar in the summer of 2014, almost a year before we received the Tata grant. That visit to

Jhalawar was one of several recces we made at that time to familiarize ourselves with the state. We saw many disturbing things in the villages—women who had no choice but to have baby after baby till they had a male child. Women, just weeks away from their due date, who had never had a check-up. Infants who had never suckled because their mothers had to work in the fields. Children who were much too small and thin. Superstitions, taboos and social norms dictated what women could and could not do. We met many committed health workers, overworked and overwhelmed, trying to balance the pressures of work and home.

We were keen to know what the collector thought of the situation. The CM's office had sent word of our visit and we easily got an appointment. But first, we had a meeting with the District Chief Medical Officer (DCMO).

$\sim$

We asked the DCMO, Irfan Ali,[1] short and portly, about the malnutrition we had seen in the villages. His philosophy of life was that human beings fell into two categories—those with whom you should be obsequious and those to whom you should be rude. He had slotted me into the first category—after all, I had spoken directly to the chief minister herself. He was less sure about my colleague Arnaz Sherwani,[2] who was also a medical doctor, though Irfan didn't know it.

Irfan said, 'Sir, we have very few cases of severe malnutrition. Please see in the government Malnutrition Treatment Centre [MTC]—the beds are empty.' He smiled ingratiatingly.

I said, 'I think that may be because it is difficult for a woman to bring her child all the way to the town and then stay here for a few weeks.'

Arnaz added, 'We noticed that many children in the villages were thin and tiny—both stunted and wasted.' Stunting is a sign of chronic childhood malnutrition.

At this, Irfan turned towards her, 'Madam, there is stunting in every village in India! Indians are stunted people, even in cities.' Then, taking a closer look at Arnaz who is petite, he added, 'Why madam, even you are stunted . . .'

Arnaz: 'I am not stunted.'

Irfan: 'Stunted.'

Arnaz: 'Not stunted.'

Irfan pressed home his advantage: 'Madam, you are stunted. I am a doctor.'

Arnaz: 'I am also a doctor.' Then, looking pointedly at his pear-shaped figure: 'If I am stunted, then you are malnourished.'

Things were heating up and I thought it was best to intervene. I jumped in, saying we had to leave now, as we had an appointment with the collector.

Getting into the car, I was controlling myself. Arnaz saw that and said, 'Ashok, you dare say it and . . .' I burst out: 'Stunted.'

We collapsed, laughing.

~

The Secretariat in Jhalawar is an ornate pink structure, a little over the top, even as the administrative headquarters of a district government. But this was no ordinary district, for it had been the political constituency of Chief Minister Vasundhara Raje for more than twenty years. A white Maruti car parked outside the entrance, with a blue beacon on its bonnet, told us that the collector was in. A polished brass plate on the door announced 'Vishnu Prasad Tulsi'. A glowing red bulb above the door said he was not to be disturbed. A showy security guard stood outside, just to make sure. The private secretary took us to a small waiting room, and assured me that he would send my card in right away.

Soon, he was back: 'Sir is ready to see you now.' Entering the collector's office at its far end, we saw six rows of chairs facing a massive glass-topped desk. The first four rows were occupied by men wearing white dhoti-kurta and turbans. I guessed that they were farmers who had come with a petition. The collector had interrupted this meeting for us. The men in white took no notice as we walked in. Their eyes were fixed on the collector.

Vishnu Prasad Tulsi was a tiny man with an ebony complexion, dapper in a crisp cream-coloured shirt. His neatly trimmed hair was parted in the centre—oiled, but not excessively. There was a large white towel draped across the back of his chair, an arcane practice followed by government officers across India. He extended his hand without getting up and nodded, cordial but unsmiling. The chairs were all taken up by the farmers. At another nod, a few got up and went to the back, making room for us.

As tea and biscuits were brought in, I asked the collector about his district. He ticked off their many achievements, enumerating the lowest, highest, biggest, smallest, broadest and fastest. I managed to interject and say that the record was truly impressive, but what about public health? The collector responded, 'Our health record is very good.'

I said, 'Vishnu ji, we have just returned from touring the district. There, we saw many cases of malnutrition and infant deaths.'

The buzzer sounded suddenly, and the collector told his secretary to put the call through. With an apologetic smile, he held his hand up with his thumb and two adjacent fingers pressed together at the tips, the gesture meaning 'excuse me'. He took the call standing up, a sure sign that the call was from someone far above his rank.

For the next several minutes, the only sound we heard from Vishnu was 'sir'. IAS officers say 'sir' on the phone in a certain way, depending on the caller's rank. The word can come out with a bang or quietly. A rapid-fire sir-sir-sir or with long breaks in between. The officer can carry on an entire conversation with this one syllable. And so it went for a while till the call ended abruptly. From the way he had enunciated his 'sirs', it seemed that Vishnu had conveyed that he had understood and would 'do the needful', which is another government idiom.

The collector sat down and resumed our conversation without missing a beat. Frowning, he said, 'Impossible; we have no such problem of infant deaths and malnutrition.'

'Not even a single case?'

'Not a single one in this district.'

'There are infant deaths in every district in India.'

'We don't have a single case.'

I turned to Arnaz, who handed me a printed sheet of paper. We had come prepared with Jhalawar's health statistics for the past few years, including infant deaths and malnutrition cases. The record showed that the district's performance was worse than the state average.[3] I slid the sheet quietly across the table to him, saying softly, 'Government data'. The collector looked carefully at the paper without picking it up. Then he slid it back without a word. He looked over our heads at the farmers and nodded, and the men at the back got up to reclaim their seats in front of him.

As we left, my colleague whispered, 'Maybe you shouldn't have entered a debate with the collector, Ashok. After all, we may have to work with him later.' I shook my head. What was I to do—congratulate him?

I met the collector eight months later in Jaipur at the ceremony to launch our work in Rajasthan. The conference hall was packed with government functionaries and media. Vishnu and his counterpart from Udaipur had been given a place in the front row, two o'clock from the chief minister. Today was their day because they were in charge of the two focus districts—Jhalawar and Udaipur*—selected for the programme.

Vishnu looked sharp in a smart blazer, starched white shirt, dark tie and perfectly creased trousers. He gazed directly at the chief minister, leaning forward in his seat. He nodded agreement as I spoke of our plans, and when RNT made his remarks. He pulled out a little diary from inside his jacket and took notes when the chief minister spoke. After the event, he came up and said, 'Sir, I am looking forward to working with you. We have many health problems in Jhalawar and must show Madam the improvement.'

Next week, he called a meeting of every official in the district who was associated with public health. He impressed upon them the need to work closely with us and offer all possible support, '. . . because honourable chief minister herself has said so.' And so, on that solid foundation, was built our relationship with Vishnu Prasad Tulsi, the collector of Jhalawar.

~

The collector is at the bottom rung of the bureaucratic ladder. Four other IAS officers, far senior, would also be crucial to our work. They were the head of the National Health Mission (NHM); his boss, the secretary incharge of wellness; his boss, the chief secretary and the principal secretary to the chief minister. They were all located at the seat of government, the Secretariat in Jaipur. We had to start building those bridges.

---

* Soon, Udaipur was substituted by Baran district.

One reason I was optimistic was that I had already built a good equation with the chief secretary, S.K. Shankar. He had ensured that my discussions with the chief minister had gone smoothly during the six months prior to the launch of Akshada. I went to see him soon after the launch to get his counsel and ask for his continued support.

Another meeting was going on as I stepped into his office. I took a seat at the conference table on the other side of the of the room. A man and a woman, evidently poor villagers, sat on the edge of their chairs, across the table from the chief secretary. The man was talking quickly, as though he was used to being cut off, hands folded in supplication. He spoke in a local dialect and used the word *zameen*, meaning land, frequently. The woman's face was covered and she was crying softly.

The chief secretary listened for a while and asked a few questions. He read their papers. The man and woman fell silent. After a few minutes, he said something and rose. The couple scrambled to their feet and the man tried to touch S.K. Shankar's feet.

After they were escorted out, I asked S.K. Shankar what that was about. He said, 'Some powerful person in their village simply usurped this poor farmer's tiny plot. He has been running from pillar to post and no one has helped him.' I surmised that the police had been paid off by the land-grabber. And perhaps the farmer was unable to get through to the collector of his district.

'So, what happens now?' I asked.

'It's quite straightforward. Luckily, his papers are in order. I'll talk to the collector and he will sort it out.'

'How do you find time for such cases on top of all your other work?'

'If someone has travelled such a long distance to seek justice, it means I am his last resort. It's part of our job, serving the public.'

I briefed Shankar about our plans. He said he would always be available if we needed his support. But it would be better from now on if I worked with the health department and with the chief minister's office. Those were the official channels, and no one should feel that I had bypassed them. I saw good sense in that advice.

I was confident of building good relationships. After all, we had the chief minister's backing, the chief secretary's support and a collector in Jhalawar who had seen the light. Now for the others.

~

Three bureaucrats had the power to block or enable any initiative we wanted to introduce in Rajasthan. That was because each one was responsible for a different aspect of the health system. To be prudent, we will refer to them as a trinity—the Father, Son and Holy Ghost.[4]

The most junior amongst the three, the Ghost, led the State Health Institute (SHI)[5] which focuses on family planning, maternal and child health as well as nutrition. Our work fell directly within his jurisdiction. I had met him briefly during the launch ceremony.

The TAF approach is to develop innovations that the government can roll out on a large scale. Every such idea, big or small, had to be cleared by the Ghost. For instance, the simplification of the ANM's record-keeping was urgently needed. The ANM was required to maintain copious daily records of her work in up to seventeen separate registers. She could either attend to patients or take hours out of her day doing record-keeping. Many ANMs kept small personal diaries because their registers were too heavy to carry around. They planned to transcribe the readings they collected during their rounds into the registers later, but often didn't get the time. Columns of perfect 120/80 blood pressure readings suggested that the numbers were made up. This was serious, because low or high blood pressure during pregnancy can endanger both mother and unborn child. The data had to be tracked accurately.

Soon after we began, we figured out how the record-keeping could be greatly simplified. If the Ghost approved, the new registers could be rolled out across the state. It would be an early win and establish our credibility.

The head of the SHI readily agreed to meet us. He came in a few minutes late, a handsome man, solidly built, with clean-cut looks. With hair swept back in a puff, he looked much like a hero from the black-and-white Hindi films of the 1950s. He took our cards, reading each one carefully and scanning that person's face. When my turn came he made no eye contact and said 'Sir', politely.

Piyush Mehra presented a set of slides, explaining what changes could be made to the ANM's registers to free up her time. He explained how we had developed this design with inputs from the health workers. The Ghost heard us out without any questions. Then he said, in Hindi, 'We are already doing all this.' I was taken aback. He added, 'We have completely redesigned the ASHA's register. Have you seen it?' He was looking straight ahead at the screen. He went into a long discourse on the ASHA's registers.

We learnt only later that he had personally championed that project. We had not done our homework. We should have started by acknowledging his work—we had not, and that would have rankled. I realized we had made a mistake.

But it was also frustrating. We were focused on the ANM, who had the most crucial and complex job. The ASHA was a different type of health worker, and her registers were not as complex. I tried pointing this out, but he shut down the discussion, saying, 'Let us see, we can discuss further [another time].'

On the positive side, the Ghost had a sharp mind and was passionate about his subject. He had spent a lot of time in the field. That made me optimistic that we could work with him. I had no doubt we would turn the ANM registers idea into something tangible.[6]

The Ghost had a boss—the Son, in the trinity. Almost everything to do with the wellness of the people of Rajasthan fell under his charge. Every decision by the Ghost would need to be ratified by him.

We secured a meeting with the Son. It had been three months since we started work and we were excited about the progress the team had made on many fronts. We had come prepared with a formal briefing. It was the lunch hour and there was already a small crowd in the waiting room outside the Son's office. All the seats were taken and some people stood along the walls. The assistant was gracious, 'Sir is still out for lunch. Please take a seat inside his room, he should be here shortly. Yours is the first appointment.'

We thanked him, went inside and settled down on a sofa. The Son came in ten minutes later. He took one look at us and said, 'I don't like anyone sitting in my room during my lunch hour.' We said that was where we had been asked to sit and he looked back at us blandly. We apologized and stepped out to join the people standing along the walls of the waiting room. Ten minutes later, we were ushered in to meet the Son.

I started to tell him about our activities and plans. He interrupted me with, 'We are doing all these things.' The Ghost had used the same blocking move when we had met him some weeks previously. But while the Ghost had been polite, the Son seemed angry. We had come all the way from Delhi for this one meeting. I took a deep breath. Then I said quietly, 'No sir, you are not doing many of these things. That is why . . .'

The phone rang. The Son went into a long chat with a lot of banter and some tittering. I waited patiently because I wanted to finish my sentence. I assumed I would have that chance because tea and biscuits had not been brought in yet and this is the usual courtesy with visitors. But when the call ended, the Son said, 'I have a few more calls to take now . . .' Astonished, I realized that our meeting was over.

As we stepped out of the Secretariat building, I said to Piyush, 'Well, I don't know about you, but that's the first time I've been thrown out of someone's office and had a the and a half-sentence meeting.' We laughed it off, but something was amiss.

~

On the way back to the airport, I thought about the difference between Jaipur and Jhalawar. Jaipur was where we went to plead, persuade, negotiate and complain. There, we dealt with big egos, trod the corridors of power. We began to understand the politics of the IAS system, their attitude towards outsiders, the tensions between departments and between people. We saw the give-and-take between the political system and the bureaucracy. It is where we learnt to play the game.

We began to understand that the chain of command of the government health system is a long one. It begins in the villages of Jhalawar and ends at the office of the chief minister in distant Jaipur. It would seem the chain is governed through a strict hierarchy, but that is not the full picture. We realized that any person in the chain could subtly stall and sometimes even stop, a directive that came from many levels above—even from the chief minister. Everything was connected and every person had influence. Perforce, we had to build good working relationships with people, high and low, at every link in the chain, to get our work done.

These people played different roles. We worked with some of them every day and we thought of them as partners. When we needed permissions, we went to the gatekeepers. We also had to contend with the blockers who created problems for us, as well as the sleepers, who chose to do nothing. And we always searched for guardian angels for protection.

People moved on. Just as we had established a relationship, that person could be replaced—at its worst, an angel by a blocker. That is why we always tried to find out how much time was left before someone was due for promotion or retirement. Sometimes, the government system felt like a jungle and finding our way through it was draining. Yes, there was a lord of the jungle and we had her blessing, but gods don't fight daily battles for anyone.

There was always an undercurrent of tension when we entered the hallowed Secretariat building in Jaipur. Indeed, my mood would be low even as I woke up in Delhi, knowing I would soon be on the early morning flight to Jaipur. When the team left by the night train for Jhalawar, however, the sense of camaraderie always made me feel better. We would gather at Comesum, the popular eatery at Nizamuddin station, before the train left. We regaled ourselves with the latest tales, wicked but never mean, hugely exaggerated, about some unfortunate colleague. We recalled incidents such as when we had hidden a colleague from the ticket collector, because he had gotten his ticket at the last minute and was travelling under an assumed name, age and gender. And there would be the friendly banter about who would get the upper, lower and side berths. Our spirits always lifted when we stepped off the train in Ramganjmandi and began that scenic drive to Jhalawar, breathing pure air, meeting real people.

~

Most states have someone who takes care of everything the government must deal with, at the highest level. In Rajasthan, he was the person we call the Father, an IAS officer in his early forties. Though only a mid-level officer in the Service, he was treated with deference by all Secretaries and Ministers. The Father came from a middle-lass family in a small town in Jharkhand and had studied at the prestigious Birla Institute of Technology. It was said that he knew everything about everyone. When the Father called, they all came running.

After meeting the lukewarm Ghost and simmering Son, I urgently needed to build an equation with the Father. He knew how important Akshada was to the chief minister and for that reason, I assumed we would have his support. I asked for an appointment. He explained that in Jaipur, his calendar was always full and his schedule so unpredictable that it was difficult to fix a dependable date and time. He suggested that we meet in Jhalawar since things were not so chaotic there—he would be visiting the district in a couple of weeks.

Piyush, Neeraj and I reached Jhalawar as usual by the Inter-City Express on the appointed day. I called Vishnu Prasad Tulsi at 8 a.m. He seemed wired up, speaking quickly, emitting a nervous giggle from time to time—not the polished collector I had met before. He asked if I would come over in an hour to the Circuit House, where the Father was staying. Ten minutes later he called back, saying he was about to hand the phone to the Father himself. I imagined him wiping the mouthpiece before handing it over.

The Father was about to set off for the field. He said he would be happy to meet in the evening if it was all right by me, adding that it might get late. I assured him that it was all right. I spent the day with the team visiting two of our programme sites in the Manoharthana block. I didn't venture too deep into the field in case the Father became available earlier. After dinner at the Krishna Hotel, I told Neeraj and Piyush that I would let them know as soon as I got a message. I set off on a walk to clear my head, turning left on the main road that runs by the Krishna. On my way back, Vishnu called, sounding exhausted. He said, 'Sir reached back only at 9.30 p.m. After dinner, he was tired and retired to his room. Can you come in the morning?'

The next morning, there was a motley crowd outside the Circuit House. Local journalists, sundry supplicants and general hangers-on milled around the lawns. An enterprising *chaiwallah*[*] did brisk business. The crowd was blocking our way to the entrance and a police constable with an intimidating look came up. Before he could say anything, I looked him in the eye and told him of our appointment. Immediately, he cried out, 'Sir ji! Sir ji!' The crowd parted and I stepped into the passage that had been cleared, followed by Neeraj and Piyush. We came into a small room occupied by a dozen men, clearly local politicians, judging from their crisp white kurta-pyjamas.

A long table on the side was laden with every manner of breakfast item, spanning the length and breadth of India. There were masala omelettes, dosas, vadas and idli, dhokla-khandvi, poha, poori-bhaji and parathas. The 'Madrasi' dosa normally would have looked with disdain at the Punjabi paratha—the

---

[*] Tea vendor.

vegetarian dhokla shudder to be seen with an omelette. Now—
the ignominy of it—they found themselves rubbing shoulders on
a politician's plate! Those men had unfeelingly heaped their plates
with everything. They ate slowly and silently, eyes fixed on their
plates. Some more men were pressed against the wall, staring at
two individuals who were seated on a sofa on the far side, also
eating breakfast, but not with the same intensity of purpose.

One was my old friend, the Son. He looked up at me, made no
acknowledgement and got back to eating. The other man, stocky
and with a handlebar moustache, was the Father. He looked up
and said the word, 'Come.' It was impossible to move forward
because the room was too crowded, so I said from a distance, 'It's
good to meet you for the first time.' The Father replied dryly, 'I
have met you several times at CMO* but you don't remember.'
There was an edge to his voice. Now I recalled that he had been
in the audience in the kick-off meeting and in the background in
one of my previous meetings with the chief minister.

Someone managed to squeeze a chair in for me. I sat down,
telling the Father that I was happy to wait. I noticed an elderly
person, grey-haired and distinguished, standing right behind me.
Someone introduced him, in a whisper, as a professor at Jhalawar
Medical College. I got up, offering my seat, which he declined with
a smile. At that moment, the Father said the word 'Cornflakes'.
The professor quickly stepped forward, stooped to pick up a bowl
of cereal from the coffee table, added warm milk to it and went up
and offered it to the Father, who waved him away.

At one point, another IAS officer came into the room. He was
clearly the Father's senior in the Service, and the Father struggled
to get up as the sofa was soft and deep. Protocol demanded a
public show of deference to a senior. He said without enthusiasm,

---

* Chief Minister's Office.

'Sir, please sit here, sir.' The senior sat down on the other side of the Father. Meanwhile, Vishnu was fluttering around in the background, excited, giving orders to anyone who came close to him. He smiled wanly at me from across the room.

As breakfast was cleared away, the Father again said the word—'Come.' We pulled up chairs near him. I opened my laptop, placed it on the small table between us and turned it towards him as I walked him through the slides. We explained why it was crucial that the frontline workers have reliable data and that they share it. I told him how the AAA platform innovation was gaining momentum.

The Father was totally focused on the slides, tiny eyes glinting. His brow furrowed as he absorbed everything, asking a few questions. I was impressed by his quickness and I sensed that he was impressed by what he was seeing. In the end, I asked if we could review this material with the chief minister and get her advice. I wanted to convey that we recognized that he was the gatekeeper. He said, 'Ultimately, there should be a tablet that integrates all the data and the workers are always connected. Till then, there would not be enough to show to Honourable CM.'

The state of Rajasthan did not even provide simple logbooks to its health workers. Lives were lost because workers wrote in rows of perfect health records. We had shown why good record-keeping and sharing of that data was the crux. And here was an IAS officer, telling me that nothing short of an advanced digital solution would do for Rajasthan.

The Father had an engineering degree and was one of 200 selected from a million, for the IAS. He had been brought up in a small town and come this far, and I admired him for that. With all his achievements, his ego should have been rock-solid—but clearly, he felt slighted. I had rubbed him the wrong way because I had not recognized his importance till then. I had come and gone from the CMO on many occasions, hobnobbed with his boss and never said so much as a hello to him. Now he would show me who really ran the show.

I saw how I had made another mistake. I knew I could probably meet Vasundhara Raje with or without the Father. But it would be wise not to antagonize him and I played the game. I told him we had already started work on a tablet solution and that we would keep him posted and seek his inputs.

The Father stood up. Everyone else in the room jumped up at the same time. They all trooped out, the Father in the front with two people on each side as he shot instructions at them as they walked. The two on his left were no doubt his staff, because they each had a small writing pad and pencil in hand. One was scribbling quickly and I figured he was the more junior, because the other one only jotted a few things down. The two on the other side looked like they wanted something—they were important enough to have got the space next to the Father's right elbow. A few more people in need followed just behind, waiting for their turn to claim the right elbow.

Behind them, bringing up the rear, was the Son, with a single scribbler at his left elbow. I got a feeling that the Son was not really needed on this trip but had been summoned. As he followed in tow, it was obvious to everyone who called the shots.

Meanwhile, Vishnu was fluttering all over the place. The Father, Son and one of the scribblers climbed into the collector's official vehicle, which already had the flashing blue light swirling on the bonnet. Vishnu came running and saw that he had lost his seat in his own car. He quickly went around and opened the door to the back of the SUV. He instinctively moved to get in and then saw an armed security guard sitting there. He quickly realized that it would be unseemly for him to be seated at the back next to the guard, as though he were a prisoner. He called out urgently for another car and drove away in hot pursuit of the Father and the Son.

~

The duo had to be in Baran, an adjacent district, by evening. They had agreed to visit one of our programme sites on the way, for half an hour, sometime between 2 and 4. We wanted the Father and the Son to see our work in the field and carry away a good impression. We hoped they would say some words of appreciation and motivate the women.

The meeting was in the panchayat building of a small village called Rojpur[7] in Jhalarapatnam block. The meeting hall was empty except for ten chairs that had been placed in a row for the visitors. The floor was covered with red and green striped anganwadi *daris*.* Twelve women were seated on the daris, wearing pink, blue and white saris. They were AWWs, ASHAs and ANMs from Rojpur and adjacent villages. The women had been given the day off from their normal duties and told to report at the panchayat office in the morning to prepare for the meeting.

The women had mounted five laminated hand-drawn maps on one wall. Each map was drawn as close to scale as possible. Every lane, house, temple, school, well, handpump, pond and major tree was represented in its rightful place. Colour-coded bindis were pasted on dwellings with pregnant women, newborns and older children. Each of the healthcare workers carried a *jhola*† that held her registers and notebooks. These preparations took them half an hour. Then the women began the wait for the

* Carpets.
† Bag.

important visitors from Jaipur, to whom they would explain their maps and registers.

My colleagues Paras Nath Sidh and Damini Nenavati worked every day with the women in these villages. Now they sat with them, chatting and laughing. I took Damini aside to ask if the women were nervous. She said, 'Not really. They know their work and can explain it confidently. Only, they are a little frustrated that they were called here so early. The ANMs have urgent cases they are neglecting by spending the day in this empty room.'

A man came in carrying lunch packets of two samosas, a barfi and a banana. Hot tea was served in glasses. Paras went to find out how much longer it would take the Father's team to reach Rojpur. He came back, 'They are saying less than half an hour.' This happened a few times and the message was the same each time: they are nearby, only twenty minutes. It was approaching four and the women were getting restless. They had been told the meeting would end by then. It would take them an hour or more to get back. They had responsibilities at home—a sick child or an ailing mother-in-law, household chores, the evening meal.

I was irritated and called Vishnu. I said that a few women had no choice but to leave because of household exigencies. Vishnu pleaded, 'Please make sure they are all there. It is my personal request.' I asked him to give me a reliable estimate of when they would arrive, and he said it would be no later than 5.30 p.m. I went back in and told the women. They didn't look surprised. They knew that even if it was six, eight or midnight, they would have to wait—leaving was not an option. It seemed like they had been through such experiences before.

Suddenly, an official burst in—the additional district magistrate, no less. He had arrived along with the samosas and must have heard me announcing the delay. Now he too was frustrated. He shouted at an ASHA worker, 'You! Why aren't you in uniform?' The ASHA wasn't intimidated and said nothing. He then shouted at no one in particular, asking why there was no dais. He ordered that a makeshift dais be quickly created so that the visitors could be given the right respect. I was also getting testy and said sharply, 'There will be no dais because this is not a ceremony.' He took one look at me and stormed off. Some of the women suppressed smiles.

At 5.30 p.m., there was a commotion outside. Four vehicles were slowly coming down the narrow village road towards the panchayat centre. The SUV in front had a whirling blue light on its bonnet. The last vehicle was a police jeep. A gaggle of urchins ran alongside the cars, laughing and shouting. Men on the roads stopped and stared. The cars pulled up and the magistrate tried to garland everyone emerging from the SUV, but without success. He looked at those coming out of the second car, decided they were not worth garlanding, handed the flowers to an urchin and ran towards the hall. The urchins strung the garlands around their necks and ran away.

The Father, the Son, several scribblers and jotters, the magistrate, Vishnu fluttering—eight men in all—came in and took their seats. I greeted the Father and the Son and introduced my team. The Father glowered, but in a decent way. The Son nodded and looked away. I introduced the women and said they had come prepared to explain their maps and record-keeping. I suggested that the visitors ask the health workers their questions directly. The women did not look impressed—it seemed they wanted to get it over with and be on their way.

The men made no apologies for being late. They started asking questions—each query was like a cross-examination. Throughout the short meeting, the Father listened but did not speak. The Son was silent but seemed distracted. One of the scribblers asked an existential question, '*Aap yeh sab abhi karne lage to pehle kya karte the* [If you all are doing this now, what did you do earlier?]' He looked around as though for approval.

The women were primed and ready to explain their maps, in which they took pride. I politely suggested to the men that they go to the wall, see the maps and look at the registers, but they stayed stuck to their chairs. Snacks and tea were brought in for the visitors.

The scribblers asked questions aggressively. The women answered all the questions with poise. I felt ashamed of the sight of eight powerful men sitting on chairs, with twelve powerless women who saved lives for a living, sitting at the level of their feet.

At one point the magistrate woke up from a reverie and asked who among the women had a toilet in their home. The women were embarrassed by the question and no hand went up. A scribbler repeated the question—again, no response. A jotter picked one woman and asked her why she didn't have a toilet—the woman stayed silent. He told her that if she didn't have a toilet, she should build one—just take the money from the government fund, the collector sa'ab will sanction. The woman looked up and said, hesitantly, that she had a small child at home and a house to run—how could she build a toilet? Another jotter was getting ready to fire a salvo at her when one of the ANMs said quickly, '*Inko mushkil hai, inka aadmi shaant ho gaya hai* [It's difficult for her—her man has passed away].'

Soon after that, the men all got up and rushed off, for they were late. We said our goodbyes and just made the nine o'clock flight back to Delhi. The women went home in a hurry.

～

A few weeks later, I met chief secretary S.K. Shankar again. He asked how my first six months had been. I told him the best part was working with the community and with the AAA workers. I expressed my optimism and my excitement. He asked if I had been facing any problems, and I told him about the lack of welcome, and the indifference that had come across from the IAS officers. I related the incident when we had been thrown out by the Son. I was laughing, because with the passage of time, I found it quite hilarious.

I described the meeting with the health workers and asked if these officials understood that they had taken an oath to serve and not browbeat, the community. Shankar kept shaking his head as he stared out of the window.

He said, 'I find this very upsetting. This is not the way it's meant to be.' I almost consoled him.

10

Where Rabbits Weep

In the poorest villages, it seemed as though calamity was always just around the corner. A pregnant woman with sepsis, a newborn with acute diarrhoea or a small child burning with malaria. Or any other everyday emergency that could have been easily prevented if only someone had intervened.

Yes, of course, each person on the TAF team understood that the mission of public health is the health of the community. They knew that if you tried to save every sick person, you will never get to serve the larger community. They had been told that they should bring dire cases to the notice of the authorities and move on. But what do you do when the authorities bring dire cases to you?

That was what happened with a tiny four-year-old girl named Dhara.[1]

~

Ashutosh Gautam was sure when he turned twenty-one that he wanted 'to do a lot for my country'. In his mind, that meant joining the army, but he didn't make it through the qualifying examination. Disheartened, he decided on a degree in pharmaceutical management in his hometown, Jaipur. Afterwards, he joined a multinational pharma company as an insulin salesman. He had no problem meeting targets, for he had a way with people. But when he saw that many salespersons bribed doctors to prescribe their company's products, he was upset. He had joined the company with the notion that he would be helping save lives, and he felt disillusioned. He quit, joined another pharma major, and quit again.

In 2016, Ashutosh heard that an NGO called TAF had started working with mothers and children in the villages of Rajasthan. He applied, and we were struck by his altruism and by how keen he was to work with us. Soon, at the age of twenty-six, he was a programme officer, responsible for a block called Dag in Jhalawar district, working to ensure the good health of more than 2,00,000 people living in 261 villages. It was a huge task and he felt a sense of purpose, finally enjoying his job.

Dag was one of the poorest blocks in Jhalawar, located in the far south-east of the district. It had none of the scenic beauty or character that we experienced in other parts of Jhalawar. Dry and scrubby, Dag looked like a wasteland. The villages were sad clusters of creaking thatched-roof shacks, standing on wooden poles held together with rope and patches of blue tarpaulin.

Ashutosh had a junior colleague, Priya Bansal, who had recently qualified as an Ayurvedic doctor. The two had taken rooms in Jhalawar town, and each morning, they set out for the villages of Dag. Today, a state highway links Jhalawar to Dag. That road was still under construction in 2016, and it took Ashutosh and Priya more than three hours to travel the 130-kilometre distance using the country road. Their routine was to visit at least two villages every day, checking on TAF's work with the health workers and local communities.

Their destination that day was a village called Unhel, located close to the border with Madhya Pradesh. As they approached the Dag boundary, the two saw thick dark clouds gathering ahead. Twenty kilometres from Unhel, the weather deteriorated. The light faded quickly, and a brisk wind picked up. Birds called out warnings.

The driver said: 'This is strange. Dag gets little rain even during the monsoon season.' Suddenly, loud claps of thunder boomed overhead. Flashes of lightning silvered the barren land. The rain came down in anger, first large drops, loud against the roof, and then a torrent. The wind howled and came at the rugged Innova with force. The wipers struggled. The driver feared that they would be ripped off, and then they would be driving blind. He switched them on for only a few seconds at a time. He scrubbed a rag against the inside of the windshield as it kept fogging up. At one point, it felt like they might be swept off the road. The driver shouted: 'We can't go on like this. There is a village ahead.'

It was mid-morning now, but still dark. They inched their way towards the dimly visible lights of the village. A board said this was a village called Dhunai,[2] population, 780. There was a tea shop on the outskirts of the village, and they tumbled out of the car to get hot glasses of country tea. As they sat down, the thunder, lightning, rain and wind ceased, as if to a director's cue.

Just across the road, they saw the village AWC. There was a small group of women with babies at the entrance. Ashutosh and Priya found that it was the VHND, when the ANM would be visiting this village. The two walked across the road to investigate.

They looked into the ANM's office and saw a small woman delivering a vaccine to a baby who was bawling his lungs out. They were surprised to see that it was someone they knew— Sister Sumitra. Till recently, she had been the ANM for a set of villages that were covered by our programme. Then she had been transferred and they had lost touch with her.

Sumitra looked up and her face broke into a big smile. She called out over the baby's yowling: '*Bhaiyya*,* please don't leave. Wait till I finish.' She completed her work, washed her hands and put away her kit. Then the nurse got straight to the point: 'There is something I want you to see.'

They stepped out. The air had that slightest of chills and that distinctive petrichor that comes after rain in the Indian summer. They wound their way through narrow lanes. People respectfully greeted Sister Sumitra in her white sari uniform as she walked by.

~

They arrived at a hut. The roof was made up of chipped tiles, broken bricks and patches of corrugated sheet. On it was a tire, some empty bottles, a plastic jerry can and part of a baby carriage. The base structure was made of mud, with a small, covered veranda, and beyond that, a dark room. A few aluminium vessels stood next to a tap in the rubble in front of the house. There was soapy water in the pans and the tap was still dripping.

Sumitra called out: '*Dadima!*† *O dadi! Hum aapse milne aaye hain. Chhoti bachchi se milne ko* [Grandma! We have come to meet you—and the little girl]!' There was no response from inside. This went on for a while. Then Sumitra changed her tone: 'You need to come out right now! I have some high-up people [*bade log*] with me.'

After a few minutes, a voice called from inside, in the local dialect, that they should leave quickly and that she did not

---

* Brother (usually used as term of respect).
† Paternal grandmother.

care who they were. Sumitra shouted back, also in dialect, and
Ashutosh and Priya caught snatches of a few words: 'Your first
granddaughter . . . allowed to die . . . this one too . . .?' Thus far,
the whole sequence of events had been confusing, but these words
had a chilling effect on them.

The door opened and a rangy woman with tousled white hair
stepped out. She said: 'I am not scared of you. I will not show you
the child.' Sumitra brushed past her. They stepped into the dark
room. There was a baby boy, nine months old, crawling on a mat.
He stared curiously at the newcomers.

Sumitra shouted at the dadi: 'It is his elder sister, Dhara,[3]
we want. Where is she?' Then she saw a tiny girl sitting in a dark
corner, legs like two sticks splayed out in front of her. The dadi
came and swept her up, wrapping her in a piece of cloth. She
knew by now that some serious business was afoot.

The child's eyes protruded from their sockets and looked
dully at the people around her. She had almost no hair, and her
head looked too big for her tiny body. Her veins stood out on a
scrawny neck. The nurse took the baby and lifted her shirt. The
ribs stood out, skin stretched like parchment. Her forearms could
be encircled by two fingers. There was no question of the child
being able to stand up on her own.

Ashutosh described his first sight of Dhara: 'A living skeleton,
sitting with a dry piece of roti she could not chew in her hand.' He
was speechless—Priya turned away in shock. The nurse shouted:
'She's four years old, and only bones! I have never seen anything
like this in my life. What have you done to her?'

The dadi looked down: 'What can I do if she doesn't
eat anything?'

The nurse was enraged: 'The whole village knows that you
killed Dhara's older sister by starving her. And now you are doing
the same with this child. All this because she is a girl?'

'It is a lie. No one was killed. She would not drink milk, things happened suddenly. People will say anything. But it is true, I come from a family of four boys. That is the kind of family I am used to.' There was a trace of pride in the way she said this.

'Dadi, open your ears and listen. Now we will call the police and they will take you to jail. We will take Dhara to the hospital. But first, where is the child's mother? Bring her.'

'No, please. I will save her, here at home. The child's mother is in the fields, working.'

'Then go and get the mother immediately! We will take the child and her brother to the anganwadi. Come there quickly!'

At the anganwadi, Sumitra weighed a baby boy who was at the centre, and then Dhara. She turned to Ashutosh and Priya, shaking her head: 'The boy is nine months old and weighs 6 kilos. The girl is three years and nine months old and weighs only 4 kilos!' She was on the verge of tears.

The Block Chief Medical Officer (BCMO) arrived. He was the doctor incharge of health for the 150 villages in Dag. Ashutosh had called him and insisted that he come immediately as there was an emergency. The BCMO examined Dhara and said the same words: 'I have never seen anything like this in my life. This child will die within a week. It is too late to save her.'

Now the dadi was back, and with her a thin young woman who had her face covered. It was Dhara's mother, Revati.[4] She was crying, for she had heard the doctor's last words—her child was dying. Priya took her aside. The mother was sobbing: '*Meri bachchi ko bachaiye . . . bachaiye* [Save my baby . . . save her, please].' Her words came out haltingly: 'She never let me help Dhara. The first one was made to die . . . and I could do nothing . . . I don't want to lose this one also . . . save her, please save her!'

Revati was a daily wage-based unskilled worker and had no choice but to leave her children at home with their grandmother.

Her husband was away most of the time, searching for work in other states, coming back to the village only once a year.

The BCMO said, 'You have to take the baby immediately to the Nutrition Rehabilitation Centre [NRC] in Dag.' He was referring to the specialized facility that handled cases of severe malnutrition. Ashutosh stepped in: 'This is an emergency. The facility in Dag will not be able to handle this case. We are leaving right away for the main NRC in Jhalawar. Priya and I will get Dhara admitted.'

Sumitra said, 'The NRC will admit Dhara only if there is someone to stay with her. The treatment may take weeks. Revati must work, and there is the other child to look after as well. The only way is for dadi to go. Otherwise, we should send her to jail right away.'

She was trying to put fear into the old woman, and it worked. Every time the word 'police' was mentioned, it had a palpable effect on the dadi. She pleaded with folded hands: 'Sir, do not take the child, I will take care of her. She will be healthy. You will see.'

Sumitra retorted: '*Bilkul nahin* [Absolutely not]. Quickly go back home and get whatever you need. You will be gone for a long time.'

~

The NRC in Jhalawar is an unsung centre of excellence. Over several visits, I had come to appreciate the cleanliness, dedicated staff and excellent record-keeping I saw there. I first visited the facility a few months before we began our programme in Rajasthan. It was a recce trip and I was accompanied by Arjun Malhotra, an Indian–American based in the bay area in the US and one of our major donors.

The NRC is located inside Jhalawar Medical Centre, a government teaching hospital in the centre of town. The main entrance leads into an enormous hall. There are always crowds of patients and their families waiting here. Most come from the villages, without an appointment, prepared to wait for days, if necessary.

The centre is on the third floor—we climbed up paan-stained stairs, stopping to catch our breath before going in. A guard told us to remove our shoes and put on the worn-out rubber slippers that he produced. The medical attendant incharge took us to see the kitchen. This is where a nutrient-rich porridge is carefully prepared every day to standards prescribed by the World Health Organization (WHO). The attendant rarely had visitors, and eagerly explained to us that the porridge was a mix of cow's milk, sugar, cereal flour and puffed rice in exact proportions, and that children loved the taste. Each child's weight was monitored carefully and the feed adjusted daily.

The dormitory is close to the kitchen. There are twenty beds, ten on each side, separated by a few feet from each other. Eight of the beds were occupied when we had visited. With the high levels of malnourishment, every bed should have been taken, but the mothers were too busy working and taking care of their homes. The walls were painted in bright colours with cartoon characters, probably as prescribed by the international agency that had provided the technical assistance to set up and maintain the facility. The character that appeared most often was Bugs Bunny, with his toothy smile. The guidelines for the NRC, posted on the wall outside, read: 'Provision should be made for loving care and play.'

There was an infant or small child, thin or emaciated, lying on each bed. Some were getting a drip through a catheter taped to their tiny arms. Each had a mother or grandmother who sat by the bed. There was a hushed silence. I softly asked some of the women how their baby had fallen sick. They all said the same thing, voices drifting away: '*Pata nahin kya hua* . . . [Don't know what happened].' The children stared out from their silent worlds with hollow eyes. Some seemed to be trying to comprehend the world around them.

I noticed that Arjun was missing. I went out and saw him standing a little distance away, staring out of the window, visibly shaken. I asked if he would like to come back in, but he shook his head.

I went back to the dormitory and stood at the door, looking in, trying to make some sense of this tragedy. It was a place of profound sadness, where all life seemed to have been stilled, and yet it felt like a place of hope. A question kept coming to me that had no logic—what had these babies done to deserve this? In their short lives, to have never felt the warmth of a mother's breast and never to have known laughter. It struck me that there is nothing sadder on earth than the suffering of a child. I looked around at the colourful comic characters on the walls, the wooden toys stacked on a table and the babies lost in their silent world.

And in the dead of night, surely, when all the lights were off, with darkness everywhere, the rabbits were softly weeping.

~

Ashutosh, Priya, the dadi and Dhara set off for Jhalawar. Priya cradled Dhara as though the little girl was brittle. They wet her lips with water regularly and counted the kilometres, praying that she would survive the journey. The dadi kept muttering something to herself for most of the drive. As they entered the town, she was silent, her eyes glued to the window. She couldn't get enough of the typical sights and scenes and the ordinary noise and bustle of a district headquarters.

They took Dhara up to the NRC. The medical attendant was speechless, then gasped out the same words that everyone else had said when they first saw Dhara: 'I have never seen anything like this in my life . . .' The nurse on duty examined the child. She shook her head, saying only the doctor could say what to do with Dhara. The attendant rushed out to find him. The nurse put Dhara down gently on a far bed. The doctor swept in. He was young, but such is the caseload in rural hospitals that he would have seen thousands of severely malnourished children in his short career.

He examined Dhara for a few minutes and said, 'We will have to do a lot of tests to see if her organs are functioning. Unfortunately, it looks to me like this child will not survive.' It was difficult to find a vein on Dhara's body to draw blood for testing, but the nurse was skilled. Giving her solid nutrients was out of the question, so she had to be fed intravenously. This time, it was impossible to find a big enough vein, so they inserted a feeding tube through her nostril. Dhara's eyes shot left and right. The next day, the test results came in. The doctor said, 'It is a miracle, but all her organs are functioning. We will do our best to save this child.'

The staff at the Jhalawar NRC were caring people. But there was another factor at work. If Dhara died at the NRC, there would have to be a full enquiry by the government. Some officials would be in trouble. Everyone was, therefore, suddenly interested in Dhara's well-being.

~

Dadi was confused when she woke up the next morning, Dhara at her side. Yesterday, there had been the car drive from Dhunai to Jhalawar, with all the new sights and sounds. The well-lit dormitory, brightly painted walls, the other babies, mothers, other grannies, the nurses, doctors, and attendants, going in and out, paying so much attention to Dhara—all left her dazed. At one point, the doctor asked dadi what she fed Dhara. He had his pad ready to jot down notes and create a case history. She said hesitantly, evading his eyes: 'We gave food . . . but she never ate . . .' He asked, 'What was the food?' Silence. He closed his pad and left.

The mothers and grandmothers in the dormitory had developed a certain solidarity sharing their misfortunes, sympathizing with each other. One by one, they came to see the new patient. That was the custom whenever a new child came to the NRC, for there was a lot of curiosity. They all said the same thing when they saw Dhara, '*He Ram, yeh kya hua* [Dear God, what has happened here]?' Then that changed to '*Yeh kaise hua* [How did this happen]?' and soon, '*Tumne kya kiya is bachchi ko* [What did you do to this child]?' No one hesitated to cast the first stone.

Ashutosh visited the NRC regularly and he could sense the tension among the women. It appeared to him that dadi felt ashamed at the scrutiny and that she was isolated in facing the queries. At the same time, she was comfortable—she had access to running water and a shower, a hundred rupees and two meals each day from the government. It was a level of abundance she could never have imagined. There was a kindness in the air, and it made her think.

Meanwhile, Dhara was fighting her way back. Her weight, when measured in the AWC in her village, had been exactly 4 kilos. She was severely stunted, just 2 feet and 5 inches tall.[5] The protocol was that a child had to gain at least 15 per cent in body weight and be in sound health in order to be discharged from the centre. Dhara's target weight was set at 5.25 kilos, a

30 per cent increase over what it was when she arrived. It all depended on how readily her system would allow her to process the nutrition-rich special food that was cooked in the kitchen.

~

For the first three days, the nurse, medical attendant and doctor focused on 'stabilizing' Dhara. Very carefully, they introduced her to the nutrient- and energy-rich food that they prepared in the kitchen, a half teaspoon to begin with. This was what they called the 'starter formula'. The little girl was not used to swallowing food, and it took time to wean her away from the feeding tube that went in through her nostrils.

Then they replaced the starter formula with the 'catch-up diet'. That had the same ingredients but more calories and protein. They increased the amount by 10 ml with each meal, until some amount of food was left uneaten. Then they increased the number of feeds steadily, till Dhara was taking eight feeds a day. After this, they introduced soft foods of the kind that should be given at home—dal, boiled vegetables and curd. Eventually, she ate only these foods, and they encouraged her to eat as much as she could take in. It was a carefully managed protocol.

Dhara had a good appetite, and seven days after she had been admitted, she weighed in at 5.1 kilos. By day twelve, Dhara had reached her target. That was two days sooner than the fourteen-day norm set for a 'normal' SAM child to recover. Some children take three to four weeks to get to their target. The staff were overjoyed and for the first time in two weeks, dadi smiled. Dhara was discharged on day fourteen at a weight of 5.6 kilos.

The NRC had saved Dhara's life and put her on the road to recovery, but the real challenge would begin now. To put this in perspective, we need to consider that a girl of four should normally weigh 14 kilos—Dhara's weight was less than half of that. Now she needed to go back to her home environment and gain weight there. The guidelines of the NRC say: 'Before being discharged from the facility, the child must become accustomed to eating family meals' (but what if the family ate only one meagre meal a day?). It further added: 'Ensure that the parent/caregiver understands the causes of malnutrition and how to prevent its recurrence' (but what if the caregiver was knowingly starving the child?).

Ashutosh and Priya were hopeful, if only because Dhara was now on the radar of the local officials, high and low, in the health system. The manual required that the ANM, ASHA and AWW pay close attention to her case. They would be personally responsible for Dhara reaching normal weight. She had to be brought back to the NRC after two months for a full check-up.

Dhara went back to her village with her dadi, and Ashutosh got busy with his regular work. In the weeks that followed, his thoughts frequently returned to the little child. He dreaded the answer he might get if he asked how Dhara was doing. Three months went by, and then he called Sumitra, his heart beating faster: 'Dhara *kaisi hai*?'

~

In 2021, four years later, with Ashutosh's help, I tracked Sister Sumitra down in Ajmer. She had been transferred there a couple of years after the Dhara episode. The nurse had stayed in touch with the child and her family after she left Dag.

It was the middle of the COVID-19 lockdown of 2021, and I interviewed Sumitra on Zoom at her home. She is a pleasant woman with a round face, given to laughter. There was a commotion in the background and a little boy showed up a few times behind his mother, peered at my image on screen and ran away.

She said, 'I was born in a middle-class family. My father always wanted me to get a proper education. In 2005, I got my degree in nursing from Jhalawar Medical College, and in 2009, I joined government service as an ANM. It was a big responsibility. I was married with two children, a boy and a girl, ages two and seven. My husband was recovering from a heart operation and he was in bed for many months. His mother stayed with us. So I had to look after the whole family.'

I asked her to describe what a typical day was like for her in those days.

She replied, 'I woke up at 5 a.m. I bathed and got ready, and then did *jhadoo-pochha*,* made *nashta*.† Woke up the children, washed them, got the older one ready for school. Saw to my husband and *saas*‡ and served nashta. At 8 a.m., my son left for school and I left for work. First, I went to the sub-centre and saw patients till 10 a.m. I was responsible for five villages. So, from the sub-centre, I would go to the first village, which is Dhara's village, Dhunai.'

I asked: 'How did you get there?'

'It's close by, I walked.'

'How far is it?'

'No more than one kilometre.'

Ashutosh, who had been listening silently, interjected softly: 'Sumitra ji walked everywhere. The villages are spread out 5, even 7, kilometres apart. She carried all her medical equipment and walked.'

---

* Sweeping and mopping.
† Snacks.
‡ Mother-in-law.

Sumitra said, laughing, 'It was not so hard as bhaiyya says. Someone or the other who was passing by would say, "Sister, you shouldn't walk; let me take you there." This way there was no problem.' Ashutosh just shook his head, smiling.

I asked her about Dhara.

She said: 'In this village, I saw from my records that one child was not being brought to the anganwadi. So I went to that house. Dhara was malnourished then, but not the way we saw her later. I told the dadi that she needed to bring her to get the mid-day meal and play with other children. She said there was no need. Then it started—I would meet her and tell her, and still she never sent the child, who became thinner and thinner. I told the supervisor, who also spoke to her, but nothing happened. No one saw the child but everyone suspected that things were getting worse, because the first girl had died. One day I even pleaded with her, "We are both women. Dhara is like us. She will grow up and be of help to you in the house." Nothing worked.'

Sumitra continued, 'After they returned from the NRC, dadi first acted angry with me, saying look what all you put me through and so on. But there was something different about her. She brought Dhara to the anganwadi regularly. She never said a word about what had changed in her, but something happened at the treatment centre. Two weeks after she came back, Dhara stood up for the first time. Three months later, she spoke her first word, "Ma". Dhara's mother cried.'

She went on, 'Then Dhara started joining the other children in the class. She was very shy, then slowly she started to play with the others. She began to say a few words. But sometimes, she becomes very quiet and keeps looking far away. She is a little slower than the others, but she is recovering. She has been through a lot. The anganwadi *behen** tells me all this because I call her regularly.'

---

* Sister.

I ask why, when she sees so many malnourished children, Sumitra continues to follow Dhara's progress, even after she has left the district and two years have passed. She laughs and says, 'Sir, there are so, so many serious cases, but Dhara was very special.'

There are pictures of Dhara in Ashutosh's records. First, the 'living skeleton' they found that fateful day wearing a red T-shirt coming down to her ankles. She sits on the mud floor, looking up with big protruding eyes, frightened and confused. One taken three months after she came home. She has gained weight, but looks no more than three years old, because she has been stunted by malnutrition. Another, taken a year later, where she is with her mother, who is combing her hair. Dhara is smiling uncertainly into the camera. And a photo taken two years after this, when Dhara is six. She is wearing a yellow frock, her eyes have kajal, and her hair is oiled and brushed. She looks like any other child her age.

~

Dhara is not the only case of dire neglect that my teammates came across. Years later, I had my own close encounter, which I relate in the opening chapter of this book. We can rarely intervene in such situations ourselves, but we always bring these children to the attention of the health authorities and we hope the best will happen, but we can never be sure.

There is a joy when we hear of cases that recover through our direct intervention, after so much damage has been done to them, body and soul, at such a tender age. That fleeting sense of joy, however, is always followed by the thought of thousands of little hungry children in unknown huts, unseen villages, as far as the eye can see and beyond.

Then we remind ourselves that this is why we are in public health to contribute to solving that larger problem.

11

Push and Pull

In India, politicians are often reviled, and it is true that many of them have worked hard and done much to achieve that reputation. Sometimes people asked me: how could you work for Vasundhara Raje? The insinuation was that she was just another callous politician. On top of that, she comes from a famous royal family. What would she know about the plight of the wretched and the poor? The fact is, we never felt we worked *for* Vasundhara. She had given us the opportunity to attend to the poorest women and children of Rajasthan, and for that we were grateful. But we always felt we served the community, never her.

Social sector programmes require the clout of government as well as the backing of the political system. In theory, the bureaucrat is obligated to implement the directive of the politician, the elected representative of the people. But there is a subtle push and pull, for the bureaucrat has control of the implementation process. They can execute well out of a sense of duty, or poorly, out of self-interest or even sheer cussedness. The politician, who seems all-powerful, needs the bureaucrat.

The outsider must know how to manoeuvre through this invisible arrangement and have a slice of luck. It was to be a steep learning curve.[1]

The health czar of Rajasthan, who we know as the Son (and met in Chapter 9) had made his displeasure apparent from our very first meeting, when he threw us out of his room.[2] It bothered me, but not unduly, for after all, we had the chief minister's backing, and we had an MoU with the state.

At that time, a well-known consulting firm was advising the government on the health system. The team leader gushed about how much they enjoyed working with the Son. So what had I done to offend him? Then it dawned on me that at the launch event for Akshada, I had talked about Rajasthan's abysmal health record. He may have taken it personally.

As time went on, the Son continued to behave as though we didn't exist. A few months later, I asked chief secretary Shankar whether he would enable an informal meeting between me and the chief minister, because I had not briefed her for a long time. As I expected, Shankar said she was bound to ask how things were going and would expect a clear answer. I explained that on principle, I didn't tell tales within the government system, as that would rebound on me. Shankar countered, dryly, that it seemed as though I had no choice.

I met the chief minister some weeks later at her official residence, which she used for many of her meetings. Shankar and I were waiting in the conference room when we heard the bustle outside that indicated that the CM had arrived. A few moments later, she looked into our room and said, 'I'm exhausted. Let's go in.' We went into a small living room that had a personal touch, with paintings and artefacts. I awaited my turn while Shankar discussed work items. She listened carefully.

After a while, she said, 'My feet are killing me,' and put her feet up on the ottoman, kicking off her sandals. There was a large diamond on the second toe of each elegant foot. They flashed, and I tried to avoid looking in that direction. I had the impression that she was aware of the effect.

I briefed her on the state of our programme. I spoke of the support we were getting at the district level and the commitment of the frontline workers. Then she asked about the Son. She may have inferred that something was amiss because I hadn't mentioned him. I told her the facts without embellishment—she said nothing, nor did she show any kind of reaction.

A few months later, the chief minister reshuffled her senior bureaucrats, but the Son stayed in place.

~

The chief minister was scheduled to visit Jhalawar in December 2015. The AAA[3] platform had gathered momentum by then, and we asked her office if we could show her how the programme worked in the field. But a few days before her visit, we were told her schedule had changed, which would not allow her to stop at the villages. We came up with a different plan: bring the AAA workers from six villages to some place that was on her route. It was decided that the meeting would happen in a government hall on the outskirts of Jhalawar town.

It was a large hall. Six maps had been mounted on its walls. Each looked like a happy scatter of bindis of different colours. In fact, they were serious public health statements, some of the bindis representing a life at risk. Each map was the result of days of copious teamwork by the health workers.

The visit of a chief minister is a huge event. Much thought goes into such details as which refreshments will be served and which flowers presented. Government functionaries, local politicians, the media and the civil society of Jhalawar began to assemble well before the scheduled time of 11 a.m.

At 10.30 a.m., I was walking up and down the walkway outside the hall when I saw the Son coming towards me with two aides. As I came up to him, I said, 'Good morning . . .', greeting him by name. He walked past as though he hadn't seen me. The stretch was such that you had to turn around to return the same way. As the Son came up again, I told him politely, but pointedly, that I had said 'good morning' a minute ago. He looked taken aback and said petulantly, 'I also said good morning.' His companions looked embarrassed. I was childishly pleased by the exchange.

People milled around the arrival area. I hung back, thinking there would be a reception line. The CM was almost two hours late. She had stopped at a dhaba along the way for tea and to chat with the locals. When word came that her arrival was imminent, people started running around frantically in all directions. Her motorcade came in, four cars with flashing lights and an ambulance.

The Son and some others greeted the CM with bouquets. Then there was chaos, everyone pressing forward. I was at the fringes. She spotted me: 'Mr Alexander!' The security people made way.

I said, 'Good morning, ma'am. The AAA workers are here, keen to tell you about their work.'

She said, 'I am looking forward to it,' and left, walking briskly, receiving bouquets all the time.

I ran ahead by the other route to get to the packed hall. Soon, the CM had taken her seat on the dais. I sat on my appointed place to her left, a minister to her right and the Son after that. To my left was a short and podgy young man in the typical politician's outfit of white kurta-pyjama. I saw the collector, pressed against one wall. The protocol is that a collector will never sit on a dais with the chief minister.

The programme began after bouquets were offered to everyone on the dais. It occurred to me that Vasundhara must handle a few thousand flowers every day. She was speaking to the minister, occasionally saying a few words to me. The man on my left was saying something to me but I missed most of it, because she was on my right and I had to be alert.

The ceremony was about to begin. I told the chief minister that the AAA workers would explain their maps. The women were nervous only to the extent that there would be a big crowd. The first ANM was inaudible because of the buzz of the crowd. The CM said, 'I'll go to them,' and stepped down from the dais. She spent a long time with each group, asking questions about the villages—she seemed to be familiar with many of them—and the process the AAA workers had followed. Excited, the women explained their maps. Their enthusiasm was not because they were talking to the head of state—it was because their work was being publicly appreciated. Now Vasundhara Raje had her arms around their shoulders.

These women worked hard for little recognition. My mind went back to that awful meeting in Jhalawar[4] when the AAA workers had tried to present their work in a public meeting to a group of senior government officials, and the latter were totally disinterested, indeed, interrogating them rudely.

While the chief minister was with the AAA workers, I turned to the person on my left. He introduced himself as Dushyant Singh, the CM's son and member of Parliament for the Jhalawar constituency. He was humble, staying away from his mother's limelight at this event and addressing me as 'sir'.

When the CM returned, it was obvious that she had enjoyed herself. I spoke in Hindi with my Devanagari script written out in

English. When I got back to my place at the dais, a large politician had occupied it and was saying something earnestly to the chief minister. The fellow had seized the opportunity and grabbed my seat. In a moment, someone came and deftly put a chair down for me to the left of the politician. The CM cut the politician short mid-sentence with a raised forefinger. Then the forefinger pointed at the seat he was occupying and said, 'Mr Alexander's seat.' The politician, as though he had expected the ejection, vacated his seat promptly and sat down on my left. He looked me up and down, smiled greasily, put his right hand to his chest and said, 'Myself . . .'

The CM was enthusiastic about the AAA platform. My sense was that she liked the wholehearted involvement of women at the frontline of health delivery. As we stepped out, the chief minister asked how the programme was going. I brought up the Skill Lab, a training facility that would greatly improve the capability of nursing staff. I explained that it would make a vital difference towards safe delivery in the district, and that it needed clearance.

She looked around and asked for someone to go and find the Son, who materialized within moments. She then asked him if he knew about 'this skill lab thing'? The Son looked flustered. She cut him off and said, with a smile, 'Please get yourself a notebook. Take a fresh page. Draw a line down the middle. On the left side, on top, write: "What Mr Alexander Needs". On the other side, write: "What Mr Alexander Gets".' She swept away. I left quietly, avoiding the Son's eyes.

~

Dushyant had some idiosyncrasies but with me, and with senior bureaucrats, he was always deferential and polite. I asked him about this once, for we had become quite familiar over time, and he said, 'Sir, in politics, humble sells.' Most Indian politicians don't seem to understand this, so he had a competitive advantage. He appreciated our work and publicly launched some of our new projects.

Our model was to work with only one programme officer for a block of 150–200 villages. In comparison, major programmes in maternal and child health had anywhere from six to over a hundred staff in a block. With fewer staff, we had to think of ways to work with and through the government—this would also instil confidence in the government functionaries that they could run the programme on their own. But it took a new programme officer at least six months to come up to speed. More staff for this start-up phase would have been useful. To some extent, necessity had forced invention on us: we did not have the funding then to add more people.

In a conversation with Dushyant, I mentioned in passing that a volunteer at the village level would give us some additional capacity and build sustainability because these people were local. He suggested that we talk to 'my man in Jhalawar', saying he was a useful person to know there. A minute later, he was speaking to his man, someone called Hasan Rahim:[5] 'You have heard of The Antara Foundation. They are doing excellent work in Jhalawar. Give them all help they need. Mr Alexander will come and see you.'

A week later, Piyush and I went to see Hasan Rahim in Jhalawar. His palatial house seemed to be made of solid granite. Jhalawar is a small town, and I had seen nothing like this there. The inside of the house also had a lot of granite—on the floors and the walls, in many colours. We weren't sure why we were there.

Rahim came in—a tall man with grey-dark hair combed back, dressed in a light blue safari suit. He took us into his office and introduced himself: 'Hasan Rahim. I'm in the granite business.' Utterly superfluous, I thought to myself, considering we were standing in a sea of granite. He took us on a short tour of his house, which seemed part factory because there was a good amount of stone lying around that had not been used in the house. It was mostly granite, though there was some marble and Kota stone as well.

We went back to Rahim's office. He got straight down to business: 'I understand you need some more people—I can get them for you.' I clarified that we were not recruiting, only looking for a few volunteers for a short period of time. He said, 'That is what I mean. How many volunteers do you need?' The conversation was gathering speed unexpectedly, and I was uncomfortable. I said perhaps two or three people to support our programme officer for a few months at the start. He said, 'No, no, no. You need much more than that. I can get you many more than that—hundreds of them in the district. I can get you thousands.' The conversation was getting out of control, and I thought it best to put brakes on it.

I told him that we didn't need so many people, that we could not afford that many staff in any case. Rahim responded, 'Sir, they will be volunteers. You need only give them a small stipend. I have all these young men, just sitting there in between elections, for five years. I don't need them all the time. This will give them something to do. They will learn something. I will have solved my problem—you would have solved your problem.'

I said that was very generous and I appreciated his concern for our work. We would think about it and get back to him. He reached out his hand and said: 'Anytime.'

In the car on the way back, Piyush and I looked at each other. I said, 'Are you thinking what I am thinking?' Piyush nodded, and we decided that was the last time we would talk to Hasan Rahim.

There was no need for Dushyant to know of the offer, and he never asked if we had met his man in Jhalawar.

~

We also developed, in parallel, the digital version of the AAA platform—the first ever such device. Through it, the three health workers and their supervisors were connected in real time. We tested it extensively and it showed excellent results. In July 2017, we got the opportunity to demonstrate the AAA app to the chief minister. A group of AAA workers showed how they used it to share information and detect high-risk cases faster, ensuring timely intervention. The chief minister immediately saw that the product could save thousands of lives and be a game-changer in public health, not only in Rajasthan but nationally. She wanted it fast-tracked, along with the AAA platform. We thought it would be easy after her endorsement.

We needed the support of five IAS officers if the app was to go forward. The key person was the Ghost (who we met in Chapter 11), the head of the SHI. Over the past two years, we had come to appreciate his genuine commitment, indeed, his passion, for the cause of mother and child. He had been wary of us at the start but had thawed as we introduced the simplified record-keeping and the AAA platform. We developed a decent working relationship, though it was never easy because his default setting was: 'We have already done this.' He was the first person to whom we had shown the app. Sceptical to start with, he grew excited as he saw the demo. Then at one point he exclaimed: '*Aaj mera sapna poora ho gaya* [Today, my lifelong dream has come true]!'

Bina Nayyar[6] was soon to succeed the Son. Before she assumed office, I called to congratulate her and to say how much we looked forward to working under her guidance. She responded warmly, saying she remembered TAF's launch ceremony in Jaipur two years previously. But soon after, the shutters came down. Her support would have been vital, but she simply disappeared from the scene.

There were three other senior bureaucrats who would play a crucial role. One headed WCD in the state and she needed to agree that the AWWs could use the product. The other oversaw information technology and he needed to sign off on how the data generated by the app would be captured on government servers. They were Secretaries, the highest level of the bureaucracy.

The most important of them all, though junior to the other bureaucrats, was the Father. It was his duty to see that the project went ahead smoothly. Being an engineering graduate from a leading institute, he understood technology and had several useful suggestions. But what he had in mind for us was something else.

The chief minster's office in Jaipur is a separate building located behind the imposing Secretariat. Past stringent security, two floors up and a left turn later, you are in the corridors of power. To the right are Vasundhara Raje's chambers. There was a large and elegant waiting room with abstract oil paintings in the waiting room opposite the chief minister's chambers, and an eclectic selection of books ranging from Wodehouse to Radhakrishnan.

The Father's office was a modest room, down the corridor. This is where the high and the mighty, the rich and even the famous, came and went—a motley stream of humanity. It was no ordinary working place—more like a durbar. The office table was very large and had nothing on it except his mobile phone. The Father's phone could just as well have been attached permanently to his ear because he was perpetually on it. From that chair, he emitted an aura, the glow of unbounded power, for here was a man who had reached his appointed place in the universe.

For the next several months, we went from one government department to the other. Every bureaucrat saw the benefits of the product, but not one of them was willing to champion it. Bina Nayyar stayed away. The information technology secretary, a decent person, pointed out the challenge of integrating the servers. The WCD secretary, an affable lady, said this would require permission from the central command in New Delhi. Sadly, the Ghost, who was outranked, kept completely quiet, even though he had said the app was his dream come true.

We made trip after trip to the durbar. There would always be a few people in the room before us. No one made eye contact with anyone else—they wanted to get it over with and leave quietly. We would await our turn as the Father fielded a stream of calls. Once in a rare while, he would laugh uncontrollably, a peculiar high-pitched staccato sound. Then, one by one, the Father would quickly dispose of the group, which would have grown to four or five, not counting us. The word most frequently heard was '*Dekhenge* [let's see]', or if the petitioner was fortunate, 'Madam *se baat karoonga* [Will talk to Madam]'. At this point, perhaps an hour after we had entered the room, one or two, sometimes even three, of the Secretaries would come in, for it was time for our segment. The Father would then pay more attention, throwing in the required 'sirs' and the conversation would go off in different directions as we tried to bring it back on course. To be fair, the bureaucrats were bringing up valid challenges in introducing the app; but if they had the will, we might have moved forward.

The biggest problem was that the WCD secretary required permission from her parent ministry in New Delhi to participate in the introduction of the app in Rajasthan. This was because maternal and child health services fall under the jurisdiction of two ministries. The ASHA and the ANM are from Health and the AWW is from WCD. At the central level, the two ministries are often at loggerheads. At the village level, our AAA platform programme had demonstrated that the three women, left to themselves, could work together smoothly. With the app, many other players had surfaced.

In Delhi, I went and saw Dr Vikram Kaul,[7] one of India's most respected public health authorities, whose opinion on everything to do with maternal and child health had influence at the highest levels. I knew him from my Avahan days and we had a relationship of mutual respect. He said, 'Ashok, this is a marvellous product. But it is ahead of its time. My advice is don't push it any further at this stage. Run it on a small scale in Rajasthan and gather hard data. In a few years, its time would have come.'

It was good to hear this endorsement, but it was also a big disappointment. The chief minister wanted the app introduced quickly, but because of the red tape and government squabbles, it was mired in bureaucratic quicksand. The Father had me exactly where he wanted. I had reached the end of my tether. I put it to the Father that the app had the potential to save thousands of lives and that I was dismayed that something the chief minister wanted was so badly stuck. He suggested that maybe I could raise it directly with her. I understood that if I took the matter to her, she would naturally refer it back to Father and we would be back where we started, with the added factor that he would be angry.

He gave me that gleaming smile and said: 'These are real problems. You are taking this too personally. *Chalo*, let us see what we can do.' He had a meeting then and I had a flight to catch to Delhi. He gave me a date for two weeks later. I asked if we could meet one-on-one without other people in the room and he agreed.

Those days, I would lie awake at night thinking of stratagems. On field trips, when I saw a severely malnourished child, I would imagine that she could have been healthy if the app were already in use. The frontline workers would have shot information to each other when one of them spotted her at an early stage. At times, a hatred for the entire system, the whole lot of them, would swell up within me. Yes, I was taking it personally.

Two weeks later, Damini and I were ushered into the Father's room. We went in at noon, but he said he was being called by the chief minister and could we return at 3 p.m. At three, he called saying he was at the chief minister's residence and she had started a meeting. More meetings would follow and he couldn't say when these would finish, maybe by 8 p.m., but that would be too late for us. He understood, 'though I would be happy to meet then'. At eight, we were back in his office. He called, apologizing, and said the meeting would end by 10, and he could definitely meet us then. I decided that we would cancel our flight, spend the night in Jaipur and await his return later in the evening. I told the Father that and he said: 'As you say.'

We needed a change of clothes and rushed off to find a shop that would be open at that time. At 10 p.m., the Father called, saying that the meeting would conclude soon but he could not be sure when exactly. He said he was sorry we had had to wait the whole day, but it wasn't in his hands. He said we would meet and discuss the whole thing undisturbed first thing in the morning, at 10 a.m.

The meeting started at 11 a.m. the next morning, almost twenty-four hours after it had been scheduled. The Father told us that even if we could not work across the state, we could introduce the app first in a few districts: 'I will put it to honourable chief minister.' He could have said this a few months ago. As we left,

Damini said she was amazed that I had so much patience. I said I was surprised too.

~

Six months after these negotiations, on 20 December 2017, Vasundhara Raje launched the AAA app and AAA platform across Rajasthan. The brand the state had decided on for both products was 'Rajsangam'. The event was held in the conference room at the chief minister's residence. The Father, Son and Holy Ghost were present. All the senior bureaucrats we had been dealing with were there, as was my team. I went up and greeted the new secretary in charge of wellness and she gave me a wan smile. No one congratulated anyone else—it looked like everyone wanted to get the matter over with. The chief minister spoke glowingly about the government's partnership with the Antara Foundation and how Rajsangam would save countless lives.

It had been two years and nine months since our programme had been launched in the presence of RNT and the chief minister. Now it would be rolled out to every village in Rajasthan—46,000 in total! This was all that we had worked for and we celebrated that night.[8]

A year later, the Vasundhara Raje government fell, losing the Assembly election. It was not unexpected since Rajasthan had an unbroken record, going back to the country's Independence, of taking out the incumbent and bringing the opposition back. We had lost our primary patron in Rajasthan. It had been a long journey together and I felt sad. The thought crossed my mind that our programme might be at risk now that a new government would come into power. I assured myself that would not happen because Rajsangam had already been officially launched.

The ball was now in the Ghost's court. As head of the State Health Institute, he would decide how the rollout would happen. This is when we saw the vast reach of government and the efficiency with which it could implement something, once it had decided. AAA workers from all over Rajasthan were trained in the entire process of the platform in six weeks. This happened through simultaneous videoconferencing to 350 regional video-conferencing centres. Our programme officers served as master trainers.

After this, a confident Ghost told us that the government would 'take the programme forward from here. At this stage, we must see if we can do it for ourselves.' It was an admirable sentiment, but we felt that another year of hand-holding support was needed from our side.[9] He demurred: 'If we are incapable, how will we know unless we try?' We agreed that we would provide thin support: just one programme officer per district, in five such districts. By April, our programme officers reported that the AAA workers in all their districts were doing the mapping exercise well. The government in its report of the time said that the AAA platform known as the Rajsangam in Rajasthan, is an 'exemplified initiative of Rajasthan' that has helped in convergence in data of different departments like ICDS and Ministry of Health and Family Welfare. It also mentions that it has led to 'creation of village level apps and identification of focus areas for each frontline health functionary.' Another progress report released in 2019 has mentioned the process through which Rajsangam works as a means of implementing effective methods for coordination among frontline workers and better healthcare service delivery.[10] The app continues to be a flagship initiative of our program, with the potential to save many lives.[11]

~

Over the past few months, the new chief minister had put his own team in place. Every person we had dealt with during Akshada was transferred. The Father, Son, Holy Ghost, Bina Nayyar were all gone. Chief secretary Shankar had retired. Those who replaced them knew little about Akshada and our partnership with the state.

Fortunately, the new secretary was a right-thinking sort. He was bright and understood the importance of the Akshada programme. But he was easily distracted and never seemed to focus. He liked me because he too had taught at Harvard, and he too had written a book—he treated me as if I were a kindred soul. I presented him an inscribed copy of *A Stranger Truth*. He always had a small stack of books on his desk, title pointed outwards—mine was somewhere in the middle. He wore a suit to work every day, even in the hottest weather, without doubt the only person in the Secretariat wearing one.

In late April, Anjali and I were in the US to see our children. I was enjoying a well-earned break when I got a call from Piyush in Jaipur. He said they had just come out of a disastrous meeting with the Ghost's replacement, Mohit Varma. My heart sank.

We knew Mohit reasonably well. He was a medical doctor who had joined the Service. He was always civil with people, but felt he knew the answer to most things. He had an annoying way of interrupting as soon as the other person had uttered a few words—as though he knew what the other person would say even before they had started speaking. His style was to quickly make judgements, shoot out directions in minute detail and move on.

Mohit was a few weeks into his new position. He had decided, quickly, that there was no need any more for us to continue the AAA programme in Rajasthan. He said his staff had told him there was nothing happening on the ground, without any data to back it up. He thanked Piyush for our efforts and that was it, meeting over. All that work over the years, sanctioned by the previous government, officially launched by the state, summarily ended by a single IAS officer who had made a lightning quick decision!

There was only one man—his boss, the secretary—who could undo this. I sent him a message and his response was not to worry, and that we would talk after I got back to the country. He conveyed this in a 'there, there' tone. Piyush and I went to see the secretary as soon as I returned two weeks later. I said, as calmly as I could, that I was surprised that Mohit had made such a quick decision without the secretary's approval. That may have pricked his considerable vanity. He looked at his calendar and said he would call Mohit in to meet us two days later.

The secretary asked Mohit why he had made the decision, using the gentlest of tones. Mohit didn't say anything and let the underling who was with him speak. The underling muttered that nothing was happening on the ground. The secretary asked how he knew that, and the reply was not convincing. He said the programme was a priority. Mohit said 'Sir' and the meeting was over. I didn't sense that Mohit was upset in any way—he had many other problems left to solve. A few weeks later, Mohit was transferred from his position, as can happen without warning in government.

We decided that we had done enough. The AAA platform had been adopted and rolled out across the entire state of Rajasthan. The government reports indicated that it was progressing well. We developed a tracking system for supervisors to use and the secretary agreed that would be included in their performance evaluation. Ideally, we should have cradled the baby for another six months, but all said and done, it was a great conclusion to our work in Rajasthan.

Proof of concept of the AAA intervention had been established. It was time to move on.

12

The Band Played On

But even as we celebrated this milestone, an internal crisis was brewing. We always assumed that the FCRA would come through, and that it was only a matter of time. Alternatively, that Indian donors would come forward. Neither of these events happened and as we looked at the financials it was apparent that we had been spending beyond our means in developing our programme so innovatively and at such speed. Calamity had been creeping up on us in seemingly still waters, and it struck suddenly through an unexpected sequence of events. Suddenly, the ship was going down, with no rescue in sight. It was just a year after the launch of Rajsangam, when the bouquets were still coming in.

~

By early 2014, we had generous corpus funding from three prominent business leaders or sponsors, as we called them: Arjun Malhotra, Shiv Nadar and Cyrus Poonawalla. Together with Bill Gates,[1] they acted as an informal advisory board for TAF.

By the end of the year, we got the grant of Rs 12 crore from the Tata Trusts for a programme in Rajasthan that would run for four years, 2015–19. It had been an arduous effort over two years to secure this funding. R. Venkataramanan ('Venkat'), the executive director of the Trusts, assured us that we could expect follow-on funding for another two years after 2019. I remembered the words a long-term grantee of the Trusts had told me, 'With the Trusts, if you do good work, you are in for the long haul.'

There was a catch, however. This was the Tatas' first major foray into the maternal and child health sector, the largest programme grant they had ever made in this sector. We were grateful, but we estimated that the funding was barely half the money we needed, and it would need to be supplemented by other donors. I mentioned this to RNT on one occasion, having heard that the Trusts welcomed partnership. He responded by saying that the Trusts didn't need anyone's help.

At this point, some would say, the prudent decision would have been to size the programme to fit the funding at hand, and build it slowly as and when more money came in. I didn't consider that an option. It would run counter to the fast-moving, experimenting, adapting pace at which we had begun to move, to have an impact on a large scale in a short time. From the very start, I believed that TAF could not be denied. It had an inherent logic and its time had come. That conviction made it easy to make some major calls.

The way I saw it, there was still enough money in the bank, including the sponsors' funding. Our experienced chartered accountants assured us that the FCRA permission was routine and would come through in the next few months. With that much money secured, and expectations of more coming in from abroad after the FCRA permission, I never felt we were taking any risk. The meter, though, had already started ticking, for I had recruited a team of seven even before the grant had been secured.[2]

In September 2014, I met the sponsors at the business centre of the Oberoi Hotel in Delhi. I described our plans for Rajasthan to the sponsors and laid out the financial outlook. I explained why the Tata funding would not be sufficient. I explained that my hopes were pinned on the FCRA permission, and hoped that as we delivered results, Indian donors would step up.

The sponsors had put their money into a corpus fund. The understanding was that this would be a buffer, to be used only if urgently needed. Now, it was urgently needed even before we started work! I asked for permission to dip into the corpus money till other funding came through. The sponsors readily agreed. They didn't want to second guess my judgement on the matter.

Later, Bill joined the meeting after this main discussion was over. He spoke enthusiastically of the work I had led at Avahan, and said he was confident that TAF would deliver on its mission. The meeting ended on a high note.

～

And so, the ship set sail into uncharted waters. A few of my teammates had worked in maternal and child health, but never on this kind of scale. I had worked on a large scale before, but not in the maternal and child health sector. Some people had done neither.

In making the transition from HIV to maternal and child health, I took the view that the principles of scaling up that I had learnt at Avahan were universal. We had done street mapping to find the sex workers most at risk—now, we were doing village mapping to find the most vulnerable mothers and children. In Avahan, we had worked with and through the community of sex workers—now we were working with and through the community of health workers. The first principles I had learnt during Avahan served me well even as work at TAF got underway.

Through 2016 and 2017, we introduced several innovations in the villages of Jhalawar. There was the flagship AAA platform[3] and work was underway on the AAA app. Simplified record-keeping by frontline workers had been adopted by the government throughout the state of Rajasthan. The supervisory cadre was trained, and government nurses been coached by our nurse mentors. We demonstrated how high-traffic delivery points had to be managed. A mobility solution for ANMs (described later in this chapter) was in the works. There were experiments involving adolescent girls as change agents, and local self-governance by village communities. All this was backed by a robust monitoring system. It was an ecosystem of linked innovations, a remarkable effort by a team of rookies.

By 2017, TAF was expanding quickly. Our programme monitoring data was showing a significant increase in the detection of high-risk cases. The pinnacle was the launch of Rajsangam and the growing interest from other states. In creating the ecosystem, we were digging into the corpus. The FCRA permission was crucial. But as the weeks and months went by, it was apparent that the permission was going to take a long time. And when the months became years, we had taken the FCRA out of our planning horizon by 2018. It dawned on us that we might have to manage without foreign funding.

We saw no cause for panic, however. After all, we had enough money in the corpus and the Tata Trusts had virtually committed to a follow-on grant. And we believed that those

Indian donors would emerge and we would get the FCRA permission sooner or later.

~

In the meantime, I was meeting potential Indian donors regularly. Nothing had changed—people lauded our work and referred me to others. I met Deval Sanghavi, the amiable founder of Dasra, a stand-out organization that puts donors and potential recipients together, not case by case, but through a marketplace approach. He said we were doing amazing work and Dasra would look out for the right opportunities for TAF to receive that elusive Indian funding, but nothing came of it.

My book had won accolades and I did the round of book festivals through the first half of 2019. At the end of each talk, I would have several business cards from corporate leaders and philanthropists, who told me, 'We would just love to support Antara.' I followed up with the most promising of these but came up empty each time. Perhaps, when the rush of emotion had passed, they decided against supporting TAF.

Why was it that our work was so widely appreciated, yet it was hard to find donors? I remembered the scores of funders whom I had approached when setting up TAF, and the two years of hard labour securing funding from the Tata Trusts. It seemed Indian donors wanted to fund more visible things—treatment or education and other causes with tangible outcomes. Many didn't understand prevention, that you could have impact by working on the invisible. Some might have been uncomfortable with disturbing issues, such as severe malnutrition or infant deaths.

I also wondered if donors had concluded that we didn't need any help because we had some famous names funding us—Ratan, Cyrus, Shiv and Arjun. And on top of that, Bill Gates as a mentor.

I had spent the past ten years giving away enormous sums of money as head of the Gates Foundation in India. I didn't know how to be a fledgling NGO, going about pitching for comparatively small amounts of money. I naively thought that I would sail through with my track record with Avahan. Honestly, if someone had told me I would spend a lot of my time raising money, I may never have started TAF. I hated fundraising.

Looking back, I believe that if I had done nothing else for a year, I could have brought in some sizeable donors. But where was the time? In the early years of our Rajasthan programme, I was involved in operations, dealt with recalcitrant bureaucracy, liaised with the donor and focused on building our talent pool. Devoting all my energies to fundraising would have been impossible.

In the middle of it all, once again, we were offered a colossal amount of money, seemingly without any conditions. An organization called Sanjot[4] contacted us to say that a billionaire non-resident Indian had put $30 million into a fund that they would manage.* Their mandate was to give it to one or several donees who would do good with it. They made a simple proposition: take the money, deal with us, you will never have to engage with the donor. The donor, though, had gained some notoriety in recent years for the damage his ventures had done to the environment. Activists alleged that thousands of indigenous peoples had been displaced because of his business ventures. Reenu, Piyush and I were quick to decide we would decline on principle. Our mission was to work with and for communities, and not for those who did harm to communities and their environment.

$\sim$

---

* It turned out that it was Rakesh Khandelwal, the same person who had offered substantial funding a few years earlier, as described in Chapter 5.

The 'mobility solution' was one of our sweetest innovations, but today I remember it with some bitterness. In Rajasthan, ANMs travelled vast distances daily to get from one village to the other—indeed, this is the case in many states. Incredibly, the government required that they use public transport. That was absurd, for a bus might come by only once every few hours in some remote areas. Many villages were located a distance away from the main road. Most nurses depended on a male family member to drive them around on their motorcycle. As a result, they lost crucial time that should have been spent with patients.

Our idea was straightforward: 'Scooties for ANMs'. The two-wheeler scooter had given way almost entirely to motorcycles in Indian cities but was enjoying a revival. A lighter product, the 'Scooty', was made just for women by Hero, the leading scooter manufacturer. Surely, the productivity of ANMs would improve vastly if the government was to provide them with this simple low-cost transport. The women would get to more villages, sooner, and spend more time in each.

I cold-called Venu Srinivasan, the chairman of TVS, the other large scooter manufacturer. I explained the idea and asked if TVS would donate some scooters for a preliminary pilot study. He agreed to donate six, apologizing that they couldn't give more since their market was largely in the south. The whole conversation took all of two minutes.

The chief minister readily agreed to launch the idea at a public event. We needed ANMs who had shown special commitment and were confident, and we recommended six names to the district government. A few weeks later, Vasundhara Raje handed the keys to gleaming new scooters to six ANMs before a large outdoor gathering, to huge media coverage. Most of the ANMs couldn't drive, but one who could drove it off the ramp to huge cheers. The rotund District Medical Officer Dr Irfan Ali got carried away and started shouting,

'*Bharat* Mata *ki jai* [Hail mother India]!' The media loved it. The CM was her usual charming self and visibly happy.

Soon, all the ANMs picked up driving and were zipping around on scooters, each fitted with a GPS device. We could track the movement of the scooters between villages and the time taken at each stop. We also saw that the scooters often stopped at the vegetable markets, but ignored it. There was some tampering with the GPS systems to avoid being monitored. These minor problems were easily overcome.

The time ANMs spent interfacing with patients had gone up significantly. But the sample size was too small. We needed at least ten more scooters to gather enough data to advocate with the government to provide scooters for all ANMs. The total cost was about Rs 10 lakh, including the running costs for the pilot period. But who would foot the bill?

We tried public sector organizations who might feel some affinity for a potential government programme. That didn't work out. Then I called someone whom I had known since my McKinsey days. He had shown a lot of interest in TAF and said he would definitely want to be a donor. He was listed among India's top ten billionaires, and I thought this would be an easy ask. He hummed and hawed and said all his organizations had used up their CSR budgets. Then he said, in a martyr's tone, 'Maybe, I can pay for one from my own money . . .' I said that would not be necessary and left as graciously as I could.

I wanted to conserve the corpus funds for the core programme. We had no option but to drop the Mobility Solution idea, and that hurt. It was a sound idea, and I hope some state government will take it up in the future.

There were several other initiatives we couldn't fund. The Tata Trusts had specified that their funds should not be spent on monitoring and extensive programme and scientific evaluation.

We could not invest in professional exposure for our staff through visits to other programmes or to attend conferences. I became increasingly aware of what we could not do, or where we had to cut corners, because we didn't have enough money.

~

Then came the first major blow as we got caught in the crossfire of an internecine war within the Tata Group.

In December 2012, RNT stepped down as chairman of the group and Cyrus Pallonji Mistry took his place. In January 2013, I seized the opportunity to begin engaging with RNT, a two-year process that I have described in detail earlier.[5] In December 2016, Mistry was sacked by the board of Tata Sons, the holding company for the Tata Group. He went to court, filing a rash of cases against the Tata Group.

The war turned ugly. Word was out that the Tata Trusts were suddenly under government scrutiny, including that of the CBI, because criminal charges had been filed by Mistry's lawyers. There were scores of lawsuits and the Trusts were spending huge amounts on lawyers' fees. That pressure kept increasing, and by the end of 2018, the Trusts stopped funding hundreds of running grants. We were told that there would be no extension of our work after April 1. That was a shock, because we had assumed the extension was imminent after all the accolades our work had been receiving. Venkat, the executive director of the Trusts, was sympathetic, but said we were lucky to be allowed to serve out our time till April 2019.

There was another problem. The Trusts had given us permission to take forward a portion of our grant into the next financial year (i.e., after 1 April 2019). At that time, we were transferring the AAA platform to the government of Rajasthan, and it made sense to wait and spend the money only after it became clear what type of support the state government needed. This is called a 'no-cost extension' of a grant and is routinely given by donors to grantees if they want it. The Trusts had agreed, and Venkat assured me that this part of the funds would be protected. But things were spinning out of his control, and we were told just before April that there would not be any no-cost extension. We wrote a cheque giving the leftover funds back to the Trusts.

And so our work with the Tata Group ended in sudden death. There would be no more funding going into the next phase, and nothing for immediate support to the government. We told the team to continue the work that they were doing even past 1 April, and we would wind things up as smoothly as possible. Now we would be running only on corpus funds.

~

In March 2019, we got a call from the H.T. Parekh Foundation (HTPF), the philanthropic wing of HDFC, India's leading private sector bank. They liked the work we had been doing in Rajasthan and wanted to talk to us. We flew to Mumbai and met Upahar Pramanik, who managed the health portfolio, and Ziaa Lalkaka, the head of the foundation. Deepak Parekh, the chairman of HDFC, joined us briefly—I had met him before. In September of that year, HTPF approved a one-year grant for work in a single district in Madhya Pradesh.

The funding was enough to give us a foothold in a major state. But it was clear to us that now the main goal was survival. The money would take us through another year of work, and we went in with the hope that the rest would come later. The grant might even be a lifeline to something big. We accepted it gratefully.

The big opportunity that came to us at the same time, however, was from TED International. It was the coveted invitation for me to deliver one of their talks. The sweetener was the possibility of substantial funding attached to it. TED had tied up with Star TV and was then in its second season in India with a series of TED talks focused on 'social changemakers'. The programme was being hosted by the superstar of Indian cinema, Shah Rukh Khan.

I looked up the speakers who had featured in the previous seasons. It was a parade of people who had done remarkable things in their life. And they all looked so utterly poised and self-assured, as though they had been born, and grown up, on that red carpet. I felt a flutter inside.

TED, in the United States, is part of a group of social investors called the Audacious Project. The business magnate Richard Branson is also part of Audacious, and had been hosting a small group of philanthropists on his private island to discuss worthy causes and NGOs that they might choose to fund. It was all done discreetly and nothing much was known as to who was invited, and who gave how much to whom. I imagined men and women in casual island attire, well-tanned and sipping fine wines, doing some serious giveaway.

TED now had the idea: why not do this in India? So they spoke to the producers, Star TV, and developed a format. The programme in India consisted of eight episodes in as many weeks, each featuring four social change leaders. Of these thirty-two, six had already been singled out as possible recipients of philanthropic funds. The expectation was that the six would get funded a few million dollars each.

The Indian business leader Gaurav Dalmia was the doyen of the Indian philanthropists' group. He didn't have an island, and the only thing we were told was that the group would meet after the TED event and view a special short film to be made on each person and his or her work. They would watch each TED talk and get down to deciding whom they would fund. I imagined them at the Belvedere, sipping single malts or fresh juice, in animated discussion.

There was a meeting at the India International Centre in Delhi where we, the six chosen ones, were invited to meet Gaurav and introduce ourselves to a small private audience. At this event, I was struck by the stellar work being done by organizations such as Educate Girls, Goonj and Khabar Lahariya.

The TED people told me I would get two coaches, one for English and the other for Hindi. I was to do two talks, one in each language. The coaching would be spread over two months. Anjali and I were leaving on vacation at the time and I had a lot of work commitments. I was a little miffed at the notion that I needed coaching in English. I said I could do no more than two weeks intensively, and maybe we could cut out, or cut down, the English portion. The organizers said it was up to me but I would be missing out on something valuable. Eventually, I agreed, of course, to do the coaching in both languages. In either language, the idea of walking down the red carpet, standing before a live audience, King Khan in the front row, was daunting.

This is where the two great coaches came in. Sujay Saple and Saurabh Nair, both well-known stage actors from Mumbai, worked their magic with us. From them, I learnt that the essence of this kind of speaking was not how well you spoke the language, but whether you could radiate your passion well enough to capture not only the studio audience, but thousands of home viewers. I saw that I had a lot to learn—in both languages—and I worked hard. By the time the big day came, I was confident and looking forward to it.

Tragedy struck on the eve of my departure for the talk in Mumbai. Our German Shepherd, Noori, was rushed for an emergency operation in the evening. I called the organizers and asked if I could be given another date for my talk. They sympathized but said that would not be possible. I knew I would not get another shot like this. In our precarious financial position, this TED event was our only big hope. I set off early the next morning for Mumbai. I got back the next day and Noori died that same night, breaking my heart and filling me with guilt. I believe she was waiting for me to come back.

In the Hindi talk, I wanted to get the audience on my side from the very beginning. So my first lines were: 'First of all, I want to say that I am from Kerala, but my wife is not. She has coached me thoroughly in Hindi and sent me here. If I make mistakes even after this, she is wholly responsible.' The audience laughed and clapped, and King Khan shouted out, 'Yes, yes. Always blame it on biwi,' adding to the atmosphere.

The event went well. I felt that I had conveyed the essence of TAF in both talks.[6] We spent the next few weeks in keen anticipation of the grant, but there was no word from TED except to say that we would soon hear from them. Then a letter came in November, five months after the talk, from TED in New York. They tried to put a good spin on it, but evidently things hadn't gone as planned. We heard later that the Indian philanthropists had funded only two NGOs out of the six. We were one of the two, and our donor was the programme's producer, Star TV.

The Star grant came through in early December. It was a small amount, sufficient to work in three blocks of a new district in Madhya Pradesh, and one block in the neighbouring state of Chhattisgarh. I was grateful that Star had stepped up to fund us, but I also wondered if the host channel had done so to avoid the embarrassment of not a single Indian donor having reached for his or her wallet.

~

In September 2019, I went to Seattle to meet Bill. It was a critical juncture and I needed to brief him. I wondered if this would be the last time we would be meeting like this, because TAF might not exist a year from now. I took him through the situation, examining all the angles. There wasn't much to discuss because it was straightforward: without the FCRA permission, we couldn't be funded by any foreign donor. And finding a substantial Indian donor seemed improbable at this point. I always came back from these meetings with Bill feeling energized, inspired. This time it felt as though I was returning from a funeral.

In 2019, the Tata Trusts grant had evaporated over the course of a few months. The one big opening we had, with TED, had come to virtually nothing. We had secured the HTPF grant but that was certain only for the next nine months. Fortunately, Star had also thrown us a lifeline. We had come down to twenty-two members of staff compared to forty, two years previously. If no other funding came through, TAF would be out of money by September 2020. Reenu, Piyush and I were talking about next steps all the time. We decided we would inform our team members and begin plans for shutdown over the next nine months.

The thought crossed my mind: sell TAF. This really meant finding someone who would fund the organization for the long term and have the final word on how we ran it. We had turned down some huge offers of funding over the years. We could have gone back to most of those at this point. But I knew we would not be able to run TAF with freedom and preserve the culture, which was so precious to us, with any of them. I would rather close TAF down than do that. Then the thought crossed my mind, It was to sell TAF to someone known as a 'white knight' in business—a friendly investor who comes to the rescue. It would have to be a person who believed in us, who I could trust implicitly, who would never interfere, but always retain the final say. It seemed highly unlikely I would find someone liken that.

Then, a miracle—we found such an investor! A dear friend and long-time supporter of TAF said he would acquire TAF. The team celebrated the last-minute rescue. But a week later, that fell through.

It had been a roller coaster. I finally accepted that the game was over and a great sorrow arose within me, as though someone very close to me had died, and as I thought of all that TAF could have been. A wave of guilt washed over me and I wondered what might have happened if I had carefully nurtured her and let her grow slowly.

A tremendous anger then seized me. Our three-month-old Golden Retriever Ruby was yelping away, trying to get my attention. I spanked her and she cried out in surprise. When I saw what I had done, I broke down. I fell asleep immediately and awoke after a restless night. I was surprised that my face was wet.

Anjali and I desperately needed a change of scene. So, in early 2020, we set off for a place as far away from Delhi as we could find.

13

Beyond Havelock

We booked ourselves at a resort on Havelock Island, two hours by boat from Port Blair. It was the perfect place to recuperate. I had all the time in the world to laze and think about the work and, oddly enough, about God.

As I have mentioned before, the great joy of our work had always been the field. There were travels to distant villages and hamlets where people lived their lives with a singular outlook. They seemed to accept whatever came their way stoically, even cheerfully. In poor communities, people ate only one meal—they had never experienced a full stomach. They had nothing to compare that with—their suffering was unrealized. To know what you are missing, and know that you can't have it, is felt suffering. It was difficult to comprehend, for these were other worlds. In that reverie, I mulled over what I did not have and realized it was very little, so why brood?

Now, sitting on the beach at Havelock, I wrote some more in my journal. I felt the joy of owning something precious that nobody could take away.

From there, somehow, my thoughts went to my uncertain relationship with God. It began in early childhood. Every evening before I went to sleep, my mother or elder sister Mariam would read to me from the Bible. In the Old Testament, it seemed as if God lost his cool very easily—his punishments seemed way worse than the crime necessitated. He tested innocent people in cruel ways. It happened in Eden and with Abraham, Job and many others. If I had a bad dream, mom would ask if I had prayed before I slept, and if not, well, *quod erat demonstrandum*. I grew up thinking of God as essentially punishing, not loving.

As an adult, I accepted the logic of 'There is a perfect order in the universe, ergo, there had to be God'. But the corollary 'If there is God, why should terrible things happen to good people?' left me wary. My childhood notion of God left me fearful—my adult conception left me uncertain. So, in times of strife, with nothing to turn to, I tended to imagine the worst.

On one of those occasions, Anjali said I should have more faith: 'If anyone has had a higher power looking out for him, it is you.' She was thinking of the many points in my life when I was on the brink and was saved in the nick of time, and the many unearned good things that had suddenly come my way. Sitting on the beach at Havelock, I counted the times, and it made me wonder.

I had been delving into the Gita. I remembered what it said about equanimity, to accept that there is a duality to everything. The good had come to TAF, and now it was the other side. I should accept it as the way of life. The question was, what to make of the situation. And then, the famous line: 'Thy human right is for activity only, never for the resultant fruit of thy actions.'[1] It was ours to work on TAF but TAF was not ours. I interpreted it also as 'You did the best you could, you could have done no more—don't grieve or feel guilty.' That gave me solace and it became a mantra.

Those halcyon days at Havelock. A series of random reflections that helped me heal.

~

I remember every minute of the afternoon of 17 January 2020. My mobile rang exactly at 2 p.m. It was a friend in the government calling from Delhi. The only word I could catch was 'FCRA'. The connection was weak. I said I would call back in a few minutes and went quickly to the reception, where there was a better signal. I feared it would be a message that our application had been rejected for some technicality and we would have to apply all over again.

The friend told me he had heard that our FCRA application had been approved. I was speechless because by then, we had waited six years. He told me not to take it for granted, and that it might take weeks or months. I ran to tell Anjali, gasping when I reached the door, 'We have the FCRA!' Holding on to her, I was jumping up and down. She was more sober: 'Look, Choki, you have been disappointed about this in the past. Now you are at a stage where you are letting things go, and you won't be able to take it if this falls through. Don't expect it, wait till it happens.'

But I was in another world. I said I had to call the team and rushed off again. The signal was weak at the reception. There was a landline around the corner. It was taken by a German tourist— five minutes, that seemed like an eternity. He finished and stepped out with apologies. Now the Delhi connection was weak. I finally got through on Reenu's line. It had been three hours since my friend had called.

The ensuing conversation should have been recorded. It went like this:

'I have something amazing to tell you!'

'Wait, there is I something I want to tell you first. It's urgent.'

'I can't talk office stuff just now . . .'

'Ashok, will you keep quiet for a moment and let me speak?'

'No, you listen! I heard from a friend that we have been cleared for FCRA. But we must lie low, not get our hopes up. It might take weeks or months, and worst case, it won't happen . . .' I was talking at high speed, almost babbling.

'Now can I speak?'

'Yes, go ahead.'

'I have it in my hand right now!'

'Have what?'

'The permission letter. It came just now!'

'What?!'

There was a huge cheer in the background. It seemed the entire office was in the room.

I sprinted back to our room. Anjali and I talked excitedly. It seemed like a miracle. I closed my eyes and enjoyed the moment, awash with gratitude.

~

NGOs in India need government permission to receive foreign donations under the FCRA. We set up TAF assuming we would get that permission within a few months of our application in 2014. As I have described at the beginning of this narrative, we had found it difficult to find funding from Indian donors and expected that it would be easier with foreign donors.

The permission had not come through even after a few years and we had stopped counting on it. After a run of bad luck, it seemed like TAF was steadily going under, but now, with the permission in our hands, it felt like someone had thrown us a lifeline.

We had a few perfect last days at Havelock Island. Back in Delhi, I was thrown immediately into the ongoing work with

HTPF. After a few weeks, we hunkered down to develop a plan for fundraising in the US. We had not thought about this in any depth till now—after all, what was the point when we didn't have the permission?

The problem was that we didn't know how to create a cogent plan. I had no experience in fundraising outside India. I had left the US almost twenty years ago and had no networks there, no feel for what US donors wanted. I didn't understand the market: who gave how much, for which causes, to whom, and who supported maternal and child health in India or which strategies Indian NGOs had used. I wasn't sure whom we should approach first: high net-worth individuals (HNIs) or foundations, create chapters or giving circles?* Which type of US organization did we need?

Early in March 2020, I went for a reunion in Dubai of the '90s group' of McKinsey's India office. I was the only one of the six 'founding fathers' who had relocated to India in 1992 from McKinsey in the US to create an India office. Some of the youngsters we had recruited then were now venerable senior partners of McKinsey and Company—many others had built funds. Here was a group that was wealthy, had wide networks and held me in high regard. It struck me: McKinsey was the place to start our US fundraising effort.

And then, even as I was thinking about which steps to take, COVID-19 hit India. Soon, the government announced a nationwide lockdown. Overnight, our staff, who had been deployed in the field, were idle. We had to carry that cost, adding to the financial pressure. We closed our office in Saket with a lump in the throat because this was where TAF had been born. Working from home on Zoom became the norm.

---

* Local groups of givers committed to a particular cause.

The clock had been running out on us. We needed two to three years of our current level of funding to reach some measure of stability.

During COVID-19, no one would be in a mood to discuss charitable funding. International flights were not operational. Some staff had left but most stayed—we decided we would lay anyone off under any circumstances. It seemed the financial pressure would continue. What a cruel joke if we failed despite the FCRA!

~

By July, the situation had deteriorated. I approached two well-connected McKinsey senior partners, both friends, and explained my plight. There was Ramesh Mangaleswaran (widely known as 'M') who lived in Chennai and was on the board of Pratham, the outstanding Indian NGO and a benchmark for an Indian company that has succeeded in fundraising in the US. Ajay Dhankhar was based in New York and had wide networks in the business world. I had recruited M sixteen years ago in India when he was just out of business school. I had been Ajay's 'development group leader' back then, shepherding his professional development. I didn't expect too much from them because they were incredibly busy people and would have other causes, and other foundations, they championed. I would have been happy if they made some introductions to a few HNIs and provided some counsel.

But both, without hesitation, said they would help. Ramesh reminded me that I had recruited and mentored him. Ajay went a step further, saying I had mentored him and got him elected partner. I could remember nothing of this kind. I had done no more than the routine duties of a partner to his wards. I asked, in all seriousness, if they were mistaking me for someone else. As if to make their point, they each put in a generous personal contribution.

The duo went into high gear. Ajay put together a McKinsey team, pro bono, to develop a fundraising strategy. There were two partners on the three-person team: Shiv Sinha and Nisha Subramanian. They had bought into our mission and were determined to see us succeed. The strategy exercise took six weeks. The approach would be to focus on HNIs first, then engage with foundations. There were names of hundreds of people and organizations we should approach. These had been sliced and diced in multiple ways, such as foundations with former McKinsey people in leadership or those with a history of supporting mother and child causes.

M introduced me to people who had been in the NGO fundraising game in the US for a long time. One of them, a seasoned campaigner, asked, 'How much money do you want to raise?' I told her. 'And by when do you hope to raise this money?' she asked with a smile. I said we aimed to reach a survival level by December 2020, and stability by July 2021—this was in September 2020. The campaigner shook her head: 'Ashok, that's totally unrealistic. It took even Pratham* the best part of ten years to raise money at the levels that you are talking about. Donors in the US are generous, but also savvy. Nobody has heard of TAF in this country. You need to tone down your expectations.'

I was not worried. We had a sound model, a good track record and a great team. I thought we were special, and placed in front of a potential donor, we had a good chance. In any case, we didn't have the option to tone it down.

---

* The stand-out Indian NGO, focused largely on education, that has been successful in raising massive funding from the US over the years.

I found an excellent person, Srividya Prakash, based in the Bay Area, to represent TAF outside India. More accurately, Vidya found us, because she had always been keen on supporting the cause of mother and child health in India. She too, was part of the McKinsey 90s group.

M and Ajay decided I should do a series of Zoom meetings with potential donors, starting with groups of McKinsey partners, present and past. They began to make calls within their networks to drum up attendance. The first meeting was on 21 November 2020. There were seven attendees from McKinsey, of whom six were senior partners and five were recent alumni. I knew only one of the participants.

I started by talking about my journey into another India— first with Avahan, and now with TAF. I described our model, our impact in Rajasthan and the plan with TAF. I tried to tell a story, to take those seven people into the villages of Madhya Pradesh, the places where we worked, getting away from the usual McKinsey mode of being utterly fact-based, leaving little to emotion. The audience seemed enthralled. Three weeks later, we did another such Zoom meeting, this time with people mainly from the McKinsey India 90s group. Vidya, Piyush and I made that presentation together. We raised almost six months' funding from those two one-hour meetings.

These two sessions, my first exposure to American philanthropy, were a revelation. I was impressed with their generosity and sharp questions, always with an attitude to try to clarify and understand. To some extent, the idea that one of their own had gone into the grassroots of the social sector might have appealed. Some asked for counsel individually on how they might think of a family giving strategy. Whatever the reason, the idea of meeting people in small groups over Zoom worked.

It wasn't all McKinsey. In October, I called Jaideep Khanna, someone I had met over lunch in Manhattan in 2010.[2] He had made a fortune as a hedge fund manager before he retired at an early age. I thought of him suddenly one Sunday evening and on an impulse, picked up the phone and called him. The conversation went like this:

'Jaideep, you probably don't remember me, but we had lunch in mid-town ten years ago.'

'Of course, I remember you, Ashok. And I know what you are doing. You help the poorest mothers and children, whom no one else will help.'

We talked for a while as I told Jaideep about our work and our need. At the end of the call, I asked if he would support us. He committed a large amount of money—two weeks later, he doubled it, and a month later, doubled that amount again! He sincerely believes we are doing God's work and if we stay steadfast, we will achieve all our aspirations and more. It was as simple as that for him and I felt humbled and moved. As I got to know Jaideep in the months that followed, I understood that he is a deeply spiritual person, a devotee of Swami Yogananda Paramhansa. He became a source of savvy advice and a mentor to our work.

It went on like this, a steady flow of generous funding going into 2021, without meeting anyone in person. We had gone well past our 'survive' target by our December deadline. Almost all the funders gave us 'unrestricted' funding, meaning that we could spend it as we thought best. That is a grant recipient's dream because it allows you to fund the varying needs of a programme as it evolves and to use the funds at an optimum time. It signifies that a donor believes that the donee knows best how to spend their money and trusts them implicitly to do that. There can be no higher appreciation.

~

There were many foundations in the US. These were the 'big-ticket' players, often funding in seven figures. They required a long track record, strong organization and more. We still didn't meet these stringent qualifications and were trying to figure out how to secure this type of funding.

One evening, I got a call from the US late in the evening. It was a woman's voice. She was polite and chose her words carefully. Her first question was: 'Have you heard of MacKenzie Scott?' Of course, I had heard of MacKenzie Scott. After her divorce in 2019 from Jeff Bezos, the founder of Amazon, she had a net worth of almost $60 billion, making her the third-wealthiest woman in the US.[3] Scott signed The Giving Pledge,[*] saying enormous sums of money should not be concentrated with a few people.[4] She would 'give till the safe is empty'.[5] They didn't take applications. Instead, her team of advisors scoured the world for deserving organizations that had 'a record of impact . . . worked with communities . . . and had difficulty accessing philanthropic capital'.[6] She married her college classmate Dan Jewett in 2020, and that year, they gave away $5.8 billion in charitable gifts.[7]

The person on the phone went on to say, 'MacKenzie and Dan want to offer you an unrestricted one-time grant.' She mentioned a sum that would put us well beyond the 'stable' benchmark. 'We have been looking at Antara for some time now and admire your approach and the impact that you are having. This is to enable you to build upon the amazing work that you are doing.'

I said something about being incredibly grateful. I was at a loss for words.

There was one condition: I could not share this news with anyone, even my senior management team, till such time as

---

[*] Founded by Bill Gates and Warren Buffet, The Giving Pledge is an invitation for billionaires to donate their wealth to philanthropy, during their lives.

MacKenzie made the announcement within the next six months. It was 11 p.m., but I must confess I called Reenu, Piyush and Vidya and told them, without mentioning the name of the giver, and emphasizing confidentiality. For a few moments, the four of us sat in stunned silence.

We didn't have to wait long. In June, MacKenzie Scott announced that she and Dan Jewett were awarding $2.6 billion to 286 organizations. Their announcement said the grants were going out to '286 teams empowering voices the world needs to hear . . . [driven by] the humbling belief that the solutions are best designed and implemented by others . . . teams with experience on the front lines of challenges will know best how to put the money to good use'.[8] I read the announcement again and again—every line seemed to encapsulate what we strove to do. I scoured the list, reading about the inspiring organizations that had been awarded this gift. TAF was considered one of the world's best NGOs!

I called an all-team meeting. The message was short. I said, 'No over-the-top celebrations, no comments to the outside world. Let's remember the communities we serve, keep our heads down and get back to work.'

By September 2021, TAF had raised enough funding to last us for the next seven years. Exactly a year ago, we were almost broke. For almost two years before that, we were desperately trying to stay afloat. Every door seemed to have slammed shut.

Now the challenge was how best to spend this money and follow our dream.

Part 3
Adult

14

Enigma

We named our new programme, in Madhya Pradesh, 'Akshita', which means 'permanent'. This launch was altogether different from that of our Rajasthan programme in Jaipur four years earlier. That had been a formal affair in the presence of Chief Minister Vasundhara Raje and RNT. All the district collectors in Rajasthan had been summoned. There were ministers and senior IAS officers from many departments. Everyone present got the message that this programme was a priority for the state.

That endorsement from the top turned out to be a mixed blessing. It made many things happen quickly but it engendered resistance from the ranks of the bureaucracy. In Madhya Pradesh, support from the government at the district and state levels was good from the start. We decided to work bottom-up, from district administration to state government. We would approach the political leadership only after we had something tangible to show.

Accordingly, the launch in Chhindwara was low-key and, well, different.

~

The programme was to be launched by the District collector of Chhindwara at the collectorate, a charming pre-Independence structure of red brick and sloping green tiled roof. There was a diverse group of government officials seated around a long rectangular table, with three chairs at the head of the table. The one in the centre, the collector's seat, was higher and had the white towel. To the left and right of him were seats for his most senior officials. Our team was on the right, with me closest to the collector.

The programme was to begin at 11 a.m. Twenty minutes past the hour, there was no sign of the collector. Then an officer came in and announced that the collector was held up on urgent business—he had conveyed that he wanted us to start and would join the meeting later. One of the collector's deputies assumed charge, taking the chair to the left. He was gracious but seemed to have little idea what the meeting was about. Ashutosh and Neeraj started their presentation. The deputy was focused on each slide, trying to understand. Almost everyone else's eyes were glazed over.

The deputy got a call ten minutes into the presentation. He jumped up and hurried out of the room, phone pressed to his ear. There was a growing buzz in the room. Ashutosh and Neeraj had lost their audience but gamely went through their slides. They finished, and there were no questions. The meeting came to an end. An officer came running in and said, 'collector sir will meet you.' That was unexpected. It was crucial that we brief him, for we would need his help. We hurried to meet the collector in his chambers.

There were about twenty men and women waiting outside the collector's office, speaking to each other in hushed tones. They all wore white dhoti-kurtas or saris. My thoughts flashed back to my first meeting with the collector of Jhalawar four years earlier, when a large group of people, also in white clothes, was ahead of us. The men and women were ushered in a few minutes later. We settled down for a long wait, but they came out in two minutes. My first reaction was that they had been summarily dismissed. But they were smiling and talking animatedly.

~

The collector had bushy eyebrows, thickly errant hair and heavy jowls. He was unshaven and abundant. But it was not, overall, an unpleasing impression—everything somehow came together.

He gestured that we should be seated. We settled down in the theatre-style rows of seats in front of his large desk. I started to introduce ourselves, our partnership with the state, what we hoped to contribute to Chhindwara and how we needed his guidance and support. I was just warming up when he gave a single head bob, conveying, but not rudely, that he understood, and I need say no more. He said, 'Good.'

He began to speak, in a soft, gravelly voice, at times almost a whisper. Sometimes, there were long silences between sentences, and at first, I would try to insert myself into those gaps. Then, from his look, I understood that those silences were supposed to hang so that we could mull over what he had been saying.

He never met our eyes and kept glancing at a point just over my left shoulder, sometimes stopping his monologue. Once, when I tried to edge in, he clicked his tongue three times and muttered the words: '*Arre yaar* [Oh, come on dude]!' I was taken aback for I hadn't said anything controversial, nor did I like the familiarity. Occasionally, he would stop his monologue, shake his head ruefully, then continue.

At some point, I stole a quick glance over my left shoulder on the pretext of asking my team something and finally understood: he was following the cricket match that was running soundlessly on the large flat screen TV on the wall opposite him, across the way from the conference table. The test series between South Africa and India was on. Rohit Sharma, India's opening batsman, was in full and elegant flow, but as was his weakness when he had crossed fifty, he would play some loose strokes and run the risk of getting out. I am a cricket fan, and I understood the collector's frustration.

It was then I noticed that the wall behind the collector was polished grey granite. The reflection of the TV behind me was on that granite, blurry but clear enough to follow. Rohit had gotten into the sixties, tightened up his game and the runs were flowing again. So I was glancing over the collector's shoulder even as he glanced over mine, though I was subtle. There was a break in play, and the collector got back to the meeting.

After a while, I heard a few words that made me sit up. He was saying something to the effect that the temple was being rebuilt and the guardians of Hinduism were doing their duty. I felt that he had no business airing his personal views—I was put off, but said nothing.

He was given to jumping topics, sometimes even mid-sentence. On one such leap, he moved back to philosophy, circuitously, and almost inaudibly, conveying that the essence of Hinduism is that there is only one supreme being—the rest of it, everything man-made, was a charade. His words were clearer now, though they required interpretation. Now I wondered if he was only being sarcastic with his opening words about the temple.

Service staff came in with trays. The collector said, 'Please.' There was green tea and regular tea, biscuits and salted cashew nuts. It was the kind of fare offered only to important visitors.

The collector took up some new topic. I cannot remember what the topic was. He grew agitated, shifting in his chair, in contrast to the slumped position he had adopted till then. Then, almost disappearing, he bent to get something from under his desk. I assumed that he was reaching for his briefcase or rummaging through it for some papers he needed to make a point. He surfaced with a sock in his hand—he had been pulling it off his foot. It was cream in colour and slightly grimy. He rolled it up in his right fist and began kneading it, as he spoke. The sock had the word 'LIBERTY' stitched boldly in red above the heel area. For an absurd moment, I wondered if it was an intended metaphor. With the sock in his fist, the collector relaxed noticeably and got back to his monologue in the hushed voice.

He was deep into an elucidation when the same deputy who had substituted for him knocked politely, then stepped into the room:

'Sir, it is time.'

'For what?' Irritably, since he had been interrupted.

'Sir, for the conference. We are already late.'

'I am not going.'

'But, sir, you are the chief guest . . .'

'You go.'

'But, sir, without you . . .'

'You go.'

'But, sir . . .'

'GO!'

The deputy said 'Sir!' in the government tone that means 'Right!', spun around and left the room in a hurry. It was the second time in one morning that he had had to officiate in place of the collector, in a meeting he knew nothing about, and both times because of us. The collector gave us a wan smile as if to say, now you see what I must put up with. He tried to remember where he had been when he was interrupted, then started again.

After a short while, I leaned over to Piyush, who was sitting next to me, and whispered, 'Do you have an exit plan?' Piyush is good at keeping a poker face, but now, even he couldn't repress a fit of titters. Hurriedly, he pulled out his hanky, covered his mouth and pretended he was having a coughing fit. The phone rang and I sensed an opportunity. As soon as the call ended, I rose and the team jumped up too.

I said, 'We have kept you much too long. Thank you very much. We look forward to your guidance and support.' He got up and said, 'Only too happy.' Ominously, he transferred the sock to his left hand.

I took one for the team and shook his hand. Piyush and Reenu did polite namastes. When I stepped out, Reenu, with a straight face, offered me sanitizer. Overall, it had been a good meeting. I glanced at the TV screen in the reception room outside.

Rohit Sharma was still batting.

15

Khoripaar

I had barely set foot in a village till I stepped out of McKinsey twenty years ago. After that, I have made up for lost time, visiting scores of villages across Bihar and Uttar Pradesh with the Gates Foundation, and then across Rajasthan and Madhya Pradesh with TAF.

In the beginning, in Bihar and UP, we were only onlookers filled with wonder—that was also the case when we began work in Rajasthan. We didn't understand the what and the why—we never stayed long enough. We went from village to village, gathering impressions. It is a necessary stage when beginning health delivery at the grassroots: you learn a lot by asking open-ended questions.

Over time, we became more thoughtful about why we should go to a particular village. We saw patterns, we had hypotheses. We sensed that there were several obstacles to health services delivery and uptake and our purpose was to see villages that typified different types of challenges. So in Rajasthan, we focused on villages that exemplified the lack of data, how difficult it was to pinpoint the riskiest cases and appreciate the problems faced by the frontline workers. That was what led us to think of the AAA solution that became our main intervention.

Then, we went on to look at the invisible barriers, such as lack of awareness, access roads and superstitions. We selected villages that typified one or more of these barriers. This led us towards a different type of solution led by the affected communities, but that will come later in this narrative.

~

It was this type of thinking that led us to Khoripaar,[1] a tiny village of about 450 people belonging to the Mawasi tribe, one of the most backward ethnic groups in India. I was with my colleagues Prerna Gopal, a programme officer, and Piyush Bhatt, our manager incharge. Our point of departure was a small town called Bicchua, not far from the southern border of Madhya Pradesh, near Maharashtra.

We travelled the country road from Bicchua for an hour. After Bicchua, we were to traverse thick forest for about 6 kilometres to reach Khoripaar. We went first to the public hospital to pick up the ANM, who had agreed to be our guide. Roshini Karmale is responsible for delivering immunization and other health services to the people of Khoripaar and four other villages.

At this point, we hit a roadblock even before we had started. Roshini said that we would not be able to travel that day. The forest road had collapsed in places because of unseasonal rain, and our vehicle would not make it through. She was evidently pregnant, and I asked her how often she travelled to this village. She said that she went to Khoripaar or one of the other villages under her charge at least once a week, riding pillion on a motorcycle driven by her husband or another male relative. I said, 'Sister,* if you can

_____
* The common form of address for nurses all over India.

go on motorcycle in your condition, we will manage perfectly well in our van.' Roshini smiled but said nothing.

Our driver Ramesh had been listening. He had the air of a man of the world, someone who had seen it all and been unimpressed. His ego had been ruffled by the suggestion that he would not be able to manage the forest road. No road had ever defeated him, and he had an acute sense of his self-worth. He said, with a pointed look at Sister Roshini, '*Aap befikr rahiye*, sirji [don't worry at all, sir],' and opened the car door. We had hired him in the big town of Chhindwara, a long distance away, and I wasn't sure he had ever ventured into this kind of terrain, but we clambered in.

The way forward was indeed exceedingly difficult. The narrow, winding dirt road was bumpy with sharp stones that sometimes protruded out of the unusual red-black soil. In parts, the road had almost completely given way. Ramesh would stop the car, jump out and make a careful study of the dirt surface. He would nod confidently, climb back into the car, release the hand brake and then we would move forward cautiously with jerks and jolts. At one place, the road dipped steeply and we looked down at a large pool of muddy water that seemed impossible to go around. I wondered how deep it was, worried that the vehicle would sink. Laughing, Ramesh reassured me. He navigated the pool with the poise of an expert with swift changes of gear. He shot a sharp glance at Sister Roshini in the rear-view mirror as he defeated the road.

I was concerned and asked Roshini if she was all right. She smiled and nodded yes, unperturbed. At one stage where the bouncing and jolting were severe, and the inclines steep, I wondered if we should turn back. Ramesh said, grimly, that it was impossible to do a U-turn—he seemed to be enjoying himself. I thought—what if the car broke down and it got dark? His attitude irritated me and I testily told him to turn off the air conditioner so as not to strain the engine. Roshini noted my anxiety and said reassuringly that we were almost there. I doubted it.

After Ramesh turned off the air conditioner, I rolled down the window and saw that we were deep inside a forest of unusually tall trees. Roshini explained that this was sagon, a variety of local teak, and that a single tree could fetch poachers up to Rs 8 lakh. We noticed the occasional boards proclaiming that the whole area was under the protection of the forest department. Many trees were almost 20 metres high, growing vertically with a single slender trunk, with short branches and large green leaves. In places, the leaves had been drained by some bug. He was clearly an epicure, taking only the tender sap and fastidiously leaving behind the veins. These veins were held together by a translucent brown papery skin, the remnant of a once juicy leaf. I asked Ramesh to stop and took a few photographs of the lush green in conjunction with the papery brown.

As we resumed our journey, I asked Roshini Karmale about the village. She said that the health condition in these parts was terrible. She estimated that barely ten out of twenty children were fully immunized. Infants died regularly and child malnutrition was high. I asked why this happened. She shook her head and said nothing, as though it would take too long to explain. Or perhaps she too was not sure why it happened.

Small towns like Bicchua look much the same everywhere, but there was no prototype for the hundreds of villages scattered around such towns. There were the larger villages, located closer to the towns. Further away were the smaller, poorer villages, and then still more distant, the tiny habitations like Patti and Khoripaar.

~

The forest ended suddenly, and we arrived in Khoripaar in bright late-morning sunlight. We stepped out of the van, stretched our backs and legs and punched our glutes. We were atop a small hill overlooking the village, which was about 200 metres away. Between us and the village was a large green pond. Beyond the village, I could see fields and forest, and well beyond, rolling grey hills. To our left and at our level just a little distance away was the government school building, coated in the characteristic yellow plaster.

A sign above the entrance to the building announced that this was the Nimn Prathmik Vidyalaya, Junior Primary School, with classes from kindergarten to Grade 4. We were greeted by the school principal, Govind Patil, and a young teacher, Mita Ghorpade. We set out with the teacher on a tour of the school.

The walls of the kindergarten rooms were cheerful in bright colours. Hindi and English alphabets had been painted in large letters along one wall. On the adjacent wall were deft depictions of various birds and animals—parrots, tigers, elephants, fish, each one named in Hindi.

We walked down the corridor, investigating the classrooms of the higher grades. Each had a spotless blackboard and unbroken sticks of white and coloured chalk in small boxes on the teacher's desk. The bathrooms were clean and dry. Everything was as it should be. The only thing missing in the school were the children.

We sat down in the principal's spare office. On the wall behind him was the famous picture of Pandit Nehru and Mahatma Gandhi sitting on a *gadda*,* sharing a hearty laugh. On either side were portraits of the stalwarts of the freedom movement— Sardar Patel, Maulana Azad, Bhagat Singh, 'Frontier Gandhi', Dr Ambedkar and Sarojini Naidu. Jhansi ki Rani, from another era, had been thrown in for good measure.

---

* Mattress.

We asked why there were no children and no other teachers in such a nice school. Govind Patil was a man with a certain dignity. Middle-aged, short and abundant, he had the carefully nurtured 'flipover' that is the vanity of many near-bald Indian men. He cleared his throat as if to speak, then nodded at Mita Ghorpade, indicating that she should do the talking.

The teacher wore a starched light blue sari and had a spot of *sindoor** where her hair was parted. She was soft-spoken and a slight smile hovered perpetually across her lips. She had the self-assurance that seems to come naturally to good schoolteachers anywhere in the world. 'No child comes to the school. The families here are poor and illiterate. They do not think it is important.' she said.

'Why do you come?'

'*Main apna kartavya samajhti hoon* [I consider it my duty]. I sit here the whole day,' she said simply. At this, Govind Patil added, 'I have to come because after all I am the principal. Other teachers are not like Mita ji; they come sometimes only.' He said that on the days that they came to school, the other teachers 'mark attendance' for all the days they had been absent. He conveyed that he was in no position to take any action against them, even for such a serious breach of discipline. 'Besides, what will they do here?' he asked.

I asked Mita Ghorpade again why she came to school every day when no one else did. She said, 'If I can get even a few to come, and I can teach them something, maybe they will stay and I will be doing my duty. After all, the government is paying me a salary.' I marvelled at her commitment and wondered where it came from.

---

* Red paste or pigment applied on the forehead, along the parting of the hair of married Indian women.

She added, 'I have even gone from house to house and spoken with families. They show me respect and say they will send the children tomorrow, but no one comes.' After a pause, she asked, 'Sir, have you gone to the village? Go and see; you will understand, these are very poor people. They need many things. School is not important.'

There was a growing din outside. It was a small group of urchins, pushing, shoving, running up the hill towards the school. One had the metal rim of a cycle tire and he skilfully tapped it along with a stick, even though he was running uphill. Mita Ghorpade said, smiling, 'They are coming to the AWC which is next door, to have the mid-day meal.'

I asked the teacher to tell us something about herself. She said, 'My husband is a government engineer. We live in Bicchua. He drops me here and picks me up every day on motorcycle.' She added with a slight blush, 'We are expecting a baby, our first child.'

Mita Ghorpade said that after the baby was born, she would come back to the school. She said her mother-in-law would take care of the baby. 'I don't want to just sit at home,' she added.

～

We stopped at the government AWC next door. The government requires all states to have such a centre in every village. Here, children under six are supposed to get a hot cooked mid-day meal, and pregnant women, nutritious THR. The centres are required to keep weight records for each child, and provide pre-school teaching and opportunities for socialization through play. It is a wonderful idea that falls woefully short in its implementation in several states in north India. That was clearly the case in Khoripaar.

The children sat on the floor, eating their mid-day meal with fierce concentration. Each had a metal plate with two rotis and katoris with a watery dal and a ladle of vegetable. The AWW greeted us warily, possibly assuming that we were government inspectors. We tried to dispel her fears, telling her we were from an NGO and had come to learn. I asked where she weighed the smaller children, and she said, nervously, that the scale was broken, but she had applied for a new one. That was shocking because without weighing the children, she could not track if they were undernourished, and to what extent. Sister Roshini said she would ensure they got the scale right away.

We asked the AWW if we could see her record book. Every child in the village under the age of six had been marked as regularly attending the centre and receiving a mid-day meal. Each child had normal weight according to the records. I estimated that there would be at least thirty children in the under-six age group in a village of this size. If only five or six came to the centre every day, where did the money charged for the others go? Was every pregnant or lactating woman getting her allocation of rations? The books said so, but I wondered if that was really the case.

On the way to the village, we stopped to have a closer look at the large pond, which was yellow-green and emitted a dreadful stench. Sister Roshini said, 'It is a breeding ground for mosquitoes and there are many cases of malaria in the village. The government rarely sprays the pond. There is an NGO that provides bed nets. But most people in these parts don't have beds—they sleep on the floor.' She added, 'The nets are put to good use though—to store onions, potatoes, all kinds of things.'

The village consisted of a single road with about thirty dwellings on each side. The road was made of white concrete, quite the opposite of the one we had navigated through the forest. The high-quality road looked out of place in a place of such obvious poverty. Roshini explained that it came through the panchayat[*] and was funded by the Pradhan Mantri Gram Sadak Yojna, which is responsible for road quality to, and within, villages that are cut off. So here the 'within' portion had been well taken care of, but not the 'to'—why? Roshini said, 'It is a big help. This was just mud and slush during the rainy season.'

Most of the huts were made of baked mud and had thatched roofs. Though modest, they were aesthetically pleasing. The front walls were painted with white *choona*,[†] bordered with red or green. Some others were indigo blue. To the side, or at the back of each house, was a covered area for cows and goats. The cows wore bead necklaces with hand-painted cowbells.

We stopped outside a hut with an old man sitting on the porch. We called out, asking if we could visit his home. He came up to us because he was quite deaf. When he understood, he smiled toothlessly and welcomed us in. There was a small porch and the old man, whose name was Ramji, brought out a mat.

Ramji's emaciated wife squatted nearby, creating something out of a sheaf of long green leaves. She worked quickly, slitting each leaf into thin strands with a piece of flint. She deftly braided and knotted the strands together, and the knots decreased in size down the length of the cord. Each braid was exquisite. Rows of these braids lay on the ground next to her. I imagined she was making something to sell as a tribal craft item in the town, and I

---

[*] Panchayats are the units of local self-governance at the village level across India. There is one 'gram panchayat' for roughly every six villages, and panchayat members are elected by the local village communities. Panchayats are funded by the state government, and there is a certain amount of money that the panchayat can choose to spend at its discretion on local projects.

[†] Slaked lime, used as whitewash.

wondered how much each string might cost. I would have liked to buy one to take home.

I asked, 'What are you making?' She looked at me, '*Jhadoo*,'* she said, and I was taken aback. 'Are you going to sell it?' Shaking her head and going back to her work, she responded, 'Why will I sell it? I will use it. *Yeh jhadoo hai . . .*'

She must have thought me an idiot. Prerna and Piyush were supressing smiles. Ears tingling, I sat down and asked Ramji about his family, to start our dialogue.

Unexpectedly, he launched into a strange tale. I struggled to decipher his mix of dialect and toothless whisper. The story started slowly, then took off at speed. The bits I followed were— the couple had only one child, a daughter—she had eloped with a boy from Bicchua town, bringing great shame. The newlyweds ran away to some big town and here the plot got confusing— someone got HIV, her husband got murdered and she got three months in jail. She was dropped back in the village by the police, bringing even greater shame. Suddenly, the old man got to his feet, motioned me inside the hut and pointed dramatically at a beautiful bed made of black lacquered wood with ornate paint work on its legs. He gave me a significant look as if to say, you are a man of the world, you will understand, and said, 'She came back with nothing, only this bed.' I had no idea what all this meant but I shook my head and made the clicking sympathy sound with my tongue.

Somehow, it didn't seem odd in that environment that Ramji should confide such an intimate story to complete strangers. The tale had reached its sad climax and he paused for a breath. I seized the opportunity, raising my voice to ask, 'How do people earn a living in Khoripaar?'

---

* Broom.

Ramji said, 'What to tell you, sir? My grandfather, and his grandfather before him, all lived in this village. I grew up here. We are forest people: the forest is like our mother. There was a time when we got our food and fruits, honey, all medicines from the forest. All that has stopped.'

'What happened?'

'The poachers came to steal the sagon tree. The forest department took over to protect the trees, but now they allow the poachers and take their share.[2] First, they made a circle and said, "This part of the forest is for you tribals."* Then the circle became smaller and smaller. Now it is almost nothing. We have nothing to eat, see the children here, so thin and sickly.'

'Then how do you live?'

'We cannot live like this. The youngsters are leaving, going to other places, looking for work as labourers. That is not easy. This village is dying; it will not be here very long.'

As we took our leave, on an impulse I asked Ramji if he knew who Mahendra Singh Dhoni was. India's cricket captain was probably the best-known name in India at the time, but Ramji shook his head. I asked if he knew the name of the prime minister of the country—he shook his head again. The chief minister? After thinking a while, he said 'Chauhan', getting it right. When I asked him whether he had voted in the last general election, he responded that he had, as had the whole village. How did he know whom to vote for? He said he pushed the button next to the symbol he had been told to push.

I received a broad education in the thirty minutes we spent with Ramji and his wife. Afterwards, Sister Roshini joined us,

---

* I use the term 'tribals' instead of 'indigenous populations', which is perhaps more correct. It would have been cumbersome to use the latter throughout the book.

having completed her rounds, as we stepped out onto the concrete road. She confirmed what Ramji had said, 'The village people have been cut off from the forest. It is true—that is why there is so much malnourishment. They do not eat more than one proper meal.' According to Sister Roshini, they were cut off from Bicchua because the forest department did not allow a proper road to be built. She said the department said if there is a pukka road, even the villagers would start poaching.

~

I asked Sister Roshini if we could visit the house where an eight-month-old infant had died recently. The mother, Dhulari, was cleaning the porch of her ramshackle hut. She was scrawny and unkempt and her sari was tied between her legs in the Maharashtrian style. Roshini asked if we could come in and talk to her. She waved her hands, conveying 'no'. Roshini called out that we had come from far to see the village. Dhulari stepped out into the courtyard reluctantly. She looked about four months pregnant. It struck me that this was the third mother-to-be I was meeting in a morning!

'How did your baby die?' I asked, gently. Dhulari was in no mood to talk. 'I don't know,' she said, in a hoarse whisper.

'What happened?' I asked. She replied softly, looking down, 'The baby was crying in the evening and would not stop. We called the ambulance.[3] It took a long time. My husband took her after midnight. She died on the way.' I asked Roshini, quietly, 'Did the baby have her *tikakaran* [immunizations]?'

She said the baby had received the first dose but Dhulari would not bring the baby back for the next one. Dhulari responded that she hadn't because the baby had fever after the first dose (even though this was normal). Evidently, the *jadi-*

booti doctor had told her not to take the injection. The doctor
told everyone that the Mata, the local goddess, had said no one
should take it.

Dhulari's baby had been delivered at home by this charlatan.
Dhulari's husband had also agreed that there was no need to go
to Bicchua. I asked, 'Will you have this baby in the hospital? It's
much better for you and the baby.' Dhulari said nothing.

I persisted, 'You will get Rs 1400 from the government if you
deliver the baby in the hospital.'[4] Dhulari asked, 'What will we do
with the money?'

Our next stop was the home of the government's ASHA
worker, Ramvati. If there was an urgent case, she ensured that
the mother or child quickly received treatment in a health facility
beyond the village. She and the AWW had the crucial roles of
keeping the ANM informed about who needed her immediate
attention. I asked Roshini if the ASHA worker was doing a good
job. She said enigmatically, 'You will see.'

There was a large black board outside the house, with hand-
painted white lettering that announced, 'Ramvati Devi, ASHA'
along with her phone number. Ramvati was sprawled out on
the stone floor under the sign. Luckily, the shade of the roof
covered her. I was alarmed—was it a heart attack? Roshini did
not seem concerned. She tapped Ramvati's cheeks and sprinkled
water from the matka on her face. Ramvati slowly came out of
her stupor and pushed the nurse aside. We caught the heady
fermenting smell of country liquor. Sister Roshini was evidently

---

* *Jadi-booti* literally means 'leaves and roots'. Rural jadi-booti 'doctors'
offer medicines made with these local herbs. These practitioners are
probably effective in dealing with simple health conditions, but wholly
unqualified to treat any serious illness.

stronger than she looked and managed to drag Ramvati to a shaded area. 'It is better if she sleeps it off,' she said.

We heard a stirring inside the house and knocked. After persisting for five minutes, we were about to give up when the door opened a crack. A thin man, ebony-skinned and red-eyed, peered out suspiciously, a scowl on his face.

I asked, 'What is wrong with your wife?' He said, '*Bimaar*' and was about to close the door. I said, 'Please show us what medicine she is taking.' Roshini was smiling to herself. The man came back with a bottle of cough mixture and a foil with six expired antacid tablets. I peered over the man's shoulder into the house. It was pitch dark except for a tiny flicker of light deep inside the hut—a television set. I wondered how Ramvati and her husband could afford a TV. I asked him what he was watching. He said, scowl deepening, 'Serial.'

Sister Roshini said, 'It gets even more interesting. The jadi-booti doctor is the ASHA's mother. I will take you to her.' The doctor's house was close by, but she refused to meet us at first. With much persuasion from Sister Roshini, she agreed to have a few words with us. The doctor did not invite us in and we talked to her standing in the doorway. She was thin to the point of being emaciated, like every woman I had seen so far in the village. Her hair was grey and wild and gave her a frenzied look, which probably made her clientele feel comfortable. The room seemed to be a small godown with bulky sacks piled up in one corner. She had a small table on one side with two chairs.

The jadi-booti doctor told us she handled only common illnesses like cough and cold. Everything else she referred to her daughter, the ASHA, who took those cases to Sister Roshini. I asked if she did deliveries and she nodded, yes. She said she cut the cord with a blade as was the prescribed practice. I asked if the blade was new and sterilized, and she said she used whatever the family gave her. I asked if the room she delivered in was clean and the water boiled, and she said again—whatever the family had prepared. I asked what she would do with a complicated case, and she shook her head.

We asked what she thought about immunization. She nodded at the ANM as if to say, 'her area'. We asked about the Mata who had issued a diktat against immunization. She said she had never heard of such a Mata. She grew silent and would not answer any more questions. Roshini said, 'The people are poor and she charges very little, often taking payment in a little bit of grain or vegetables.'

I should have been angry with her, but I was not. She was herself a victim of the acute poverty that hung like a dark cloud over the village—she was only trying to survive. Perhaps she was not even aware that she was doing great harm.

Towards the end of the road, we came across four merry young men, tipsy on hooch. We walked up to them, while Roshini hung back. I asked them if the mahua was good. They said that it was, and then added that none of them drank. I said I didn't believe it and we had a laugh. The men made mahua, which they sold for Rs 40 per bottle in town. We walked some distance into the fields and one of them showed how the distillation was done. They packed the mahua berry into covered matkas and the fruit was left to ferment, a process that could take up to ten days, depending on the weather. The raw fermented liquor was boiled in a large vat. The fumes went through a plastic pipe, and at the other end emerged pure distilled mahua! He said, with pride, that mahua is a high-quality liquor, 'From the trees to your glass. There is nothing added, no colouring or chemicals. Much better than

English liquor. No headache the next day, nothing.' I said I was impressed, but politely declined a drink.

On our way back to the van, we witnessed an unusual sight. A dozen women were waiting for their turn to get water from a handpump. Their buckets were strewn around the pump and no one was drawing water. Behind them stood a tall metal structure with solar panels on top of it. We walked over.

The women ranged from adolescent girls to grannies. I asked some of them to explain what was happening. They said that the sun gave *dum** to the batteries and that enabled the water to be drawn from deep in the ground into a storage tank just below ground level. When there was enough water in the storage tank, the women could draw on it with the handpump. It seemed like a complicated way to get water. I was told that an NGO, the same one that had introduced bed nets, had introduced the solar pumping system.

I asked how long they had to wait before their turn to draw water. One of the women, laughing, said it depended on whether it was a sunny day and how many people were already waiting their turn. When I pressed for a more exact idea, there was more laughter and I got different answers ranging from two hours to eight hours. Hours at a stretch—to get two buckets of water! It occurred to me the alternative was much worse—walking several kilometres to a stream, filling their buckets and walking back with a bucket on the head and some more water in a lota on the hip. We walked away, leaving the women sitting in the hot sun—some engaged in banter, some nursed babies, all were in good humour.

~

* Strength.

On our way back, Sister Roshini asked if we would like to make a small detour to visit another village, Majinapaar. She said it was about twice the size of Khoripaar and very different. About halfway down the forest road, she told the driver to turn left onto another, even rougher, path. Thankfully, we bounced along this route for only another fifteen minutes before pulling up just outside the AWC of Majinapaar village. It was located at the centre of the village, where the houses converged in a cluster.

We were greeted by Mamta, the AWW. She was cheerful and energetic, and Roshini greeted her like a friend. Mamta looked about thirty, which is much younger than most women are in this cadre. It was late afternoon and the school would close soon. The children were at play and some started milling around us. They plucked at our clothes and ran away laughing. The growth charts Mamta maintained were accurate and there was a well-stocked and clean kitchen.

Mamta told me that she too was from the Mawasi tribal community. Surprised, I said, 'We just came from Khoripaar, which is also Mawasi. The AWC was barely functioning. Health didn't seem important to the community. Your village is just 3 kilometres away. Why is there such a difference?'

Mamta said, 'There are two reasons. The first is that there are several tribes in this village. Besides Mawasi, there are Bhil and Gond. Their houses are in different sections, but everyone gets along. There is a pride, a friendly competition. If your child is doing well in school, then mine must also do well, that sort of thing. This is the most important thing—the attitude of the community.'

'And the second reason?' I asked.

'Sir, I grew up in a village like Khoripaar. But my parents wanted to see me educated. I went to school and then to college.

That makes a difference too.' One educated woman in a village could make such a difference!

We dropped Sister Roshini Karmale back at the hospital in Bicchua. During our visit, there had been instances when she seemed unaware that there was a problem, with the broken weighing scale, for example. At other times, she seemed powerless to change things, for example, to enforce immunization or institutional deliveries. The situation must have been similar in many villages under her charge. It was a tough job involving a lot of travel and frustration. Over the course of a day together, we had come to admire her sense of duty and her good humour. We were sorry to say goodbye.

On the way back, my mind was racing, trying to make sense of Khoripaar's desperate situation. I ran through all the clues that suggested that a solution was possible—the road, teacher, NGO, youth. I imagined how the future might look:

> *From Bicchua we take the new concrete forest road. Sister Roshini says, 'The trip to the village now takes less than fifteen minutes. The new road has saved many lives because emergency cases can now reach the hospital quickly. The government is laying more such roads after Khoripaar as part of a new scheme.'*
>
> *It is time for the lunch break in the village school and there is the familiar clamour of little children at play. The teacher, Mita Ghorpade, proudly shows us a brass badge pinned on the pallu of her sari. She says, 'There was a good collector. He visited the village once and said, "Mitaji, you can teach just as well outside the classroom." He said I should become a "social change agent".' She takes us to a classroom where a few men and women are waiting for her. She says, 'I teach adults how to read and write. Each of them must take up a project for the village, like making sure the road is clean. This is not all—I make sure the ASHA and AWW*

are aware that I am watching them.' Sister Roshini adds, 'Mita ji is the first person I talk to after I reach the village.'

At the anganwadi, a women's group meeting led by the ASHA worker is in progress. The women pick a health topic: today, it is 'care of the newborn' and there is a group discussion in which new mothers, mothers-in-law and grannies are all participating. They develop action plans based on the discussion. The ASHA tells me the group has a lot of confidence and their demands are taken seriously by the panchayat.

The village lake reflects the blue sky above. Women wash clothes at the far bank. The cleaning of the lake is a village project led by the local community, supported by the local NGO. The staff person from the NGO says, 'Earlier, we used up our funding on solutions like solar pumps and bed-nets—now we ask the community what they need most and how they can solve the problem for themselves. We only support them. We hire a few young men from the village for our projects. Malaria cases are much fewer now.'

We visit the new community centre full of people watching a popular serial. In between, the NGO plays short entertaining videos on such topics as sanitation and hygiene.

As we stroll through the village of Khoripaar, change is evident in every direction.

16

Jad

The great joy of our work is that it takes us to many far-flung villages and hamlets. These journeys teach and inspire, and there is the camaraderie that springs from shared improbable experience.

I have trained myself, after each day in the field, to describe what I have seen in longhand in a personal diary. Fleeting images, sights, sounds and smells are imprinted in its leaves.

It is in the nature of our work that there are periods of great joy, and sometimes of heartache. It is then, that I can delve deep into my diaries, pull out a memory, to be restored again. And it was on just such a day, that I remembered a trip we had made to a place called Jad, deep in tribal Madhya Pradesh.

~

Our small group was led by an ebullient young man named Atul Deep Sinha. He was secretly envied because he was responsible for Tamia block, a place of ineffable beauty. I asked Atul how long it would take to get to Jad from Chili, the small town from which we would start out on foot. 'About thirty minutes,' he said. Nikita D'Souza, our creative person, shot me a look and shook her head imperceptibly. Atul caught that and frowned, because Nikita was all of twenty-two, four years his junior, and this was not her turf. 'It depends on the weather,' he said tersely.

On the way to Chili, Atul told us about our destination. 'Tamia block has 140 villages. Jad is part of Harrakachal sub-centre, which has eight villages. It is a hamlet of 144 people from thirty-three families and their houses are spread out far from each other. It is in a valley, and you can go only on foot.

'The people are from the Bharia tribe,[1] one of the seventy-five government classified "Particularly Vulnerable Tribal Groups [PVTG]". All babies are delivered at home since the village is completely cut off. There were two births in the last six months, and currently there are two pregnant women, two lactating mothers, and fifteen children under five.' Atul was new in the job and seemed keen to make a good impression. Paras and Harhini, his seniors, nodded approval.

After he finished, I quietly googled PVTGs.[*] The government site said these are peoples with 'primitive traits, distinctive culture, shyness . . . and isolation'. There is '. . . dependency on hunting, gathering . . . pre-agricultural level of technology, zero or negative growth of population, and extremely low level of literacy'. More 'developed and assertive tribes' often took a large share of funds allocated to these tribes, and so the government had a separate allocation and special schemes for the PVTGs. Roughly 21 per cent of Madhya Pradesh's 72 million people are tribal, and 1 per cent of these are Bharia.[2]

On the way, we passed a small nondescript town with the unlikely name 'Newton'—a fleeting mystery. We began the climb to Chili, which is at an elevation of some 1000 feet. We stopped at a curve in the road to eat bhutta. Our driver asserted

---

[*] Earlier named 'Primitive Tribal Groups'.

that these were the best you would find anywhere in India. There were several vendors along the curve. The one we stopped at was more enterprising than his competitors, with six plastic chairs and a tarpaulin roof on sticks. He charged Rs 15 for a bhutta—in nearby Betul district, we paid Rs 20 for three. The man had a take-it-or leave it attitude, but in a nice way.

We moved on, climbing the winding road through dark, green-velvet hills speckled yellow with sagon in bloom, branches laden with blossoms. The trees of Madhya Pradesh have a certain attitude, with their insistent rustic beauty. There were many varieties of trees and I took photographs to look them up later.[3]

There was a fast-moving stream below. Women washed clothes, knee-deep in the water, red *ghaghras* tied above their knees. At a decent distance, a young man washed his motorcycle in water that seemed too deep.

We reached Chili, the small market town hub for the surrounding villages. Soon, the tarred road ended and we took to a flat dirt road leading to the nearby hills. Harrakachal sub-centre was near the closest hill. It had the town's AWC and was the delivery point for the eight villages.

Sister Pushpa Parani, the person responsible for the centre, joined us, wearing her white sari uniform. She was short and stocky, with straight features and an open face, pleasant but reserved, a woman of few words. Her answers were clipped but we understood that of the eight villages, four, including Jad, were cut off entirely. She visited four villages on foot, and the others using her own scooter. She did two village visits a week, not counting visits for emergencies.

Her husband was a teacher and stayed, together with their two children, in Chhindwara. She went home every weekend. Her attitude was that she was a government servant doing her assigned job as best as she could do it. It was a tough sub-centre, but maybe her next posting would be an easier one. That was it.

Pushpa put on a bright green raincoat with a hood. She clarified that it was her own, the government didn't provide it. She picked up her vaccines cold-box and set off wearing flat open sandals.

The road petered out. We were in a large corn field and then on the undulating trail to Jad. It was clear from the outset that I was slowing the party down. Nikita was a high-altitude mountaineer—Paras, Harhini and Atul serious trekkers. Sister Pushpa had important work to do in Jad and had left us behind, a green dab in the distance, moving quickly. We were going into the valley though I felt as though we were climbing. It must have been because there was so much going up, then down, and probably the up was tougher than the down.

We stopped a few times to look at the spectacle around us, an endless, ever-changing pas de deux of cloud and hill. Sometimes the clouds were a mist, entering the hill forest in one place, emerging somewhere else in wisps. Then a big cloud would envelope a hill up to its chest, and as the cloud shifted, bits of deep green would show up here, then there, and be covered again.

That scenic panorama was to our left. The hillside was to our right. High above, near the very top, was a gushing waterfall, but too far away to appreciate fully. We didn't have enough time for me to linger and be soothed. We went forward, eyes down on the ground, which was either soft or rocky or completely wet. Nikita tested which rock to step on and I followed her footsteps, grabbing her forearm if I lost balance, for her wrist was sprained. It was only mid-way that I noticed that Nikita was carrying an enormous load on her back—she was training for an expedition six months later. She is tall and thin, looks almost frail, and it was beyond my comprehension.

The rain started to come down in steady, sharp drops. Like a magic trick, Nikita began to pull umbrellas out of her bag. I needed my hands free so I didn't take one and got steadily drenched. I learnt that jeans are the worst thing to wear on a trek because they get all heavy and soggy. My shirt was one of those outdoors things, so it wasn't so bad.

Going up a slope, we entered a cornfield again, a sign that habitation was near. We came out on a small elevation above a rugged green plain that had hills all around. We saw a small brick structure in the distance, on the perimeter of the plain. Spotting a tiny figure in white outside, we knew that was Sister Pushpa and this was the AWC.

We walked a short distance. The plain was rough and uneven, covered with long bladed grass, shades of green with a touch of yellow, wild but smooth. The range of hills in front of us had another range behind, close enough to see the trees on it. Again, the clouds were teasing the hills, pure white gossamer inching down the slopes.

There were all kinds of trees on the plain closer to the perimeter. There again was our friend the sagon, which blooms briefly at the first onset of rain. It was August, which is monsoon time, and the tree was flaunting its blossoms, standing proud. The trees were at a distance but I thought I saw mahua, kamar and mainhar, which have distinctive canopies.[4] They stood aloof from the brazen sagon.

At the base of the hill, at two o'clock in the far distance, was a single house, a tiny red speck against the massive green hill behind it. There was a smaller speck at eleven o'clock, embedded a little deeper into the hill. Perhaps the reason why the houses were near the perimeter, and the plain uncultivated, was that the hill forest provided most of the sustenance.

The valley had a unique silence. The silence of a forest is broken by birdsong and the occasional calls of its creatures—that is a known charm. On the floor of the valley of Jad, absolute silence reigned. No sound of cows lowing in the distance, roosters crowing, goats bleating, the familiar sounds of village India. Not even a rustling of leaves or the sight of any human being. But it was not an eerie quietness, nor the emptiness of a place deserted. It was the pure hush of an empty cathedral, evoking a feeling akin to reverence.

~

We came to the AWC, a tiny room about 12 feet by 8. There was one window, a weighing apparatus hooked to the ceiling and a height measurement stand. Our AAA programme's digitized village map, marked with coloured bindis, stood against the far wall. Each dot on the map represented a house with a pregnant or lactating woman or a child under the age of five. The protocol is that the high-risk cases are marked in red. Here, that was inapt, for the entire cycle, from conception to childhood, was fraught with risk, given the circumstances of this village.

There was no ASHA present. On the far wall, the young AWW Durga checked that her records were in order. She wore her green patterned sari uniform. Sister Pushpa sat on the floor, taking out the equipment and supplies she always left behind in the centre locked in a steel trunk. She wore a spotless thin white coat.

A man, his wife and their four-year-old son were waiting for Sister Pushpa to finish her preparations. The woman and her son squatted nearby, staring into the distance—the mother looked one way, the child, the other. The man sat on his haunches, wiry, and his eyes had a certain light. We introduced ourselves as health workers who had come to learn about Jad. That didn't have any effect on the man. He said his name was Bholu and he talked freely with us. The conversation would be truncated as soon as Pushpa was ready, and we had many questions. So we talked without dwelling too long on any one topic.

Bholu was a subsistence farmer, mainly cultivating makka (corn). He also grew small amounts of seasonal vegetables, such as cauliflower and brinjal. They kept hens and would eat eggs and meat after making an offering to God. He said the main problem the village faced was of road connectivity to the town. The only time most of the adults went to the town was during elections. They voted because they had been told they would lose all their government entitlements if they didn't vote. They pressed the button next to the symbol they had been told to 'choose'. Bholu didn't know the names of anyone outside his village, whether Narendra Modi or Amitabh Bachchan. He had never watched television, though he had heard the radio.

He said marriages were arranged by the families. ('First the *daaru*,* then quick *haan ya na* [yes or no], and then the feast,' he said, eyes sparkling). There were elopements from time to time, 'But they always come back and get married—but then no feast, that is only for betrothal'. Speaking deadpan, he had a wry sense of humour.

I had heard the Bharia were experts in the herbs and roots that grew in the forest and that they followed their own medicinal practices, able to cure many ailments themselves. I had just asked the question when Sister Pushpa called out to the AWW that the child had to be weighed.[5]

The little boy was lifted into the weighing harness. He was suspended above head height, but the child neither cried nor laughed. He had been sitting quietly so far, taking no interest in his surroundings. I sensed something was wrong with his

---

* Alcohol.

development. Paras said the child was severely underweight at 10.3 kg—a four-year-old should weigh 5 kg more than that. He had been stunted by severe malnutrition before he was two years old. The ANM had made sure he was treated at the NRC in town and he had recovered weight. Now, back at home, he was losing it again. Bholu had been saving face when he talked about the eggs and chicken and healthy vegetables.

Childhood malnutrition was probably endemic in Jad. It struck me that we are happy or otherwise only when we compare ourselves to a normal. If most children were sick and many died needlessly, and that was happening all the time, why would the parents think anything was wrong? That is the unique tragedy of places that are isolated. What was the solution?

In the meantime, Paras had been going through the AWW's records. He is an expert at spotting faulty entries in record-keeping. He said her records were perfect. A frontline worker's registers are not simple to manage and mistakes are inevitable. What did her perfect records tell us?

By this time, the room was full of pregnant women, new mothers and babies. They sat on the ground in front of Pushpa, who was first attending to her priority, which was vaccinating the babies. It was an assembly line where an unsuspecting tot was brought and jabbed, sometimes even as the infant was suckling. She did it so quickly and skilfully that the baby usually didn't know, but not always, so there was a continuous bawling in the room.

The women were lovely, slim with chiselled features, glowing dark complexions and enviably white and even teeth! I read later about the beauty of Bharia women. They were shy, to the extent that they would not speak or even look at anyone in our party. It seemed to me that this was not the shyness that comes from being wary or lacking confidence. I could see them talking animatedly and laughing with each other. It was just that talking to strangers was not something they were accustomed to.

Atul had to talk to the community as part of his job—here, he did it through the men. Like Bholu, men were not shy. But Atul was conversing easily with Durga, the AWW. He explained later that she was Bharia but had been brought up in another village that was not isolated. Shyness was not the norm there. She had come to Jad when she married someone from here. What opportunity did that suggest?

The next woman was Ashwati, pregnant with her third child. Pallu over her head, she sat quietly in front of Sister Pushpa, eyes cast down. She said in a soft voice that could barely be heard that she did not want to take the TT vaccine.* Atul had convinced Mahesh, her husband—that must be why she showed up.

Pushpa asked—why? Ashwati said she had fever. Pushpa knew that was not true and looked around. Durga said she had checked and there was no fever. Ashwati whispered that she had a lot of pain and fever the last time. Pushpa looked at Atul, who gently explained that the vaccine was for her and for her baby—you want your baby to be safe, right? Throughout, Pushpa was holding the needle in her palm, unopened in its wrapper, Then, at precisely the right moment, she said, 'I will give you some tablets to prevent any pain—don't take this vaccine after this if there is pain and call me yourself if there is pain this time.' She unwrapped the needle and waited. Durga rolled up Ashwati's sleeve.

~

---

* The tetanus toxoid vaccine is mandatory for all pregnant women to prevent maternal and foetal tetanus. 5 per cent of neonatal deaths in India are because of tetanus.

There was a huge clap of thunder. I went to the door—a thunderstorm was underway. The rain was coming down in torrents and the sky was dark, though it was just 3 p.m. The rain would abate, then come back with force. After a half hour of this, the thought crossed my mind that we might have to spend the night in Jad, and I wasn't entirely comfortable with that possibility.

I asked Paras what the plan was. He said in his usual smiling way, 'The rain may not stop and we may have to stay here tonight.' Meanwhile, Sister Pushpa was packing up—Ashwati had been her last patient. She put on her green raincoat and was zipping up the hood. I figured that she must know the weather in these parts and asked if she thought the rain would stop. She said, stoically, 'Who can tell what will happen with nature?' After that bit of philosophy, and Paras' almost spiritual acceptance of circumstances, I decided to take matters into my own hands. I shouted out to the team in as calm a way as I could, 'We are leaving now!' Everybody started packing up.

Sister Pushpa was in a hurry and set out—no doubt she had patients waiting at the sub-centre. Nikita ran after her, getting drenched in the process. She came back with the ANM's cold box. I asked what she was doing. Nikita said, 'Oh, my load was not enough for the practice, so I asked if I could carry her cold-box back for her.' Speechless, I stepped out with an umbrella.

Luckily, the rain calmed down in a while. The trip back was easier till I came to what looked like a flood to me. We had reached the place where we had looked up and seen the waterfall on top of the hill. That was overflowing after the storm and we had reached a point where it was rushing across our path, going left to right. On the right, the path was curving down in a way I did not like. Nikita called out that you couldn't be swept away if the water was less than waist-deep. I stepped in, heart in mouth.

I have experienced two types of journeys. In one, you learn a lot ('all my questions got answered'). In the other, you learn just a tiny fraction of what there is to know, but that fraction provokes countless questions. That makes you want to return. I planned to come back to Jad for sure.

17

Dai

As our programme gained momentum, we worked with many of the tribes of Madhya Pradesh. These included the Bhil and the Gond, which together made up more than 70 per cent of the state's tribal population, and tribes such as the Korku, Mawasi and Bharia, which were less than one per cent each.

This time, I was travelling with my colleagues Kakuli Baidya, who is a nurse mentor,[*] and Piyush Bhatt, the district manager. We were in Betul district and heading to a village in Bhimpur block called Saudar,[1] home to 1100 people belonging to the small Korku tribe, which is labelled as 'backward'.[2]

The purpose of our visit was to understand why there were so many home deliveries, and by implication, great faith in the *dai*—a traditional rural midwife.

It was said that the Korku believed that spirits possessed some women and children during the crucial '1000 days' period. People had faith in 'babas' who practised black magic and believed that they could counter all manner of ailments, from conjunctivitis

---

[*] These are highly skilled nurses in our nurse mentoring programme who focus on the skills and attitudes of government nursing staff.

to evil eye. Childhood pneumonia was sometimes treated by inhaling the fumes of burning chillies. However, we had also been to villages where home deliveries had come down despite the local superstitions.[3] We conjectured that some other factor must also be at work.

~

Travelling in rural Madhya Pradesh, my eyes are always drawn to the car window to see what nature was painting today. Today's theme was green, shade after shade as far as the eye could see, sometimes with a speck of brown just to enhance the green, an endless canvas. Maize, paddy, soyabean and varieties of trees, including palm, contributed with bold strokes and subtle accents of green.

As we approached the village, which was at an elevation, we turned a bend and saw a herd of goats approaching us, perhaps 50 metres away. There were some hefty fellows with horns, their genteel mates and a few youngsters. A hefty one was in front, obviously the leader. They were a disciplined group, noble in brown and white, striding purposefully without straggling. One goatherd was at the back, another in the middle of the herd. The men wore white dhotis and turbans and each carried a long stick and open umbrella, for it had started drizzling.

I wanted to capture the sight on my phone camera. The driver pulled up by the side of the road and I stepped out. The herd was now about 30 metres ahead and I clicked a few images. Then the leader goat saw us and stopped in his tracks. The herd pulled up behind him—even the goatherds, respecting his decision, stopped. The leader glanced at me and then looked straight ahead without moving. The word 'sorry' came out of my mouth involuntarily and I climbed back into the van.

The road to the village was in good condition. We stopped some distance away and walked towards the village, which was laid out in the shape of a large comma, a single road with houses and fields on both sides. We entered at the base of the comma, passing ramshackle houses on both sides. We were soon joined by a very thin and sickly-looking ASHA, and a quiet and dignified AWW. They were expecting us.

Saudar, at first glance, seemed like just another poor village. But between the shacks we counted three kiosks. They were selling packaged junk food, local savouries, cigarettes and paan. There were urchins outside each kiosk, taking their time, consulting with each other, agreeing on swaps, as children everywhere do when they have some coins and must choose between treats.

Behind that front row of shacks were some solid structures as we progressed up the neck of the comma. One such house was narrow, painted with choona and with a tall door, the kind that joined at the centre. Three tykes were hiding behind the door, giggling, ducking away, reappearing—they were making fun of us. I waved at them and took a step forward, at which they scuttled into the house, only to come back soon to resume their mischief.

A woman carrying a large metal vat on her head came up to the front door. The woman of the house appeared from inside. After a brief conversation, she held out a vessel and took something—perhaps grain of some kind—that the other woman ladled out. The visitor collected her payment and left, to knock on the next door.

A little further on, the main road veered off to the right and smaller pathways led into the fields on both sides. We asked if we could see the AWC, even though it would be closed because of COVID-19. Silent till then, the AWW perked up. She explained that there had been no anganwadi building for years. The government still had to build one. Instead, the centre was being run from someone's house. We stepped into the house, the front of which was a closed veranda. A weighing scale hung from the low ceiling. A pie dog sleeping in one corner looked up at us and went back to his dreams, unimpressed. Two doors led into the dark interior of the house.

Kakuli said the centre had been working well till COVID-19 struck. The ANM visited the village regularly and used the house to provide health services. This phenomenon of a functioning AWC being run from someone's house was not uncommon.

Back out on the street, a local sidled up to us, a small man of about forty. A torn, dirty white turban sat loosely on his head. He had a grey stubble and a crooked smile that never left his face. He was curious to know who we were and what we were doing in his village. His attitude was politely cocky and our conversation went like this:

What do you do? Farmer: *Nothing.*

What do you mean 'nothing'? *Nothing much.*

What work do you do? *Work on the land.*

Whose land? *My own land, of course. Why should I work on someone else's land?*

How much land do you have? *Very small, about three bighas.*

Do you sell your produce? *Why would I? It is for my family.*

I had started feeling a little silly. The man's smile had become a grin. I tried to change the topic, to make it more of a conversation between adults.

Have you taken the COVID-19 vaccine? *No.*

Any COVID-19 cases in this village? *No.*

Would you take the vaccine if we offered it to you? *Why not?* I was slightly flustered.

We have the vaccine right here in this bag. Will you take it? *Why not? But not here on the road. You will have to come to my house.*

And where is your house? *Oh, just nearby* (pointing down the road).

Do you know that if you get COVID-19 you can die? *Life or death, what does it matter? Are they not both the same?*

This bit of existential philosophy had me stumped. I wished the farmer well and urged him to take the vaccine as soon as possible. He assured me that he would.

~

From here, we went to see the *patel*. This person is akin to a village headman. It is an informal position and is there in only some villages. The patel becomes especially important if the panchayat is ineffective. A good patel is respected by the village and so we look at patels as potential allies in our work.

We were directed to a small hall used mainly for panchayat meetings and visits by senior government functionaries. There were two long benches that faced each other in the covered area outside the hall. Six locals were already seated quietly on the bench to the left. Across from them, on the other bench, the patel sat alone, a dignified man of about fifty in a spotless dhoti-kurta, with hair that was entirely white.

Piyush and Kakuli joined the locals on the bench to the left. There was no space left and, in any case, I thought it would be unseemly for me to squeeze in at a time when COVID-19 was still a threat, and gawk at the patel, as everyone seemed to be doing. So I stood at one end of the bench on the left. My teammates did all the talking. We introduced ourselves and thanked the patel for meeting us. The patel talked about the village, how people were doing better than they had ever done before. I didn't get the sense he was trying to paint a rosy picture—he was telling the truth as he saw it.

The patel took long pauses before answering each question and then delivered his words slowly and carefully. You could frame the next three questions in your head even as he answered the first one, so the stack of unasked questions would build up in the mind and you never actually caught up with him. The patel was in his own zone, enjoying the art of fine monologue.

My feet were aching after half an hour of standing in one spot, listening and stacking questions. After a moment of hesitation, I walked over and joined the patel on his bench, but at a respectful distance. It didn't seem like he had noticed or that I had given offence.

Now closer to the headman, I asked about the health situation. He thought a bit and said that the biggest problem the village faced was water, and he talked about that. I asked about health again, and why there were so many home deliveries when in other ways, the village was making progress. He thought a bit, agreed that health was a problem and said something had to be done.

~

Farther down from where we sat, a truck stood at the bend in the road. People were coming and going at the rear of the truck and we went to investigate. The back was open and a burly, fair-skinned young man was sitting cross-legged before a weighing scale. Behind him, a helper was moving large sacks of grain around. A woman came up to him with a small bag of grain. He weighed it, opened a cash box that was at his side and pulled out a big roll of notes secured by a rubber band. He peeled off a few notes, added some coins and handed it to the woman, who left without counting the money. The man with the cash handed the bag of produce to his helper, who examined it, selected one of the big sacks and poured the grain into it.

A little later, a little girl came up with some toor dal, barely enough to fill a paper envelope. The man did the same thing with this tiny amount—weighing the dal carefully and paying her from his cashbox. The villagers came in a regular stream, mainly with small quantities of grain.

The man had the cheery, affable air of a successful salesman. He said he drove his truck from village to village in this area, paying people for whatever amounts they brought in. The villagers sold small quantities, whatever was extra beyond their own needs. He claimed that if he got Rs 1500 for a quintal (he didn't say for which product), he would make only Rs 50 as his margin—it sounded as if he was running a charity. When his sacks were full or when he had covered all the villages on his beat, he would sell the produce in the local mandi.

He explained that his relationship was based on trust. 'You can see that they don't ask for the rate or even count the money,' he said. I asked him about competition. He explained that no one else came to this village because these villagers trusted him and would not go to anyone else.

A little farther up the bend of the comma, another truck was parked on the road. This one was bigger than the one we had just seen. It was open at the back and the tarpaulin had been pulled back from the roof. The back of the truck was filling up with men and women going to the mandi to buy provisions. The men were standing on the left and the women to the right. The women wore colourful saris, heads covered but not their faces. They were in a happy mood with lots of chatter and laughter—a festive atmosphere.

Our next stop was to meet the dai who delivered the babies. The problem was that the truck that would ferry people to the market had almost entirely blocked the road. The driver had parked the truck off the narrow road and on the side as best as he could. But there was still barely enough space for people to get past the truck on the other side, even walking in single file. We let a few people who were coming our way pass, and then I stepped into the narrow passageway, my team and the ASHA behind me. The AWW had stayed behind at the AWC.

I was taken aback to see a herd of goats coming from the other side, heading for the passage. Another close encounter with a herd of goats in the space of a few hours! But it was all happening—they were coming straight towards us at a steady pace, led by a goat that had pointed horns. I knew right away that he was not a gentleman like his cousin who had deferred to us on the road.

Had the leader-goat from that encounter spoken to his cousin in Saudar? Maybe goats could communicate telepathically. Who has the right of way in such a situation —humans or goats? Now the leader had his eyes fixed on me and he was trudging forward purposefully. He wore a baleful look and his message was clear: *do you really want to do this?*

Soon, he had reached the other side of the narrow pathway. Without breaking step, he entered, and then his followers, one goat at a time. I quickly backed up. They streamed past. Then I led the way forward, with a newfound respect for goats, to go and meet the dai.

~

Saudar village stood out for a single health metric—almost every delivery happened at home, twenty-eight of the thirty in the previous year. Here, it is necessary to make a small digression to understand why home deliveries, and the subject of 'Traditional Health Attendants [THA]', is so important in the Indian public health context.

India has had a tradition of dais since ancient times. These are women in rural India who perform home deliveries. They have no formal training but have the benefit of knowing ancient practices for safe delivery. They are ill-equipped, however, to deal with complex deliveries, including those requiring a C-section. At the turn of the new millennium, India's maternal mortality rate (MMR) was 370,[4] one of the highest in the world. There was a fervent appeal at that time from global health agencies, such as the WHO, UNICEF and the World Bank, for India to encourage institutional deliveries and put an end to home delivery by dais.

In 2005, India launched the National Health Mission, a visionary programme that had several elements aimed at addressing India's high MMR. The ASHA position was created at this time—young women from the village who would go from house to house, detect high-risk pregnancies, prepare that woman and her family for institutional delivery and accompany her to the facility. This led to a marked improvement in India's MMR.[5]

~

There were dais in many villages, but most made themselves unavailable when we came around. This dai's name was Bifru,[6] and she lived in a hut on top of a slope at the very end of the village. Beyond that, a dirt road led to green fields that stretched into the distance. Grey and slightly stooped, she stepped out into the small courtyard wearing a frayed red *choli* and *chunri*, and a ghaghra* with bold pink stripes. She had on the traditional thick silver bangles and anklets. The old woman must have dressed her best to meet us. The ASHA would have told her that we were not

---

* Regional attire consisting of a skirt, blouse and shawl.

from the government and that she could trust us. Perhaps she saw it as an opportunity to tell her side of the story.

We stood in the courtyard of Bifru's hut. Behind her, three children—a girl of about twelve and her younger brothers—peered at us through the bars of a window. They called out a few times to Bifru—it sounded like they were warning their grandmother not to speak to us. I guessed that they were being prompted by grown-ups offstage. Bifru shushed them and soon, they disappeared.

We spoke for a long time, the discussion jumping between topics She talked freely, with a sharp wit. These are some snatches, as I noted in my diary:

After the delivery, how do you cut the cord? *Blade.*

Is the blade clean? *I suppose it is. They provide the blade. It's their baby. I only come to deliver it* (laughing).

How do you keep the place of delivery clean? *I told you, that is not my responsibility, the family must take care of those things.*

How do you know if the baby's head is pointed the right way for delivery? *I pour a special oil on the mother's stomach. If the oil comes straight down, the head is pointed the right way.*

Do you ever have cases you can't handle? (She laughs, shyly, covering her face. We ask again) *We send her by ambulance. I went with her a few times. They didn't let me go into the delivery room. Kept me out.*

Suppose the government paid you for every case you send to the government hospital, and you don't do any case yourself? *Of course, I would! But now they don't even let me in* (this clearly rankles). *It's money, isn't it? Now I am getting old, I can't do this for ever. Sometimes someone else does it, and I sit there, telling them* (sounds like she has a helper).

What do people pay you? (Again, she laughs—a habit when she is uncomfortable) *These are poor people, what can they pay me? Maybe 40 rupees, or 50 or 20. Sometimes nothing. I still must do it, no?*

Why don't they all go to the government hospital? They will also get the Rs 1400 incentive. *They are treated badly in the hospital because we are tribal people. They make them wait, often no bed. Why should a woman leave her home and go someplace like that?*

So, if they treated her with kindness, she would go? *Of course.*

I could understand how Bifru must have felt. She had been doing two deliveries a month for more than thirty years, for a tiny amount of money. The villagers respected her. There had been a time when she was also respected by the government, who had even trained her. After the government insisted on institutional deliveries, they gave her an incentive to bring the women to the facility, even allowed her to be inside the labour room. Now, it was as though she was a criminal. She would give up the work happily if she had a choice.

The rate of infant mortality with home deliveries is twice as high as the rate with institutional births. There is a greater risk of neurological and physical damage. There were about twenty-six births every year in Saudar. About 15 per cent of deliveries generally require a C-section—that means three or four of the deliveries that happened every year in Saudar could have needed that emergency attention.

Home deliveries often happen when a village is physically cut off. That was not the case in Saudar, where there was a good road connecting the village to the town. The burly truck driver plied that road every day—we had used it to get to the village.

We met a local who came up and talked confidently to us and witnessed door-to-door sales, women going off to the market, surplus local produce being sold and a strong village leader talk about the village. This community was linked to the rest of the world, not cut off.

Saudar did not look like a village where almost all deliveries would happen at home. The answer was absurdly simple: *home deliveries were high because the villagers were disrespected and treated callously at the government facility.* The poor accepted the risk of death and illness of mother and child rather than go through all that.

So, why not make the dai an ally, and not a problem to be eliminated? But what if the village community came together to get what they needed—respect and decency from the government? The possibilities were immense.

18

Baba

They say that there are all kinds of babas in rural Madhya Pradesh. I was fascinated and asked people who might know. One cynic said every good baba will do the impossible for you. Or convince you that it has been done, though he has not delivered. Others said no baba is the same as any other, they all have their favourite methods: concoctions, talismans, rituals or mantras. Then there are the shadow babas who see visions, do black magic. But everyone said: no baba takes money, for he is serving God and man, that is its own reward . . . but he will accept an offering.

These views were a bit cynical and none of the people I talked with had any first-hand experience. I was captivated—I had to find out for myself.

Early into our work, we saw that babas were consulted on matters of love, marriage, conception, birth, death, money and—for us, the most crucial one—health. It was well-known that when the poor fell sick, they had more belief in babas than in the public health system. They readily accepted dubious or dangerous advice on blind faith. It helped that there was a sense of the unknown and an aura of fear about babas.

Dealing with babas was not part of our strategy. But I wanted to understand if there was a way to work constructively with these men of mystery rather than condemn them outright. Could their power over people be used for good? But once again it was sheer curiosity, in large measure, that sent me out in pursuit of babas.

I thought it would be easy to find a baba because it was said that there is one for every village. But my teammates could not find a single one. I have been on sorties where we were told, 'There is a baba in that village over there, just around the tamarind tree, by that pond and in that house, go there, we just saw him go inside,' and we hurried on our tired feet. And when we got to that house, his family would tell us, 'He is not at home, he has just left, we are not sure when he will return'.

Then I turned to Paras Nath Sidh, a TAF manager who has the reputation of being able to achieve the impossible if it is put to him as a challenge. And, lo and behold, Paras called a few weeks later, saying he had shortlisted thirteen babas. He had simply sent out a message that I was a writer from Delhi looking to interview well-known babas for a book I was writing. This must have appealed to the babas' vanities because many were now willing to meet me. Paras said about his curated set of babas: 'Some are good, some are bad, but all are excellent quality.' I had no idea what he meant by that, but immediately said that three would suffice for now, thank you. I had never picked a high-quality baba and left that choice to Paras.

~

And thus, it was that I met shiny baba, wiry baba and burly baba over the next few weeks. I mean no disrespect—it is just that babas rarely use a common name. It is always baba ji, or sometimes *bhagat* ji. I used the appellations in my trip notes, and now in this narrative, so as not to mix up the babas.

The meeting with the shiny baba happened in a poor village in Barwani district.[1] We were with a few community members in the AWC when a lanky man, this side of fifty, with a drooping moustache, came in—he wore a brown dhoti and a light blue top with a long white cloth tossed carelessly onto his head. I was told that he was the village baba. He went to the far side of the room—someone quickly brought him a chair. I got up and went over. The baba had very dark skin that glowed because he had oiled himself lightly. Everything was normal about him except his eyes. Red and bleary, they suggested that he was on a trip. Over the course of our conversation, the baba would occasionally shoot a glance at me, but he never looked me in the eyes. He wore a perpetually bemused look and had an air of self-assurance.

A baba rarely goes out to meet people—they must come to him. It was a signal honour that he had come to see me. I thanked the baba and asked him to tell me about his life and his profession. Here there was a technical problem, for he spoke in pure dialect that we could barely follow, and there was no one there who knew Hindi well enough to translate fluently. My colleague Nagesh knew a bare smattering of the dialect and we went ahead with that.

The baba said there was nothing much to say about his life except that he had been born, and had grown up, in this village. He never exorcized spirits or did black magic—he shook his head vigorously as he said this, as though such kinds of things were beneath his dignity. He said he was a healer who used traditional herbs to treat all types of ailments. As we delved into this topic, he became progressively excited, waving his hands as he explained his method.

The baba collected herbs, carefully, from the nearby forest. He always did this himself, for picking the right herb was all-important and required skill and experience. Many herbs looked similar and could be mistaken for others—some herbs were reticent, and a pinch was all you could get—and sometimes he would bring back a large clump. The baba would mix the herbs in precise proportions and grind them into a paste. Some blends were for common illnesses—others were designed for specific ailments. The paste would be applied on the affected body parts or consumed with water. He said certain people brought him herbs from far away, the ones that did not grow in these areas. When we enquired, he was vague about who these people were.

At one point I asked what would happen if he gave someone the wrong paste—the baba saw that I was joking, and laughed out loud. I asked if he would treat me for a chronic ailment I had—he shook his head and made as if to move away, clearly unwilling to take me on as a patient.

Soon, it was time to leave. I extended my hand—he paused, puzzled about what he was supposed to do, then he flashed a smile and we shook hands. Shiny baba was an altogether charming fellow. I believed he was a good herbal healer but I also had an inkling that his talents went beyond pastes—that we would never know.

~

A week later, I found myself sitting in front of wiry baba in a village called Rojdha, set amid the picturesque forest hills of Betul. I was with programme officer Sonu Rai and Ankita Pandey, our new district manager. Rojdha has a population of 637, distributed across many small hamlets. The people are from the highly marginalized Korku tribe and are famously shy of outsiders. It was my second visit to Rojdha—the first had been on non-baba work six months previously. I will always remember how, on that occasion, everyone scattered as soon as we walked into the village, taking shelter in their homes. We stayed a while and then left because there was no one with whom we could speak. Since then, our team had established a modicum of trust with the community, at least going beyond minute zero, when everyone had run away from us. Today, there were people in the narrow lane that ran through the village and they took no notice of us.

We had come to meet the village baba, whose house was at the end of the lane. We were told to wait because the baba was having his bath. We stood outside and watched life in a small village go by—two women helping each other collect water in buckets, a man herding goats that were busily nosing bushes to find the freshest leaves, men and women working in the fields below, two dogs idling under a tree. There was not a shop of any kind to be seen in this poor village. And yet there it was, at the end of the lane, the travelling van selling packets of junk foods just Rs 5 each, in a village where most people ate only one meal a day. A man went by with several packets of potato chips in his hand and a child on each side, each munching from their packets.

Someone from inside the house called out that the baba was ready. We stepped into the narrow, covered veranda just as the baba entered. He looked about sixty and wore a long-sleeved white shirt and dhoti. The baba (locally known as 'bhagat') was very thin, with tight dark skin that looked as though it had been stretched across his thin bones. He had a thatch of black hair, and like shiny baba, bleary red eyes. He squatted in one corner of the narrow room, which had a motorcycle parked in the other corner. The three of us squeezed in around him, but at a respectful distance.

The baba had a hoarse, high-pitched voice. He told us that both his father and grandfather had been babas, but they had truly been touched by God. They would go into trances, see visions and had the gift of prophecy. He said, modestly, that he had inherited no such powers, only learnt *tantra-mantra* from his father. 'I am just a farmer,' he said, indicating the patch of green behind his house. He volunteered that he had only one child, a daughter who had a severe mental illness and stayed at home, unable to be useful in any way.

The baba specialized in exorcism. He referred to a person who was possessed as '*hawa lag gaya*', meaning that an evil wind had affected them. He clarified that no one had cast a spell on the person but there are certain areas where the spirits gather at times, and if someone then walks though those areas, the spirit, or several spirits, might enter them. After this, the victim would fall sick. Often, it would be a '*haddi ka bukhaar*', an illness of the bones. With a malnourished child, he said this had happened when the mother had visited her *maika*—parents' home—and '*usko* hawa lag gaya' out there. So the mother had to be treated in order for the child to recover.

He said that illnesses were of two types. The first was spirit-induced, as he had explained, but there were also some non-spirit illnesses that were genuinely '*sharir ka*'—natural, physical ailments. In such cases, he would tell the afflicted person to go to the government hospital as it fell outside his specialty area. Sonu asked respectfully how the baba knew if the illness was spirit-induced or not—Ankita explained gently that malnutrition was often because the child was not eating enough.

At this point, the baba said that he was a Shiva *bhakta*.[*] He pointed towards the top of the hill behind his house and said there was a Shiva temple up there. He went there to pray and to meet those who were sick—he never saw people at home. He would

---

[*] Devotee.

ask Lord Shiva which category the illness fell into and receive the answer. I asked, 'What if the answer was wrong?' The baba said, 'If it comes from God, how can it be wrong?' There was no arguing with that. He ignored Ankita's malnutrition statement.

The next step was that the baba would exorcise the evil spirit. He would recite a few mantras and do *jhaad-phook*,* which entailed tapping the victim and the ground around with the holy jhadoo. He would ask the spirit if he, or she, was hungry, and if so, what the spirit wanted to eat. He said that sometimes it was just a lemon, but it could also be a whole chicken.

The baba said that he never took money, 'but if they wanted to offer something to Shivji', there was a holy place at the back. He said we were free to go and see it. We walked through the house, which, like every tribal house I have seen, was spotlessly clean and almost bare. There was a prayer spot at eye-height recessed into one wall. At the back was an altar to Lord Shiva on the ground, with a *trishul*.†

We came back in and asked the baba if he would take us to the Shiva temple. He said that he had been there already today, but we were free to go there if we wanted—it was only a little way up the hill. We thought for a moment about the spirits that might be hanging out on that route and had no wish to get felled by the hawa. We politely declined, thanked the baba and left Rojdha, the town that put itself in wiry baba's hands.

~

Driving down a country road in Mokhed block in Chhindwara district, flat corn fields on both sides, we spotted burly baba's

---

* Exorcism.
† Trident, the divine weapon of Lord Shiva.

house in the distance, a tiny red spot on a vast yellow canvas. We were heading to a village called Gubrel, which had a population of 1000. As we approached, we saw that the house was a small structure painted jade green, with fire-brick red borders, pleasingly assertive.

We went through a small veranda and stepped into a room that had walls the same shade of green as the outside of the house, but the red borders of the inside rooms were much thinner. The entrance to the adjacent room had no doors and there was a glassless connecting window. The baba conducted his community meetings, referred to as the darbar, in this adjacent room, which could accommodate perhaps thirty people. He sat on a small flat stool, a small desk of sorts lay in front of him and behind that, a raised bed with an ornate *chaddar*[*] on top of it. Those in the audience would see only his head and torso. A darbar was in progress, and we settled down to eavesdrop and await our turn. We heard the baba telling someone to drink no more, in a kind way, not as an admonishment—we saw him tie a red thread on the drinker's wrist, telling him never to remove it.

My colleagues on this trip were Shreya and programme officers Shashwat Mishra and Punam Dhobale. Shashwat had made a recce trip to see the baba the previous week. He had given us a graphic description of that visit during the drive to Gubrel.

The darbar that Shashwat had attended was absolutely packed. The audience consisted of poor villagers—very respectful, they sat on the floor with folded hands, heads bowed. There was pindrop silence in the room. Shashwat, despite his city look, didn't stand out in the darbar audience. Many city-based 'seekers' came to the darbar and the baba would have assumed he was another such supplicant.

---

[*] Blanket.

The baba asked people from the audience—individuals or families—one by one, to come up and sit on the ground to his right. Shashwat had come in late and heard only the last few cases of the day.

The first patient was an elderly lady, probably in her mid-fifties. Her son said that his mother was hearing voices in her head. The baba poured some oil on her head. Then he took some powder and put it in a piece of paper that he folded four times, to make a *taveez*, a talisman. He tied it with holy string and told her to always keep it tied around her neck, and to come back after a month. The woman and her son left with bowed head and folded hands.

The second patient was a girl, aged about sixteen, with her parents. The girl wore a white top and jeans, unusual for a small, conservative village far away from the city. The parents said the girl had no interest in studies—in a lowered voice, the father said they suspected she was seeing boys. The girl looked down, thoroughly embarrassed, because the village folk were listening: a teenage girl meeting boys was scandalous. The baba gave the girl a similar taveez with the same instructions.

The third patient was another elderly woman—her son had brought her and said his mother hadn't spoken in seven years. The baba said the woman was possessed by an evil spirit. He told the woman to have a bath in the house well and come back—the well had been blessed by him. She came back after a while, hair and sari still wet. She was muttering something to herself—then she went to the baba, and her son, and whispered something in their ears. The baba blessed her by putting the jhadoo on her head and gave her a powder to drink with water. He said the woman was now healed.

The woman's son was overjoyed. He kept proclaiming 'yeh *chamaktkaar* hai'—it is a miracle. He said he had never thought his mother would speak again—this was baba ji's blessing. Meanwhile, the crowd sat silently, heads bowed, numb, fearful.

After the meeting, Shashwat introduced himself to the baba and told him that I was an author writing a book and wanted to meet him. The baba was suspicious. He was hesitant at first, then agreed, but reluctantly. Shashwat and he had struck up a friendly conversation, during which the baba confided that his name was Najibullah[2] and he had a good side business going in mangoes.

There was a pleasing fragrance of attar in the air when we came into the darbar room. It was the off day for the darbar, so no one else was present. The baba was a big man and struggled to get up and meet us. He had a stubbly grey beard and wore a crumpled white shirt, baggy black pants and an ornate flat Muslim topee. On darbar days, the baba would wear a full-length green gown. I saw that he had the same red, bleary eyes as shiny and wiry babas. The stuff was seriously strong, judging from the eyes.

The baba made as if to sit on the ground with us. We insisted on his going back to his modest throne and I went and sat on the ground to his right, as had all the supplicants. This put him completely at ease and he rolled out his life story.

Burly baba was the seventh child in his family, after the birth of six sisters. The turning point in his life was when the thirteenth-century Sufi saint Khwaja Moinuddin Chishti[3] of Ajmer presented himself to the young Najibullah in a dream. He told the boy that he had the *ilm*—knowledge—to help mankind. The baba explained to us that this was the same as having goddess Sarasvati within him. In the dream, the Khwaja told the baba to go forth, do good deeds and spread the word to all mankind. He said this was his mission as a baba. Everyone came to him, he said, more Hindus than Muslims—he blessed them all and did what good he could for them. He said he owed everything to the Khwaja and went twice a year to Ajmer to worship at his dargah.

The baba's father had married off three of his daughters before he died. Burly baba had taken on the responsibility of getting his other three sisters married. He said he was married himself, but lived alone in this small house—worshipping, doing good, sleeping in this room, as he put it. I asked about his family and he said he had two sons in the village. I asked why he had not passed his learning and powers over to them. He shook his head, saying it was not possible because they didn't have Sarasvati inside them.

The baba spoke of the miraculous deeds that he could do. For example, if a woman who had been pregnant for more than four months came to see him, he could tell immediately if the baby would be a girl. I looked suitably impressed. Seeing this, he groped inside his desk and pulled out a small but wicked-looking knife. It was gently curved and just about a centimetre wide. There were two lemons pierced by the knife, one on the tip, presumably as a stopper, for safety. I thought the knife was only an artefact and the magic was in the lemons, but I was wrong. He carefully took the lemons off and said that if he gazed long enough at the blade, he would know if the person in front of him was good or bad, lying or telling the truth. I should have been alarmed as I was the person sitting in front of him and he had the knife in his hand. Thankfully, he put the lemons back on the knife and put the knife away. I nodded my head, wide-eyed.

Groping again inside the desk, he produced a sheaf of papers, each about 6 sq. inches in size, tied together by a string. Each paper had some odd symbol drawn on it in ballpoint pen—he had visualized the symbols in a trance. He explained that in some cases, he would pick out a particular piece of paper, make a taveez out of it and drop it in a glass of water. Then he would remove the taveez and tell the patient to drink the water, and her wish would come true.

By now the baba was on a roll, willing to disclose all his methods. He must have thought that he had found another trusting soul, a *lekhak*,˙ no less, ready to sit at his feet and be filled with wonder. I pushed my luck and asked whether he did exorcisms, and he said he didn't do that sort of stuff.

It was finally time to leave. The baba asked me: 'Do you get pain in your feet?' It was a reasonable guess about someone my age, and I said that indeed, yes, I did. He reached into the desk and produced a bottle of fragrant oil. He said the pain would go away forever if I applied it just once.

I had a Rs 500 note in my hand to place on the chaddar as an offering. The baba shook his head. Instead, he produced several currency notes and gave one to each of us, which we accepted with both hands, quite confused. They ranged from a hundred rupees down to ten—mine was a fifty.

As we stepped out into the fresh air, I wondered why I had not been given the hundred.

˙ Writer.

19

Down Below

I sometimes wish I had a record of all the dreadful roads that I have traversed in Madhya Pradesh. The national highways of the state are first-rate all-weather roadways. The state highways are robust. It is when you branch off onto the country roads, which lead deep into the interiors, that the picture changes. Many of these roads are charming. But lurking in the shadows are the other kind of country road, the roughnecks, who can be harsh, even brutal. It is as though their intent is to show the traveller, who has arrived so far on roads that are first-rate, robust and charming, what a real road is all about. However, it must be said in their favour that they always introduce themselves decently—the thuggery happens suddenly, after the traveller has been lured.

~

And so, unsuspecting, I set off with my colleagues, programme officers Aditi Revankar, Mihika Bapna and Punam Dhobale, on a sunny and surprisingly mild December day, heading for the tiny village of Dhana* Chariya[1] in Tamia block of Chhindwara district. The main road was smooth and we climbed steadily up the hills. The GPS system which, amazingly, can lead you these days to even remote villages, indicated that we were only two kilometres from Dhana Chariya. We turned left onto the country road as instructed, and promptly, the GPS shut down. We didn't pause to consider if it was safe to go forward without navigation because the road before us, winding gently, bordered by leafy trees, was altogether captivating.

The vehicle came to a sudden stop after ten minutes. The hard road had come to a clean end—the road-building project must have been abandoned at that point. Ahead of us lay a meandering, declining stretch of brown-orange dirt, littered with rubble, rock and the occasional boulder. There was a bend in this road a little way ahead—we didn't know what surprises might lie beyond that curve, or, for that matter, we were not even certain that this road would take us to Dhana Chariya.

We asked the driver for his opinion. On my travels in the state, I have found that there are three kinds of drivers in rural Madhya Pradesh. The first is the macho, bring-it-on-baby type who is not fazed by any road. Then there is the cautious, don't-blame-me-later type who will say that the very same road is impossible.[2] And there is the third kind, who will say nothing. Ask him and he will be silent, maintaining a distant, ruminating look. Our driver fell into this most annoying of categories.

So we made the decision ourselves to go forward. The driver muttered something to the effect that making a U-turn would be very difficult, which was no doubt true, not only because of the rubble, rocks and boulders, but also the steep decline. But we were determined to take our chances, for we had important work

---

* Dhana means 'small village', typically a hamlet.

in the village. The road was treacherous and we inched forward, the driver wrestling with the wheel and managing the brake deftly, all concentration. I was no longer annoyed; indeed, I was full of admiration for he was clearly an expert. The vehicle went forward, then sometimes backwards, as he reversed seeing that we would not be able to get past the sharp rocks ahead. Or it was up, stop, then down, as we navigated a large boulder. Or swerving to avoid the craters that we had not seen before. It was scary not knowing if indeed this would lead us to our destination or peter out when we were deep in the forest. We remembered the driver's words that a U-turn would be difficult—now it seemed impossible.

One of my colleagues had partaken of a good breakfast and was looking uneasy. And through it all, we were laughing our heads off as we bounced our way forward, for our situation was both precarious and ludicrous. After a long time, we spotted, through the dense trees—could it be?—a lone hut at a distance, bang on the outskirts of Dhana Chariya. 'Ah,' I said, 'I was looking forward to sleeping in the forest tonight,' and we laughed ourselves silly.

~

Dhana Chariya has ninety-four houses and 590 residents. About 70 per cent belong to the Bharia tribe and the rest are Gond. The village is divided into four dhanas. We had arrived at School dhana, the biggest, with twenty-five houses. The other dhanas were scattered across the steeply sloping hills that led down from where we stood.

We had come to learn about the women's self-help groups (SHGs) that had been established in villages in the area by an NGO named Parag Samiti. These SHGs worked on savings and livelihoods—we wanted to understand if health could also be on their agenda. The other reason was to understand why the village had such poor health outcomes, with three recent infant deaths. We took a walk around the village. The houses were solid structures. The one that stood out was a large building with a signboard that announced that it was a boarding school for girls, for grades 1–5.[3] We stopped at the AWC and met the worker incharge, a slight woman, who answered all our questions deadpan. She reported that almost all deliveries were institutional—in the last year, only two out of twenty-five deliveries had happened at home. This seemed highly unlikely, given the state of the approach road— surely it would be difficult to get a woman who was in labour safely to a hospital via that road—and in the monsoon season, almost impossible. As we talked, it became evident that the ASHA and she rarely met—we were to find out more about this errant ASHA over the course of the day. I wondered if the ANM came to Dhana Chariya on a regular basis—we didn't get a straight answer to that question either.

The AWW said that sixty-two children were enrolled at the centre. On that day, a dozen children were sitting outside in the bright sunlight, playing games. Some were animatedly matching name cards with pictures of different kinds of animals, calling out the titles loudly. Others pored over a rubber mat and were pushing English alphabet letters into the empty spaces on the mat, using brute force when the letter didn't fit. The children wore clean clothes and shoes—their hair had been neatly combed and oiled before they had left home. A little girl with pigtails, self-appointed leader of the group, was giving instructions all around.

A boy, about five years old, came up. For a moment he stood outside the circle of children, barefoot and scowling, sizing up the scene in front of him. He wore a loose shirt with rolled up sleeves—once white, now it was covered with dirt and hung loose over white shorts. I guessed he was wearing the old school uniform of an older brother. The lad had a grimy face and scruffy hair. He observed the coloured cards game for a while before inserting himself confidently into the centre of it.

I have rarely seen children playing with toys that aid learning at anganwadi centres. Most centres did not even have these toys, even though they were required by the government as part of the required protocol for early childhood cognitive development.

Three older girls in uniform pushed their way into the group. One disrupted the game, grabbing some of the cards and letters, but she soon threw them back. The AWW looked up and explained that a few girls from the boarding school always showed up at the time the mid-day meal was served. 'It isn't meant for them,' she said, 'but how can I say no? They are children, after all.' The anganwadi helper appeared and started handing out steel plates.

~

We set off to visit the smaller dhanas. A local said he would take us down the slope as the way was tricky. He said something quietly to Punam, looking in my direction. She told me he was asking if I would be able to make my way down with them. I told him with just a hint of sarcasm, yes, and if I found it too tough, I would turn back. After my trip to Jad, my confidence was high when it came to these kinds of small excursions. As it turned out, the descent was steep and uneven but I managed well, my hand firmly gripped by one of my companions when they thought there was a risk.

We arrived at a clearing with two adjacent huts. We introduced ourselves to a matriarch who was squatting on her haunches, halving a nut-like green fruit. She would remove the seed and throw the halved pieces onto a large mat in front of her.

She told us the fruit was called harra and they sold it in the market in Tamia town at Rs 20 for a kilo. That was about a third of the price at which it would finally be resold. The fruit is valued in Ayurveda for its medicinal properties.

A girl who looked barely sixteen was spreading the nuts out on the mat. Her hair was tied in a braid and she had the sweet face of a child. She was wearing a sari and looked as though she was not used to it. The girl had a *mangalsutra** around her neck and Mihika said '*badhai ho* [congratualations]', and asked her when she had gotten married. The girl glanced at her mother and said, eyes averted, that she wasn't married. Mihika asked, gently, why she was wearing the mangalsutra then and the girl said, 'I just wore it for fun—*vaise hi*.' Her mother nodded.

I asked the matriarch's permission and went around the side of the house to get a sense of the property. It was surrounded by steep slopes on all three sides. Under a tree next to the house were stone *murtis*† of three figures—a man and two women. They looked lifelike, wearing everyday clothes. I had heard that in some communities, the custom was to have murtis, not of the Gods, but of family members who had died.

We asked the matriarch and her daughter if they knew of two women, Salwa and Dhanvati, who had lost their babies in recent months—we had seen that from the AWW's records. The older woman pointed to her left, saying the two lived just a short distance away. As she was speaking, a small boy, perhaps twelve years old, came up the hill carrying an enormous load of firewood on his head. He was making good speed past our group when the matriarch, addressing him as Sonu, told him to take us to Dhanvati's house. The boy paused for a moment, sweating in the

---

* An auspicious thread or chain worn by married women.
† Idols.

winter sun. He thought for a bit, threw the load down, turned around and set off.

It took us a few moments to understand that the boy expected us to follow him. Mihika decided to stay behind and talk to some more people in that area. Aditi, Punam and I set off after the boy. It is impossible to keep up with someone who is more than fifty years younger than you, especially when the track is steeply downhill. I had been feeling quite pleased with myself after the first descent. I hadn't expected another one so soon. Meanwhile, the boy had disappeared into the brush, and we were on our own.

A few slips later, we were on level ground again and came out at a fork in the road. Two tiny scamps were playing some kind of game using twigs to make marks in the dirt. We came up and asked the way, smiling. They both stared at us for a moment. Then they each let out a howl and one ran left, the other right, at full speed. The hut on the right was a lot closer than the one on the left, so we set off in that direction.

We stopped for a few moments to take in the sight on our left. The land sloped down to an olive green corn field. The winter sun was beating down and lent a golden sheen to the crop. There was thick forest, deep green and black, behind the field. Someone along the way told us that the first house, further down, was Dhanvati's.

It was a sturdy structure with a roofed front porch where a man was chopping firewood. On the far side, a woman was shushing her baby to sleep. The second man lay on a charpoy just outside the porch, covered in a *razai*.* There was a chulha, embers still glowing, at the far corner of the porch.

---

* Quilt.

Punam said, 'We have come from Chhindwara to see your village and learn about it.' The man didn't seem surprised to have three people from the city show up at his doorstep. He just nodded and we stepped into the porch. His name was Danat and he was Salwa's husband—Salwa was the woman whose babies had died. His brother Gopal lay on the charpoy while the latter's wife Dhanvati looked after her baby. Gopal was sick—he didn't speak at all while we were there.

A bawling started from inside the house. It turned out that the little boy who had run away from us belonged to this house. He must have looked through the window and seen that the ghosts had landed in his front porch. Someone inside was pacifying him, probably telling him that we were just human beings.

We explained that we worked with mothers and children to improve their health, but that we were not doctors. Dhanat informed us that he had lived in this place ever since his childhood. He and his brother were agricultural labourers tilling their own land, which was part of the stretch of green that lay in front of the house. They grew peas, fenugreek, corn and spinach, depending on the season. Dhanat would go regularly to Tamia to sell their produce. The yield was good but getting to Tamia was treacherous—earlier, only a tractor could traverse the hill! Dhanvati listened carefully as she rocked the infant in her lap.

We asked Dhanat about his wife Salwa. As if on cue, a woman walked in from the fields. She was beautiful, with sharp features and smooth ebony skin. She covered her head and settled down on the ground. She too didn't seem surprised at seeing us. Danat had been doing the speaking thus far—he spoke shyly and in a hesitant voice. Salwa took over the conversation, speaking very softly but clearly, always with a smile on her lips.

We talked about her family and generally about bringing up children. Unexpectedly, and in a matter-of-fact way, Salwa said, 'I have no children; they both died.' We asked what had happened. Salwa said she had been carrying twins without knowing it. When the contractions began, they set off for Tamia on a motorcycle. The babies were born soon after they reached Tamia—they were stillborn. She had had no ante-natal check-ups during her pregnancy. We told her why the check-ups were important, as was one's diet during pregnancy. Salwa said the ASHA had come to their house only once, early in her pregnancy. She had seen the ANM once around that time as well. Her smile had disappeared by this time and her eyes were moist.

Dhanat asked a few questions, eyes wide. He repeated the answers we gave, each time, under his breath—he really cared for his family and wanted to take care of them. How ironic that the community wanted to know but the frontline workers were not available for them!

We asked Dhanvati about her family. She said that a few months ago, her baby had died when he was ten days old. She wasn't sure what happened. He had developed high fever and died within a few hours. She too had rarely seen the ASHA or gone for check-ups. She admitted that there was a baba whom they had gone to see—she seemed a bit shy about revealing this piece of information. Danat added that many people in the village went to this baba. It appeared to us that the baba's word and his prescriptions carried more authority than the medical system in the village.

My colleagues are not doctors, but they knew enough to gauge that Salwa was severely anaemic. Aditi explained to her what anaemia meant and what its consequences could be. She urged her to see the ANM when she next came to the village. The whole family, including Nandlal, listened carefully. We asked if they were aware of the women's SHG in the village—they barely knew of it. We told them that they should try to attend the meetings of the SHG because they would get support there. They looked uncertain.

Before we left, we gave Danat the number of Atul Deep Sinha, our programme officer responsible for Tamia. We went back up to the previous dhana and the house with the matriarch. A young man was leaning against a wall, watching disinterestedly. He was the brother of the girl with the mangalsutra. His wife was sitting behind the matriarch. She had all the signs of a newlywed— bright red sari, glass bangles, heavy sindoor, new silver for her ankles. We asked if she planned to go to the SHG meeting that would start in just a little while in the school dhana. The bride showed no interest in us—she looked bored. We asked if anyone in this dhana went to the SHG meeting. The women shook their heads. We told them the SHG would help them save money and improve their crop. They looked uncomprehending.

This time, there was a litter of four very cute and boisterous puppies there. Their mother soon appeared and the puppies all flocked to find a teat.

~

We climbed back up to the main village. We joined Mihika, who had talked to other people from the community while we were with Salwa and her family. Everywhere, it was the same story of abject lack of awareness and risky health practices. In one home, there was a twenty-two-year-old who had already had three children—two had been delivered at home in the middle of the night. Her youngest child was four months old and had not received his vaccinations yet. Neither the ASHA nor the AWW had ever visited her, even after three children. In another home, a seventeen-year-old girl was pregnant and was seeing only the baba to ensure a safe pregnancy.

A local NGO had organized women's groups in several villages in the area. Two young men from the NGO were facilitating the meeting. They had just started the meeting with an ice-breaking exercise: each woman held a twig in her hand, and when they put the twigs together, they saw that the bundle could not be broken. The agenda for that day included seeds and different crops, how to improve yields and get better prices by combining their produce. The women were comfortable with each other and there was much laughter and camaraderie.

There was that special something in the air that is almost palpable in an active women's group meeting. We were thinking the same thing: if such a group also had health on its agenda, they could develop the collective influence to ensure that the ASHA did her job or was replaced. Salwa and Dhanvati would then have attended group meetings, met other mothers-to-be—perhaps their babies might even have been alive.

The village, in effect, had two very different levels. The one on top with the women's groups was a place of sunlight and good cheer; the place deep below, where we had met Salwa and Dhanwati was was dark and tragic. I felt something stir inside as I thought of the courage and quiet dignity of Salwa's family in the middle of all their adversity. I felt anger thinking of that wretched ASHA and the callousness of the entire system. How were such contradictions possible? It was not as though the people down below were much poorer. Nor was it that they were unexposed—the men travelled regularly to Tamia town. This trip had been a sad one, but we were still full of hope after seeing the women's groups.

We left, for it was getting late and the road was waiting.

20

Gwalior

So far, our work had been entirely in the tribal areas of Madhya Pradesh, on the state's southern border with Maharashtra. We knew that we also needed to work in some states where the context was different, especially the issues of caste and community. That experience was important if we were to develop a model of work in maternal and child health that could ultimately be introduced state-wide. We had therefore recently begun work in Gwalior and Morena districts, about 600 kilometres due north, on the border with Rajasthan. I was headed on this visit to Gwalior to learn what was different.

~

Gwalior has been the seat of five major kingdoms from the tenth century onwards.[1] Many monarchs reigned from the Gwalior fort, which dates back to the sixth century.[2] Surrounded by industry and commerce, renowned for its music and arts, it is being developed today as a government-designated Smart City.[3] Gwalior the city is confident and assertive. But we would soon see that rural Gwalior is as underdeveloped and deprived as the shy, impoverished districts in the tribal south.

I travelled with our district manager, Izhar Qureshi, to a small village called Adivasi Pura in Gird block. We drove the 30 kilometres to the village down a good highway, with green and yellow fields on either side. The trip took forty-five minutes because the last section, the village road, was almost impossible to negotiate. Overloaded trucks would routinely swerve off the highway and take this route to avoid paying the road tax at the toll booth farther down the highway. The trucks wreaked havoc on a road that was not designed to accommodate heavy loads.

Three lanes branched out from where we stood at the entrance to the village. The path to our right led to the section where the Banjaras lived, nomadic peoples originating from the Mewar region of Rajasthan. The middle section was occupied by the Nath community, worshippers of Lord Shiva from ancient times. The section to our left was taken by the Sahariyas, the only major northern tribe. It is another age-old community, concentrated for hundreds of years in Shivpuri district, close to Gwalior.

The Sahariya people are a notified Scheduled Tribe (ST), classified as 'primitive and backward' by the government. The Naths belong to the Scheduled Caste (SC) category, the lowest rung of the caste system. The Banjaras fell under the broad category of Other Backward Classes (OBC).[4] These three communities, considered socially backward and economically underdeveloped, lived in harmony in the small village of Adivasi Pura.

~

Our programme officer, Dipika Roy, had assembled about twenty women from the Sahariya and Nath communities in the Sahariya section. She had been with us only three weeks and had already won the respect of the local women. She introduced us to Ram Rathore, a tall, amiable fellow with a grey-black stubble.

He was a small-time power broker from another village, reputed to know every man, woman and child for miles around. He had gratuitously adopted our team when we started our work in that area, and always showed up whenever we had any community interaction. I soon saw how Ram Rathore could be both asset and liability, sometimes at the same time, but on balance he was useful. He helped us understand the local context and learn who was who in any village.

We sat on a dari that had been spread out on the narrow lane in the centre of the Sahariya section. It was one of those days you sometimes experience in December in central India when a golden winter sun blends perfectly with the slight nip in the air. We settled down in its pleasing blaze to talk to the womenfolk, who were a mix of older mothers-in-law and young married women. Their heads were covered, except for one woman whose sari was new—she stayed silent throughout the meeting. Dipika whispered that the uncovered head was her privilege because she was a daughter of the village, as opposed to a *bahu*, one who had married into the local community.

Their men were mainly agricultural labourers. The local wage rate was only Rs 200 per day, and so young men and entire families migrated for eight to nine months in a year in search of better wages. They went mainly across the border into Rajasthan, where they could earn up to Rs 400. The women told stories of their men's wages getting delayed or even going unpaid, and of brutal beatings, when they migrated. The women were loud, argumentative, even aggressive. There was none of the reticence that we had seen among women in the tribal areas.

Water was a big problem, with only two handpumps, one in the Banjara section and the other in a common area. The closest source was a kilometre away and the women would walk there with their buckets to capture some of the water that was being released into the fields, or to plead for water from people with private wells. One woman said the government was building a pipeline that would lead to their village. As soon as she made that statement, several women shouted her down, for the pipeline was much awaited and long delayed, and she had touched a raw nerve.

As designated backward communities, they were entitled to certain privileges from the government, such as reservations in public sector employment and higher education. Many had lost the Labour Cards required to claim these benefits. Getting a new card was a cumbersome process.

About 40 per cent of deliveries were done at home by family members and dais with little experience. This was because it could take two hours to get an ambulance and reach the nearest health facility, the Primary Health Centre (PHC), which was in poor condition, with callous staff. All this time, Ram Rathore was interjecting with his comments, needlessly interpreting the women's statements, which made them even more belligerent. It turned out that he was the husband of the ASHA—she was present, looking as though she had nothing to do with him.

The women knew what was required for good maternal and child health. They understood the importance of breastfeeding, but they had bigger problems on their minds. They knew that antenatal check-ups were important and that institutional delivery was essential. There was no lack of awareness—the problem was a justifiably strong mistrust and antipathy towards the government system. We had seen this in many tribal communities as well.[5]

~

We headed towards the Nath section of the village next. It was located on the other side of a lush field. At a distance, we could see an old man labouring his way through a sea of green, his hand on the shoulder of a young woman in front of him. Ram Rathore said the old man was almost blind and dependent on the woman, who was his daughter and the village dai. I asked if we could talk to her. Ram Rathore called out to the woman that we wanted to talk to her, and his authoritative tone made me cringe. We were approaching the village along the horizontal side of the field, and the old man and his daughter were walking across it in parallel, so we had to speed up to catch them. But the meeting never happened, because as we came closer the woman hurried, calling out over her shoulder that she would take her father home first and then meet us—we never saw her again. It was yet another missed meeting with a village dai. I intuited that if only Ram Rathore had been softer, the woman might have been willing to speak to us.

The village was a haphazard assortment of densely packed semi-pukka houses, built on either side of narrow lanes. As we made our way forward, we saw several urchins and men with dabs of cobalt blue on their faces, hands and clothes. We came to an open space with more houses just ahead, and we saw that the wall in front of us was being painted. It was a messy job, half completed. A handwritten message, not yet painted over, reminded people of the virtues of good health and Vitamin A.

There was a sudden hue and cry. An elderly man with blue face, white hair and stubble was telling all the world about the injustice that had been done to him. Ram Rathore was stepping forward to talk to the elder, and I was worried we would lose the chance to speak to him. Izhar intercepted Ram Rathore, gently leading him away by the elbow.

The elder's name was Babu Ram and he was incensed because he was being relocated. We explained that we were not from the government, at which his voice came down several decibels, and still further down when he saw that we were sympathetic. It turned out that the government had given notice, claiming back this section of the village because it was public land. The villagers would be relocated some distance away to better plots. Babu Ram's voice started climbing the scale as he said that this land had belonged to his forefathers and no one else had any right to it. He said that those who had been relocated early had been allocated the best plots, even though they had come to live in this section much later. It was unclear how all this had happened. Ram Rathore came up, now in his asset mode, and somehow placated the elder.

~

We moved on, passing a group of huts where the *Sappera* people lived—traditional snake charmers. Ram Rathore said that it was not occupied by the Sappera anymore—the profession itself was almost extinct because of the animal rights movement. He shook his head, disgusted that these do-gooders were denying someone an honest livelihood.

A little further on, two kids were playing with that homemade children's toy popular everywhere in India—the wheel on a stick. A third, however, had an ingeniously devised steering wheel in the form of a twig at the top of the stick. The boy showed how he could twist the stick one way or the other and the tiny wheel at the bottom would turn in that direction thanks to a system of wires. I don't know what got into me, but I asked the little boy if I could have it. Of course I was joking and I expected the lad to say a fierce 'no'. Instead, he stood there frozen, uncertain. Before I could reassure him, a passer-by who had been watching admonished the little boy gently and coaxed him into handing the toy over to me. The boy, lip trembling, held his stick on wheels out to me. I told him it was a beautiful toy and he should keep it. The boy took the toy and ran away. I felt awful.

The Banjara section was almost empty. Men and women had left to work in the fields. We went on to our next destination.

~

At Adivasi Pura, we saw how three backward communities lived together, confident and assertive, yet poor and marginalized. We were headed now to a village called Chait, also in Gird block, where the caste mix was very different. Two communities lived in this village of 1260 people. These were the Gujjars, who were well-off, and the SCs, who were utterly poor.

The Gujjars are classified as OBCs. They have a fascinating history that dates to 630 CE. The Gujjars are not a single community. They are present in many states, Gujarat, Rajasthan, Punjab and Madhya Pradesh being the main ones. They are present even in Pakistan! It is predominantly a Hindu community, but there are also Sikh and Muslim Gujjars. They have many livelihoods—a broad generalization would be to say the Gujjars are a nomadic, agricultural community who rear cattle.

We were met in Chait by Girja, the AWW who was from the Gujjar community. She wore a colourful red sari and stylish sandals, and possessed a smartphone, carrying herself with panache. Girja's husband was a landowner and they had their own bungalow in the village. She said she did the job not for the money, but because it gave her satisfaction.

She said Gujjars had good health and their babies were all born in a hospital— SC people had bad health and most deliveries were done at home. The Gujjars owned land and were wealthy— the SCs worked on the Gujjars' land and received measly wages. Many were in debt to the Gujjars and had no option but to work for them.

We strolled through the village as Girja gave us this orientation. Little barefoot children, some with bellies swollen by malnutrition, played in the dirt. Girja pointed out that these were the children of the SCs, and that community's awareness about the basics of health was low.

We arrived at a kirana store in the middle of the village. It was well-stocked with all types of home products and consumer foods. An older woman, ample and unsmiling, sat on the stoop outside the store. She was the village dai, supremely self-confident. She said she conducted all the home deliveries in the village and never had a problem. We asked what she would do with complicated deliveries such as a breach or caesarean. The dai said, inscrutably, that she would do what she always did. She said she did her job as a form of social service. She took no payment except the Rs 500 that she gave the sweeper to get rid of the placenta and the umbilical cord after each delivery.

We stopped outside a modest SC family's hut. Girja said the woman of the house had a wonderful kitchen garden. She took us into the tiny courtyard and showed us a small patch of green abundant with brinjal, tomatoes and cauliflower. The owner stayed in the background. Girja asked if we would want to try some of the vegetables, and I demurred—that offer surely should have come from the person who owned the garden. Girja snapped off a couple of tomatoes and handed them to me. She said, smiling, that they are all like one family in this village. Anyone was welcome to help themselves to another person's fruit or vegetables. The woman of the house stayed in the background, silent.

Our last stop was the village AWC. An old couple sat under an even older tree in the courtyard. They told us that most people in their community had faith in babas, though they did not. The woman told us how their neighbour had given the baba two goats and bottles of liquor to save their sick child. That had cost them Rs 20,000 but the child had died.

~

From Chait, we drove north to another TAF district—Morena, on the banks of the Chambal River. Our destination in Morena was one of our programme sites, Jalhada. On the way, we navigated the once notorious Chambal ravines. These are the gorges where, for fifty years,[6] the dreaded dacoits of the Chambal valley took refuge from the law. The ravines today are as they were in those days—brush, mud and sand, twisting and turning up and down.

After that heady drive, we arrived in Jalhada.[7] There we were met by Rajvir,[8] a wiry young man with the air of a potentate. We were in front of his house, a large plain structure with a courtyard. Rajvir told us there were six to eight houses more. There were many such small clusters scattered across the region, all parts of the village of Jalhada, with a population of 650 people.

This, too, was a Gujjar community, but different from the ones we had seen earlier that day. Rajvir said that people depended on fishing for a livelihood, but there were crocodiles, so it wasn't easy. They were also farmers, but the land was scrubby and not suitable for cultivation. In any case, during the monsoon there would be the *baad* * destroying all that came in the way. And yet there were solid houses and no signs of great poverty, suggesting there had to be some other means of livelihood. We had seen a couple of tractors as we entered the hamlet—something didn't add up.

Charpoys were produced and soon a silent group of about eight gaunt men materialized, in white tunics and dhotis, mostly

---

* Floods

the old and the very old. They gazed silently at us, curious. Some young children were idling nearby while others played ball, barefoot.

We had been told by Sameer Ahmed, our programme officer responsible for this area, that women played a very subservient role in these parts. They had to wear a ghunghat, and stand, if a man was sitting nearby. They never ventured outside the home, without a relative. Shelly Datta, our Morena district manager, asked if the women in our group might talk to some of the women. Rajvir conferred briefly with the elders and said we had their permission.

We went to a medium-sized house close by. Two women in ghunghat stepped into the verandah. One, whose name was Kamla,[9] perhaps in her mid-thirties, did all the talking, words coming out in a torrent. She made a striking figure even with face covered with the ghunghat, standing tall in her deep blue-black sari. After a while, Rajvir decided I was harmless and said I could join the group of women. I went and sat quietly in the back.

Kamla was brought up in Gwalior and studied till the 8th grade.[10] She knew the importance of education and said there was no possibility of a child from their village getting an education, because the teacher came to the village barely once in two weeks. The parents didn't do anything about it, she said, because no man had seen a world outside the village. Most boys began to work alongside their fathers from a very early age, falling into the same rut.

Throughout our conversation Kamla said nothing about the restraints on women. It was as though she accepted that as being in the natural order of things.

By this time, the elders who had been sitting at a decent distance, came and settled around a charpoy at the far end of the verandah. There was a subtle shift in Kamla's's tone after that. Till now she had been angry with the men. Now it was about the fact that they were all—men and women—hapless victims of a rotten system.

She switched to the topic of health, pointing out that there was no AWC nearby. The PHC was far away and dysfunctional. It was easier for them to go to Morena with their husbands when the weather allowed. The ANM came regularly but 'why does she have to go and sit somewhere, and I go to her? She should come to my house instead'.

We had noticed a young woman, about twenty, inside the house. She had been following our conversation. We asked if she would join us and she came forward hesitantly. Her head was bare, indicating that she was a *gaon ki beti*.[*] Rajvir was alarmed at this turn of events—he told the elders to leave immediately, rather than be exposed to a woman without ghunghat. Rajvir followed the men out but lingered in the area just beyond the verandah.

Free to speak candidly, Shelly asked Kamla if it was true that no one wanted to marry their daughters into this community and it was because the men were seen as too backward. Kamla had just begun to answer when Rajvir ran up, very agitated—he had been listening in. He wanted Shelly to get off this whole topic of marriage. He said he had heard her ask the same question earlier, with the elders. The meeting was clearly over.

It had been a long day, and I was trying hard to sort through all that we had seen about the complexities of caste and communities between Gwalior and Morena

$\sim$

---

[*] We saw this earlier that day at the Gwalior village.

Before we left, we walked down to the banks of the Chambal River. It was breathtaking, the river pristine, majestic, as it flowed slowly from east to west. The dark blue of the river and the white sands on its banks made a soothing contrast. Two lone boats were moored on poles far away. Across the river were the green slopes of Rajasthan—the white marble tips of a distant temple could be seen. Close by, a gaggle of urchins took turns jumping into the river, seemingly unafraid of crocodiles.

In the foreground, a young girl wearing a vermillion red tunic stood watching.

21

Return to Khoripaar

By the second half of 2021, the COVID-19 pandemic began to decline and our programme was ramping up again. I had been cut off from the field for over a year and was excited about going back.

As I have mentioned before, while almost all our work in Rajasthan had been in non-tribal areas, much of our work in Madhya Pradesh is with tribal communities. On this tour, I planned to visit villages that were the most difficult to serve. In that context, there was a small village, Khoripaar, in Bicchua block in Chhindwara, that I had visited two years previously.[1] This was where ninety families of the Mawasi tribe lived. Their situation seemed hopeless, with regular infant deaths and a high level of malnutrition—the root causes included a dysfunctional ASHA, corrupt AWW, mostly home deliveries and a village that was nearly isolated. And yet, at the end of the field visit, I felt that there was hope for Khoripaar.

I wanted to see what changes might have happened in the past two years. We had begun work in Khoripaar very recently.

I set off together with Yogesh Kochle, our programme officer responsible for the village, and Prerna Gopal, a programme officer who had accompanied me on the earlier trip.

~

We drove two hours from our base in Chhindwara to Bicchua, the small town closest to Khoripaar. From there, we took the country road to Majinapaar village, located at the mouth of the forest that we would have to cross to reach Khoripaar. We had met the local AWW for Majinapaar, Mamta, on our last visit. She was still in that position and familiar with Khoripaar—she kindly agreed to take us there.

The road forked at Majinapaar, with one branch leading into the forest. It was a dirt road and the forest was dark. Gopal, the driver, was quite the opposite of the cocky charioteer who had taken us into the forest without any qualms on our last visit. He stopped the car even before entering the forest and said: '*Raasta bahut kharaab hoga*, sir ji [The road will be very bad, sir]'. We assured Gopal that the road was not all that bad and that we should go forward.

Little did we know! The forest road was in as bad a condition as it had been two years ago, perhaps even a little worse. Gopal gamely managed the sharp turns and steep ups and downs. At one point he said grimly that if we went farther, it would be impossible to do a U-turn to get back. We reached the point where the road dipped steeply—last time, we had managed to go forward because of the skill and bravado of the driver. This time, that was impossible because part of the road had caved in with the monsoon. Already there was a faint smell of burnt rubber, and we decided to walk the rest of the way. We told Gopal to turn the vehicle around somehow before we got back. He looked relieved.

Mamta said there was a shorter way. We clambered up a small slope on our left to arrive at a rough track that would lead to the village. We had stepped outside the dense part of the forest on which we had been driving. Bright sunlight filtered through the trees. The trail was narrow and we walked in single file. I remembered someone telling me on my last trip about the problem of leopards on this route. Mamta said we were quite safe, and in any case, leopards did not attack in bright daylight.

It was a straight, rocky pathway with some ups and downs where you had to be careful. I found some fascinating rocks along the way. A few were rounded, others jagged, in shades of grey and coppery red. Many had serrations, and I wondered if a river had run through this part of the forest ages ago. Some rocks had microscopic, embedded sparkles that glinted as I moved them around in my palm—it was mystifying. They say you should never take anything away from a forest, but I couldn't help it. Today, three of those stones, now old friends, sit twinkling on my desktop, even as I write these words.

On the sides of the track were wildflowers and greenery, a rustic beauty. They also say you should never touch forest shrubbery as it might be poisonous. Still, I plucked a leaf that looked like mint, crushed it and inhaled deeply. It had an incredibly strong and pleasing minty smell. Mamta assured me it was not pudina,* and not to chew it.

~

The track ended suddenly. We stood upon a small hill, looking at the village a distance away—dilapidated shacks with brown thatched roofs. Between the village and where we stood was the

---

* Mint.

lake. It had been green when we came last, and now it was clear. Mamata said this was because of the monsoon—the lake would soon revert to its green, fetid version. Turning right, we saw the school, shuttered because of COVID-19.

We headed to the AWC, which was close by to the right, beyond the school. Between the school and the centre, there was a small gathering of men, idling. They watched intently as we walked past. I did a namaste, and they looked back silently, not hostile, just undecided. One toothless old fellow struggled to his feet, gave a lopsided smile, and did a namaste. He was obviously drunk, swaying in his own breeze.

On our last visit, the tiny AWC had been dark, dank and almost dysfunctional. Now the same space could barely be recognized—freshly painted in bright colours with English and Hindi alphabets. It had all the requirements—new weighing scale, clean kitchen, adequate supplies. There was an AWW and an ASHA in their patterned sari uniforms. A gleaming new village map, populated with coloured bindis, stood against the wall. It told us that there were four pregnant women, four lactating mothers and one high-risk pregnancy in the village. Yogesh said that in the past six months, there had been three deliveries, of which two had happened at home.

Eight women sat on the ground, not counting the ASHA and the local AWW. Most were older women, a few were young. One was obviously a bride, in a striking gold and red sari, head covered by her pallu. Sindoor had been generously applied in the parting of her hair. She wore bright red lipstick and her skin was dark and smooth. She was beautiful. The bride must have come from a village that was much better off than this one. I wondered how bewildered and lonely she must be feeling.

We tried to talk to the women but it was difficult. Some of the older women answered in monosyllables, the younger ones kept their eyes down. The ASHA was sprightly and active, but a woman of very few words. The AWW was not shy and answered our questions readily. The room began to fill up as the men outside filed in and sat near the doorway—they were mainly the same men who had been idling outside. Those who couldn't find space looked in from outside. They had come to the centre because they were curious. With the arrival of the men, the women fell completely silent, and so we turned to the men. The drunk was in the second row. He attempted to get up and say something but tumbled down.

Ram Nath, the sarpanch, did all the talking. He chose his words carefully and carried himself with a certain dignity. We asked about the health situation in the village. Ram Nath paused a while, with a slight smile on his lips. It looked like he had two ways to answer our question. Then he said, 'What does it matter? If the road is bad, the health will be terrible.' He gave an example, 'A pregnant woman had bad pains in the middle of the night. Her husband tried to take her on a motorcycle. It was dark and the road very bad—it was impossible. We carried her on a charpoy to a point the motorcycle could reach, and they took her to the hospital from there. Luckily, mother and baby survived—not always.' He said he had taken up the matter of the road long ago with the panchayat and had filed a petition, but nothing happened.

The drunk managed to stand up and began a long rambling statement. He was made to sit down. Then, little by little, a few others began to express themselves. They spoke of the other big problem that the village faced: water. The women walked more than a kilometre every day to fetch water. In the height of summer, the river went dry, and it was almost impossible to find water.

～

We walked through the village with the ASHA, AWW and Mamta. We planned to come back to the centre later, hoping that the men would disperse and we could speak freely to the women.

On the way out, the drunk came up to me, reeking of mahua. I liked his cheery attitude and was curious to know more about him. But it is difficult to start a conversation with someone who is totally smashed. For a start, I asked what a bottle of mahua cost in these parts. The drunk perked up: '*Assi rupya.*' I said eighty was much too high because I had seen it sold for twenty to forty. He looked evasive and kept mumbling: 'Assi.' I told him firmly that I wasn't interested at any price, and joined my colleagues, Mamta and the ASHA, for the village walk.

The drunk joined the party, trailing a few feet behind. Soon, a scrawny dog, limping, with a half chewed-off ear, came up, wagging his tail excitedly. The drunk tried to kick the dog away and lost his balance. He must have thought the dog would make a poor impression on a potential customer. The dog saw his master was not in a good mood and kept a safe distance behind but stayed with our party.

The village was worse off than before. The houses, mostly made of mud with thatched roofs, were dilapidated. As we strolled through the village, I asked Mamta about the wonderful teacher, Mita Ghorpade, whom we had met on our last visit. Mamta said she had been transferred to another school. The village school was closed but the headmaster came down to the village every day and gave lessons to four to five children who showed up regularly. A little later, we were introduced to a young man, a local who volunteered his time to teach children, supporting the headmaster. We asked him why he did it—he smiled and said nothing.

We came to a junction in the concrete road that ran through the village. I remembered turning right and going to the house of the village ASHA who was passed out outside her home in the mid-day sun. I asked Mamta what had become of the ASHA's mother, who was the local jadi-booti practitioner and the only dai in the village. She said that the old woman had died and that now, nearly all deliveries happened at home. 'The saas or some older woman does it,' she said.

I asked what had happened to the ASHA. Mamta said in a whisper, nodding towards the ASHA who was walking with us: '*Wohi hai* [It is her]'. I could hardly believe that it was the same person, recalling the woman who was passed out the last time we were here. Mamta explained that the ASHA had gone away for some festival, where she met a baba. His magic cured her overnight of her alcoholism. She was now a model health worker, regularly doing the rounds of houses.

The drunk must have felt there was too much superfluous conversation going on, and he sidled up. He brought up the mahua topic again, still sticking to his price, but in a tone that suggested he was open to negotiations. I again made it clear I was not interested, whereupon the drunk suddenly fell at my feet, crying, 'Dada* ji!' Prerna burst into peals of laughter while I tried to maintain my composure. The wretch was at least ten years older than me.

We passed the place where an NGO had created a water pumping tower that ran on solar electricity. Two years ago, we had seen women gathered around the tower, waiting hours to fill their buckets. Today, the project had been abandoned. There was solar power, but nothing to pump.

Meanwhile, the drunk sensed an opportunity. He announced that his 'real' wife—whatever that meant—was now the village dai. He claimed that she had been doing deliveries for a litre and

---

* Grandpa.

a half of mahua each time. I turned to Mamta, who said quietly that it wasn't true. The drunk invited us to come to his house and meet his wife. We thanked him, but said it was getting late and we had to be on our way. He asked us to wait for a few minutes and stumbled away.

His hut was within sight of where we stood. Through the window we could see the drunk inside the hut. He was shouting at an old woman who was lying face down on a charpoy. It was obvious that she was knocked out by hooch. We could hear him yelling '*Jaldi utho . . . bade log aaye hain* [Wake up fast, some big people are here]'. He was threatening her with dire consequences if she didn't get up and meet the 'big people'. Then he started pummelling her on the back, but the old woman barely moved, absorbing the blows. He was doing it all for our benefit and we thought it best that we move on quickly.

~

We saw some more of the village, then made our way back to the AWC. The drunk had got there ahead of us. He was sitting against a far wall, sulking. Only a few women were left, and some of the men.

The ASHA spoke haltingly about her job and how she went house to house, looking out for illness in the family, reminding them of the next visit by the ANM. The AWW described her routine—providing mid-day meals for the children and take home rations for pregnant women and new mothers. They both explained how they kept their data in their own registers, how they made sure it matched and how they stuck bindis on the village map to mark households with different types of health conditions. The few remaining men listened quietly. Yogesh, whose job was to guide this process, said their record-keeping was almost perfect.

Suddenly, the drunk's wife crashed in through the door, grey hair wild, eyes glazed. She looked around the room, seemingly unsure of where she had arrived. Her husband seemed not to have noticed. No one made a move to help her. They glanced up and returned their attention to the meeting, as though all this was entirely normal. The old woman slumped against the wall and stared fixedly ahead.

We got up to leave—it had been a long day. The drunk came up and said he had a bottle. I told him again that I had no need for a bottle. He asked, '*Nahin loge kya?* [Will you not take it?]'. I said no, I would not take it, wished him well and turned to go. Disappointment was writ large on the drunk's face, but he was not upset. Setbacks were part of his daily life and he took it in his stride. He walked with us right up to the spot where we had entered the village from the forest. He said goodbye with folded hands and a toothless smile.

~

We went to meet Sister Roshini, the ANM responsible for Khoripaar, who had accompanied us on our last visit. We had been impressed then by her commitment to her job and this village. Roshini was honest about the situation in the village. There had been some improvements after she had formed a team with the other two health workers. But home deliveries were still the norm, infant deaths still happened and malnutrition prevailed. I asked her what could be done and the reply was immediate: '*Sadak theek karna*'—Fix the road. The road—of course, the road.

On the face of it, the village looked hopeless. But over the course of the day, we had seen many reasons to be hopeful. There was the well-intentioned sarpanch, the committed health worker, the young volunteer, the transformed ASHA worker, a well-functioning AWC and accurate record-keeping. The people of this forgotten village were spirited in their quiet everyday way.

But the single biggest reason for the poor health record of the village, and probably the easiest to fix, remained untouched—sadak theek karna!

22

Ghansour

The pool of fresh blood lay glistening at the entrance to the PHC. A trail of drops curved away to the right. Rahul and Anuradha were the first on the scene. The young man froze, eyes widening—Anuradha reached out to steady him. Then she began running—she knew already where the trail would lead.

The labour room at the PHC in Ghansour block of Seoni district is located at the end of a long corridor, to the right of the entranceway. Stepping over a splash of blood at the doorway, Anuradha, the nurse mentor, moved quickly to the inside door. She stopped for a moment, shocked.

A young woman lay on the bare floor—she had given birth to a baby girl just moments ago. The four people in the room were in panic. Clearly, no one knew what to do, including the junior staff nurse. The ASHA, between sobs, explained that she had brought Kamala[1] to the hospital from her village—she had been bleeding throughout the half-hour journey on a rocky road. Kamala had given birth to a healthy child on the way—that baby's twin sister was born minutes ago on the floor of the labour room a little later. That was because they had no time to lift Kamala onto the birthing bed. Mercifully, both babies were healthy.

Kamala moaned faintly—she was losing blood rapidly.

~

Anuradha was born in Roorkee, a small town in the hill state of Uttarakhand. Her father, Shashi Kant Sharma, was her hero. He had worked all his life in the clerical cadre of the Indian Army, retiring with the rank of Junior Commissioned Officer (JCO). His job entailed frequent changes in postings. Consequently, Anuradha studied in a series of modest government schools in small towns as well as big cities across northern India. She excelled in singing, dancing and sports.

When she was in Grade 12, Anuradha's father, who was a man of few words, said, 'If you don't get good grades, we will get you married right after you finish school.' She doubted he would do that because she was his favourite and he doted on her—surely, he wouldn't want her to get married and leave home so soon. But taking no chances, she worked hard and did well in her final examinations. Soon after that, one day, she overheard her grandfather telling her father that this was enough of studying, you should get Anuradha married now. She knew that an arranged marriage was inevitable, sooner or later—what she most wanted then was to be independent. They were living in Dehradun, a small place with few options for a higher education. So, on that pretext, she applied for all kinds of courses in bigger towns and got admitted into a four-year undergraduate degree in nursing in faraway Jalandhar. She had no understanding or great love of nursing—it was just a ticket to a larger world.

Shashi Kant loved the values of the army. Two military mottos hung on the walls of their government flat: 'Service is our Creed' and 'Vigilance and Valour'. All this translated into the exhortation he had always given his daughter: 'Always challenge yourself'. Anuradha took that very seriously. He was broken-hearted that his beloved daughter would be leaving home. But he was true to his principles and saw that, indeed, his daughter was challenging herself. He gave her his blessings in tears.

After completing her BSc in nursing, Anuradha taught for a year, then spent the next two years getting a postgraduate degree. But by now, the pressure to get married was mounting and every time she went home to Dehradun, she would be forced to consider marriage proposals that were coming to her parents. She told her parents that she would be willing to get married if it was the right person—she never spelt out what that meant to her. But as the proposals came in, she found that there would always be two conditions: that her family would pay a dowry, and that she would give up nursing and become a homemaker. Both conditions were unacceptable to Anuradha. She made it clear that she would not consider any arranged marriage offers from then on.

Anuradha taught nursing in Dehradun for five years after that and then joined TAF as a nurse mentor, responsible for three blocks in Seoni district of Madhya Pradesh. She lived in the district capital, two hours away, and travelled a bad road both ways every day for her work. It was her first real job, ensuring that the government ran the busiest labour rooms as models. It is a massive responsibility, overseeing seven such facilities, together amounting to more than 2000 deliveries. She trains the government staff nurses in every aspect of labour room management—technical knowledge, equipment and record-keeping. At thirty-two, she was much younger than the senior nurses whom she taught, but she commanded respect and had won their affection. Finally, she had the kind of job that she had always wanted: full of challenge.

But nothing she had done so far had prepared her for the kind of trial she faced that day with a poor woman, who was rapidly losing blood, lying on the bare floor of a labour room.

~

As Anuradha ran to the labour room, Rahul, still in shock, went to look for help. There were few people around since the outpatient crowds came only in the afternoon. He visited these facilities routinely in his job as TAF's programme officer responsible for that block of 150 villages. He knew his way around and searched for the old peon, Phool Chand, who worked in the OPD. Rahul said, 'Phool Chand ji, there is blood at the entrance, a lot of blood—do you know that?' The veteran gave Rahul a look as if to say: of course I know, because I know everything that happens in this hospital, from long before you were born. He nodded, muttering, 'A case has come. Two babies. Lot of bleeding.' He turned to get back to his work.

Rahul told him it was an emergency and that Kamala needed to be taken immediately to the Community Health Centre (CHC), forty minutes away. Voice rising, he told Phool Chand to call the government's 108 ambulance service right away. Even as Phool Chand said, 'It will take some time to get here . . .' Rahul replied, 'Just do it, now!' He spun around and ran towards the labour room.

Kamala's mother-in-law and husband stood outside the room, terrified. The husband spoke in a low, hoarse voice, avoiding Rahul's eyes, saying they had delayed bringing Kamala to the PHC for too long. He said his *jeth* (husband's elder brother) had forbidden him from calling for an ambulance. Their first baby had been delivered at home and was healthy—he saw no need for his brother to take his wife to the hospital. It was the practice for the ambulance driver, staff nurse and other attendants to extort as much as Rs 1000–2000 each for their troubles. Their father and his brother were poor labourers and they couldn't afford that kind of payment. Later, when Kamala's situation became dire, they called the ambulance but that took far too long to reach.

Rahul was only twenty-six and had never experienced anything like this calamity. He is from Chhattisgarh, a small, heavily forested state adjoining Madhya Pradesh's eastern border. The state is rich in natural resources but the rural and forested areas lack even basic amenities. Rahul was brought up in such an environment, in a small village called Lacchanpur, in Lormi block.

His earliest memory is of being taken by someone's hand to the AWC. His brother, Rohit, was two years older and was qualified to go there. The authorities allowed Rahul to accompany his brother so he would stay in the centre with all the older children, every day. From there, a deep bond was forged between Rahul and Rohit. His elder brother become both friend and mentor, guiding him at crucial stages in Rahul's life. 'He is my idol to this day,' Rahul says.

Rahul's father was a small farmer with a few acres of land, enough to feed the family and generate a small surplus that he sold in the market. He believed that his sons should get an education if they were to move ahead in life. He was a gentle person but was strict about studies—two hours every evening was compulsory. One day, he got emotional and said to his boys, a quiver in his voice, 'I want you boys to study. So long as I live, even if I must sell my land, I will see that you get an education.'

Indeed, Rahul and his brother were set on studying and got good results in the village school, which then had classes from 1–5. After that, he started studying in a private school close by and that took him through till class 12. Rahul and his brother formed a study group in the village with their neighbours' children and they motivated each other. Rahul had a natural ability for mathematics and he tutored some of the other children. The class 8 test is crucial because it is a State Education Board exam—he came out in the top ten students in all Chhattisgarh, and this was a turning point.

Rahul went to college, 75 kilometres away, to pursue a degree in forestry management. The medium of study was English, and on the first day, the teacher asked each boy to stand up and introduce himself. When Rahul's turn came, he stood up and wept because he couldn't understand the question or speak a word. Three years later, he emerged with a college degree and was admitted to the Tata Institute for Social Sciences (TISS), one of India's most prestigious social development institutions. His life had been built around academic excellence and sheer grit.

By this time, Rahul's brother had joined a prominent all-India NGO. He decided to follow his brother's example and take up a career in the social sector. He joined TAF in late 2021 as a programme officer responsible for 170 villages in Ghansour block of Seoni district. Life had prepared him for challenge, but not the kind of emergency that confronted him and Anuradha at the door of the PHC that morning in Ghansour.

~

There were three people in the labour room: the ASHA who had brought Kamala from the village, a lab technician and the staff nurse who was on duty that day. As is typical in most PHCs, there was no doctor available in the hospital. The regular nurse was on leave and the one on duty was a novice, only twenty-one years old—she pleaded with Anuradha to help, saying she had no idea what she should do in this emergency.

The bleeding woman was pleading for water, her voice barely a whisper. She was closing her eyes occasionally and the worry was that she would become unconscious. Anuradha said, pretending to be stern, 'I will give you water, but only if you don't close your eyes.' Kamala took the water in small sips.

Anuradha needed to check if there had been a tear in the wall of the uterus. She wanted to confirm that the placenta had been discharged completely and that no part of it remained in the uterus. The problem was that only government nurses were allowed to do internal examinations and the staff nurse said she had never done this kind of thing before. Anuradha told her to quickly sterilize herself and put gloves on. Then she demonstrated the procedure to the nurse, moving her hands in the air and speaking slowly so that the nurse understood. Soon, there was good news—there was no tear and the placenta had been discharged completely. The bleeding, however, had become profuse, and Kamala needed to be taken immediately to the CHC if her life was to be saved.

Word came from Rahul that they had called the government's 108 emergency ambulance service, but no ambulance was immediately available. The person at the other end said they would send one as soon as they could—it eventually arrived ninety minutes later. Kamala was sinking fast and likely would not last another hour. Rahul and Anuradha had a hurried consultation.

TAF's policy is clear that, in emergency situations, our team on the spot should get in touch with the government authorities and get their permission to take life-saving action. Here, there was no time—they decided that they would rush Kamala to the CHC in the TAF car. There was a risk: if Kamala died on the way, there would be an inquiry by the government. Pending the result of that enquiry—which could take months—all TAF work across Madhya Pradesh could very likely be shut down. That would be catastrophic for our programme.

Rahul ran ahead to alert the driver to stand ready. They sanitized the inside of the vehicle to the extent that was possible in a few minutes. In the meantime, Kamala was lifted carefully onto a stretcher and was brought out from the labour room. They had reached the entrance to the PHC when Kamala's eyes closed briefly. Her saas, on seeing this, began a loud wailing. Anuradha lost it and shouted at her, 'Amma, *khamosh! Varna* . . . [Amma, shut up, or else]! She is still alive—this is not the time for you to make a loud noise!' The saas subsided immediately.

Kamala was lifted and placed gingerly across the laps of her saas and husband. The husband looked shocked by all that was happening. Anuradha and Rahul climbed into the narrow third row of seats. The SUV set off, going as fast as possible on the bad road. The vehicle bumped and jolted, and Anuradha prayed that Kamala would survive. In the meantime, Rahul got through to the Block Medical Officer (BMO)—the doctor responsible for all the villages—and apprised the doctor of the situation. He asked him to ensure that the CHC was ready and medical staff standing by to receive the emergency case. Rahul knew the BMO well and the doctor immediately assured him that they would be standing ready.

With every bump and jolt, Kamala moaned. Her saas and Anuradha would sprinkle some water on her face and tap her cheeks to make sure that her eyes stayed open. The CHC was still twenty minutes away, and Anuradha was losing hope. At that point, she let out a fervent plea: 'Dear God! Please save this poor woman who has to support her family. Take me instead. I am alone, and she has two babies and a family . . .' Rahul turned in surprise and assured her that they would all be well, but he was also losing hope. Anuradha was repeating her plea continuously under her breath.

The drive seemed endless, but at last the vehicle turned in at the gate of the CHC. The BMO and all his key staff were standing at the entrance. They rushed Kamala to the emergency room. Two hours later, she was out of danger. Anuradha came out of the emergency room to tell the distraught husband and the family that Kamala was safe and recovering. The husband was weeping. He kept saying the same words to Anuradha and Rahul: 'If it were not for you, she would not be alive today.' Rahul was emotional and whispered to Anuradha, 'This is why we work for TAF.'

~

That was the story of how two young TAF members tackled an emergency, saving a life. But it is not an unusual story—indeed, stories like this abound in the day to day lives of our programme officers and nurse mentors.

We are focused on our public health mission, which is to deliver services that will avert death and morbidity among large rural populations. We do not get involved with individual lives, for that would only detract from our larger mission. Our protocol is to bring each needy case to the attention of the government system. But there are times when that is not possible and when you cannot walk away. That is when our team at the front does all it takes to avert tragedy, going well beyond the call of duty.

23

Beyond the Call

We do serious work.
But we don't take ourselves seriously.

Yes, laughter abounds after the serious work is finished. Some in our team are prone to making gaffes—others have idiosyncrasies. They are fodder for the team's many mimics and raconteurs. For example, there is the teammate who likes to climb tall trees—once even a coconut palm—after three drinks; the one of unusually rosy complexion and imposing goatee, who was mistaken for a Russian; the person who comes up with all manner of devious stratagems to secure the upper berth whenever we travel by train; and another who always sleeps with his boots on when travelling by train ('otherwise someone might steal them').

In most workplaces, colleagues pretend they have not seen or heard the gaffes—they certainly never make light of personal idiosyncrasies. But at TAF, eyes and ears are wide open. Howlers and peculiarities are quietly noted, artfully embellished and brought out when the time is just right.

$\sim$

They are a diverse group* from small towns and large cities—they have studied in modest as well as better-known universities, including from abroad. They have studied, or have work experience, in social work, public health, liberal arts, business and government. They have come from almost every Indian state and between them, speak twelve languages. Two out of three staff are women. They are young, most of them are in their twenties and it is their first job. They are conjoined by a single overriding passion: to save lives and prevent morbidity among the poorest mothers and their children. Support staff at every level are deeply involved in the field—our role is to support our frontline colleagues.

We have three types of field staff. There are the block officers, typically in their mid-twenties, who manage a block of 150–200 villages, a population of 1,50,000–2,00,000, and the fellows, who apprentice with a block officer. Finally, the nurse mentors, are each responsible for five to seven high caseload delivery points,† training at least fifty nurses in how to smoothly handle almost 2000 deliveries every month. At the time of writing this, we have a little more than a hundred field staff.

Collectively known as programme officers,¹ these three grades of staff play a crucial role in our field programmes. They are TAF's frontline warriors who work directly with the government supervisors, community health workers, village women and children every day.

~

---

* Of about 140 at the time of writing.
† We give this name to health facilities—usually CHCs—that have the largest number of deliveries.

These members of the TAF team fan out to their field locations every morning. The block officers and fellows go to the villages for which they are responsible, nurse mentors to their assigned facilities. There, they review progress, troubleshoot problems and train government staff. They are back in the office by the evening and settle down to review the day's work and plan for the next day.

It would have become evident from the preceding narrative that we work in beautiful locations. But seasons change, and the same places often have extremes of weather. Summer temperatures are in the high forties centigrade, monsoon rains so heavy as to cause flooding; winters, bitterly cold. The programme officers' job is, therefore, a physically demanding one. Irrespective, the work goes on without break. The job can be emotionally draining. Take, for example, a programme officer who has oversight of 150 villages and a population of approximately 1,50,000. That translates to more than 3500 births every year. In the normal course, more than a hundred of these newborns would die before they reach the age of one, and at least five women would have died in the birth process. Almost a third of the newborns will end up malnourished, of which more than 150 will be severely malnourished. There would be about 20,000 malnourished children under the age of five at any point. It is a lot to absorb.

~

Our young programme officers take on this enormous responsibility for their blocks. Their commitment goes very deep. It is as if they feel personally responsible for saving the lives of a hundred babies every year. There are also the dire emergencies, when the programme officer must make the call whether to get personally involved or refer the case quickly to the authorities. And it is a lonely job. The programme officer is far away from family and friends. There are no avenues for entertainment. They are virtually cut off from the mainstream of life.

So why do they do it? Why would a young person choose to take on such a physical and emotional challenge? I ask this question of our programme officers all the time. At the interview stage, I tell them what to expect and ask if they are prepared to take it on—some back out, and that is entirely understandable. When they have been in the job a year or more, I ask what makes them stay.

Certain reasons come up, time and again: the chance to make a big difference, enormous responsibility, steep learning curve, self-discovery, deep friendships, adventure and laughter, freedom. I realize that this is an extremely sterile description of a unique job. Perhaps their own words would serve the purpose better. At different points, on being asked this question, our programme officers have answered as follows:

The most important reason is the chance to make a big difference. We are working with some of the poorest and most overlooked mothers and their children. To see a child dying from severe malnutrition, restored in a matter of weeks, is to experience a miracle. If I saved a single life in my entire lifetime, I would be so happy. I am getting the chance to do that for hundreds of children and mothers.

I am given enormous personal responsibility. It is not as though I am working on some big government programme that sets out to save a million lives—then I would be a small cog in a huge machine. Here I am, not even thirty, and I am accountable for 150 villages! There is nowhere else I can do that at my age—or even in an entire lifetime

It's about learning new skills. I took this job thinking that I would learn about something called 'maternal and child health'.

And I had no idea what that meant. In just two years, I have been given the chance to begin learning how to think strategically, use data, communicate with all types of people, understand a very technical field and so much more. It's not classroom stuff, it is apprenticing with a master trainer, someone far more experienced, in each of these fields.

It's about discovering myself. This work has given me a clearer idea of what makes me happy, what I can do well, what I must get good at. I am learning the meaning of what were just abstract concepts—like 'compassion' and 'giving' and 'poverty'. It's given me not one but several options for what I want to do in life.

It's about making deep and different friendships. We are a bunch of very different people on one ship. Normally, I would have gravitated towards people from my sort of class, education, childhood, wanting the same thing. Now I am with people from totally different backgrounds—therefore, we make particularly deep friendships. I have made friends with people from the communities—we have active WhatsApp groups! That is a different view of people and life that I would have entirely missed otherwise.

It's about adventure. It feels like we have made a huge leap into another world and we must figure out the way forward using our wits and asking people along the way. It's incredibly exciting!

It's about laughs. Where else would I find a job where I laugh out loud every day?

And it's about the culture: complete freedom, the obligation to challenge and dissent, humility.

Really, it's an experience that sets you up for life, but it's not for everyone, only a few.

24

Abida

We have worked closely with the triad of frontline health workers for almost a decade. We have seen their shortfalls, but much more often, witnessed their deep commitment to duty. Often, these women have had tough personal lives and yet, they give freely of themselves, administering to the needs of the poorest mothers and children. The everyday heroism of the frontline worker is largely unheralded.

As we come towards the end of this narrative, let us find a window into their struggle, suffering and triumph, through the life story of one such worker.

~

Abida[1] Sayyed, the AWW, sat to one side, observing the meeting. We were in a village called Devni (pop. 2100) in Pati block[2] of Barwani district and had come to the AWC to meet the community. It turned out to be a short meeting because no one was ready to speak to us. We had heard and respected that people in this tribal community are shy of visitors. My colleague Kritika Pandey—our programme officer in Barwani—and I, were the ones intruding into their lives.

The ASHA was proud of her village and must have been embarrassed. She said: 'You must speak to Abida khanum. She has been working here for thirty-seven years.' I was amazed that a health worker could be in the same position, and place, for so long. The woman who had been sitting to the side smiled and came up. We sat down in the airy veranda and I asked Abida Sayyed to tell us her life story.[3]

Abida was tanned a deep walnut brown, with wind-blown hair and a heavily wrinkled face. She was fifty-seven but looked much older. She spoke confidently and in flashes, revealed a wry sense of humour. She was born in Rajpur[4] town in Barwani, the eldest of six girls in a very poor family.[5] Her mother did jhadoo-ponchha and her father did odd jobs, mostly using his rudimentary skills in sewing.

Their combined earnings amounted to an income of barely Rs 100 a month,* wholly insufficient to run a family with six children. Every day, Abida woke up at 5 a.m. and fetched water from the handpump. She then ground the day's atta. Sometimes her father and mother would both go out on work, leaving her in charge of five younger siblings.

Abida's parents pulled her out of school after third grade. Her mother gave them a lot of love and was very clear about her priorities—and money was on top of the list. ('Education doesn't give us food today—money does that.') Abida and her two younger siblings would run small chores for neighbours occasionally and

---

* This and some numbers that will follow, may look like a typo to this generation of readers. Allowing for inflation, a hundred rupees would be about Rs 3000 in today's terms.

bring home some money. Her mother would attach great value to whatever they brought home, however little.

At times the family had to go to bed on an empty stomach. The children, aged four, six and nine, would not understand why their mother hadn't give them food and cried themselves to sleep. Every time, their mother's heart broke into pieces. Nearby, the father lay staring at the dark ceiling, trying to harden his heart. Their mother always reminded them of the right attitude to life: 'Make do with whatever you have'. That was the only way to survive.

As a child, Abida had no time for play, except occasionally with her one good friend, Prema. They devised all manner of games, their favourite being to skip with an old jump rope. Prema was from a lower middle-class family. Her mother was kind and whenever Abida came home, she would give her things to eat and, always, a glass of milk. She never let the child feel pitied.

As time went on, Abida's family's fortunes worsened. Food became even more scarce. Her parents were ageing prematurely. Years of unremitting struggle had etched deep creases into their faces, though the spark had not died in their eyes.

Abida accompanied her father in selling pakoras that had been made at home in the morning and sometimes glass bangles. Sales were poor in Rajpur—it was a large town and there were many shops selling pakoras. They started travelling to nearby villages as far as the neighbouring Pati block, walking for hours, a *tokri** on their heads, full of pakoras. They also carried old newspapers and string, which they used to pack the pakoras after a sale. They had a rusty *tarazu*[†] and weights for 50 gm, 200 gm and, ambitiously, one for a half kilo.

---

* Basket
[†] Handheld weighing scale

There were well-trodden paths within the forests, but it was not altogether safe because there were regular sightings of leopards, sloth bears and wild boars. Their pakoras sold well in these interior villages and they started making longer excursions, as far as distant villages like Tora Mal and Devni. Darkness would be setting in when they returned from these longer treks. The little girl would be frightened, imagining the eyes of a leopard peering through the bush and hearing the unfamiliar screams of strange forest birds at nightfall. She clung to her father and these daily excursions forged a strong attachment between them.

The two became a regular sight in these interior villages. Abida was popular with the children who envied her for being able to go on such long excursions. The elders understood the hardship the child endured and were affectionate with her. Every evening, father and daughter returned with a few small notes and loose change to hand over to Abida's mother.

It was a tough upbringing. But Abida says she was never unhappy—they were one unit, parents and children bravely facing everything life would throw at them.

All that was about to change.

~

Abida said, 'In those days, in our community, girls were married off very early. There was stigma if she was married after her first period.' Abida had just had her second. Kritika asked how old Abida was then, and she giggled, covering her face with her pallu, saying, 'You will get me put me in jail . . .' Kritika asked again, softly, and Abida said, seriously, 'I was thirteen. By the time I was fifteen, I was a mother of two.'

She was but a child whose childhood had been snatched away from her even before it had begun. But it cannot be assumed that she was unhappy, for she was with her family and they had a deep bond forged in shared suffering.

I asked how she felt, when she was told by her mother that they were getting her married. She said that above all, she was afraid. She was going to her new home in an unknown place called Khargaon. She had no idea what it meant to have a husband and stay with another family. Her parents and her sisters wept as they said goodbye. The younger siblings had always thought of her as shelter and her parents saw her as their child-adult, close to them in a special way.

In our work, we see many things that should not be and we try to avoid judgement. But I had to wonder why these parents would marry Abida when she was just a child. And it occurred to me that they must have suffered for they had no choice but to do that, for there would be one less mouth to feed.

Abida said her husband, Munnawar Ahmed, was a 'much older man'—he was twenty. From the beginning, he was physically and emotionally abusive. He would drink heavily and meet her only for violent sex. It was never clear what job he had, or if indeed, he had a job. He had a peculiar way of disappearing from their home for weeks and sometimes months.

Apart from her saas and *sasur,*[*] there was no one else in the household. She was in purdah all the time and her mother-in-law gave her many household duties. They were a poor household, but not as poor as Abida's family.

Abida missed her period during one of Munnawar's absences—again, she was pregnant and didn't know it. She knew nothing about the cycle of menstruation, conception and pregnancy. When Abida missed her second period, her saas found out and screamed at her, that Abida was infertile, not realizing she

---

[*] Father-in-law

was pregnant. As her pregnancy advanced, Abida would always feel hungry but didn't have the option of asking for more food. She experienced a grinding loneliness and she wept every night as she thought of her family.

A year later, to Abida's absolute delight, who should show up but her father! He had been receiving reports about the abuse. He had decided to take Abida home. Her saas and sasur immediately agreed and Munnawar nodded, looking away.

Soon, Abida and her father were back at the old, familiar home in Rajpur. There were squeals of delight from her sisters and mother and tears all around as they smothered Abida with kisses. She was pregnant, probably by five months, and nobody knew it, including the mother-to-be.

She started to go with her father again on his pakora-selling trips. They went to the same villages and people were happy to see her. After she had gotten married and left, they had thought that would be the last time they saw her.

Eventually, it became evident that Abida was pregnant. Now Munnawar's family wanted her back immediately to deliver the baby in Khargaon. The only way to get from Rajpur to Khargaon was to walk 37 kilometres to Barwani town and from there, take a bus to travel 88 kilometres to Khargaon. In these rural areas, people walked vast distances routinely—indeed, Abida and her father had walked 50 kilometres and back in a day on several occasions when they were selling pakoras. The only complication was that Abida was by now nine months pregnant and her family assumed she had a few more months to go. There had not been a single antenatal checkup.

Abida and her father set off for Khargaon. Abida's mother packed a bag of moongphali for the journey. Midway, they had to wade through a river and as they came out onto dry land, Abida felt the first contraction. Fortunately, the contractions were few

and far between at this point. Finally, they reached Barwani where
father and daughter should have rushed to the nearest medical
facility. But they had no knowledge of these things and in any
case, their money was just enough for two bus tickets to Khargaon.

They arrived safely in Khargaon. Munnawar was away on one
of his disappearances. The next day, a baby boy was born, a home
delivery by a local dai. The baby's father showed up a few months
later. He mellowed after the baby came and his attitude changed
for a while. But he soon fell back to his old ways with the drinking
and beatings.

~

One day, there was a surprise visitor to meet Abida's father in
Rajpur: his *samdhi** from Khargaon, who exuded a warmth no
one had seen in him till now. He got straight to the point, 'Abida
is a very capable girl. She will be good in business. Why don't we
set them both up to run a shop, make some money?' He had in
mind a village not far from Rajpur. He added that Munnawar had
changed his ways. The question of Munnawar's family meeting
the cost, or sharing it, didn't arise.

Abida's father was simple-minded and did not question the
proposition. So, Abida, her husband and their baby moved to a
village not far from the town of Devni which was 30 km away.
Abida's father managed to put together the Rs 65 needed to buy
a very tiny space, enough for a kiosk. There was a small room
behind the kiosk where the family could stay. Abida took a loan
for the money needed to set up the shop.

It looked nice, with bottles containing biscuits, sugar and
gud. They also kept beedis. The only items that sold were beedis

---

* The person whose son/daughter is married to your son/daughter.

and sugar. People bought beedis individually, not by the packet, and they took sugar in tiny quantities. Whenever something sold, Munnawar pocketed all the money. Abida had no option but to close the shop. The money was not even enough to pay back the loan.

Abida had become pregnant again when they left Rajpur, and the second baby, also a boy, had arrived soon after they started the shop. Munnawar disappeared twice during the two years that they lived in their new home. While he was there, he would look after the children while Abida went out on her own, once again selling pakoras. The local people had seen her last as a ten-year-old and now she had come back as a young woman, married with two children—no one could have imagined the pain she had endured.

As soon as she could pay back the loans, Abida went back to Rajpur. Something had snapped inside her. She set out to build a house made of mud and poles with a thatched roof. It cost her nothing because the house was made by the village people. The girl—she was now almost twenty—was popular in the village. The sarpanch said that Abida is a '*gaon ki ladki*'—daughter of the village—and they would take care of her. Every person provided something: some a pole, others thatching and many their labour.

Her parents watched the house come up, relieved. It would have been impossible for them to accommodate their daughter, two babies and a scoundrel husband.

~

Abida began to sell pakoras again, sometimes with her father but mostly on her own. She had absorbed all the hard blows and kept her upbeat spirit. The villagers, who had endured much hardship themselves respected, and were fond of, her.

It was difficult. She could leave the younger one at her parents'
home and have no option than to take the older child with her,
going only to the villages located closer to them. Her husband
would show up occasionally and she could leave the children with
him. She could go to more remote villages then, often ending up
at Devni village, about 50 km away.

One day the sarpanch there said, 'You have been coming here
for the past ten years. You are like a daughter to us. If it gets late,
you are welcome to stay with us.' So, when her husband was back
and minding the children, she slept a few times on a mat in the
closed veranda of the sarpanch's house, secure in the knowledge
that the children were safe.

On one of her visits to Devni, a Multi-Purpose Worker*
approached her. The MPW, as he is called, said, 'You are well-
known and accepted by all in these villages, you should become
the AWW in Devni. If that post becomes available, you should
apply for it.' He was aware of her dedication and that she was
good at making friends.

The MPW shared his proposal with the Lady Health Worker
(LHW), responsible for all anganwadi centres for five or six villages.
The LHW had also heard of Abida and she readily agreed. She,
in turn, spoke to her supervisor, the Child Development Project
Officer (CDPO). He liked the idea, and in a few months had
secured the approvals. In 1985, Abida became the AWW for the
village of Devni. She was now a government health worker and
she would have a secure income for the rest of her life. It had
happened because three government functionaries—the MPW,

---

* The government's grassroots functionary, usually a man, responsible
for the control of communicable, sanitation-based diseases who also
made sure that the health system was working as it should in the villages
under their charge.

the LHW and the CDPO—and an elected representative of the village, the sarpanch, had been impressed by her abilities and her attitude.

The LHW saw to it that a makeshift AWC was built in the village. Abida's starting salary was only Rs 125, which was less than what she had been earning selling pakoras and insufficient to raise her growing children. Still, it was a permanent job with the government and she had no intention of letting it go. So, she continued with her business, selling pakoras after the day's work at the anganwadi.

She took what was left of the anganwadis mid-day meal dalia porridge, back home to Rajpur. Devni village is scattered across the hills in tiny hamlets, separated by large distances.[6] The idea that children would be brought to the centre to avail of the prescribed hot mid-day meal, made no sense. The prescribed Take Home Ration (THR) that was to be given to pregnant and lactating women was also being wasted.

Abida began taking the cooked dalia and the THR to the main road at a distance of a few kilometres from the village. This way, the people who lived near the road could come and collect their ration. She introduced a day every week to serve the people who lived farther away or uphill, when she would have the ration and dalia made in bulk, for the women to take away their portions.

As we have seen before, the ANM is critical for a healthy delivery in the village, especially immunizations. Her visits were irregular because the people of the village mistrusted, even feared, the government health system. Most children didn't get even the basic vaccines—inevitably, many children died. Abida began going door-to-door to spot cases that needed to be examined by the ANM, especially children who needed immunization. She tried her best to persuade the parents, and gradually a trickle of parents with children came forward, and then it became a steady flow. She made sure the ANM visited regularly. She also ensured that the government's ambulance service came when summoned. This meant that all emergency cases, such as festering wounds, snake bites and caesareans, were taken to the primary health facility on time.

Before the vaccination drive, there was an outbreak of measles in the village. People consulted the baba, who assured them that a vaccination was not necessary because he could exorcise the angry spirit-causing measles with a seven-day course of treatment. Abida went to each house where there was a measles case and managed the child's fever with the standard paracetamol. When the fever came down, some parents agreed to send the child to a health facility. Abida cautioned adults in the household to isolate themselves, because measles in an adult could have dangerous consequences. Abida's home visits were aware that she was taking the risk of getting infected herself.

Abida shrewdly made friends at the local police station with her sincerity and charm. Then she began to implement a three-warning system. If the parents refused to get their child vaccinated, she would sit down, all day in front of the house. Passers-by would notice and the parents would be put to shame. On some occasions, she kept sitting even as dusk set in, making it clear that she would accept no food from this house and keep sitting there the whole night, if need be, till they agreed to get their child vaccinated. It happened once that the parents, in desperation, told Abida that they needed to discuss the matter with their elders and that they would tell her their decision the next day. Abida told them to go ahead but did not move from her vigil. In such situations, people would gather outside the house and shout at the parents to take heed of the poor woman and the welfare of their baby. If even this failed, Abida would not hesitate in playing her trump card: calling the police, which would ensure an immediate change of heart where the father's child was concerned.

~

These are some of the changes that Abida introduced in the village in the first couple of years after she became the AWW for Devni. They are not remembered today except by some of the elders. But there is one incident that has gone down in village legend—the case of the dead woman brought back to life.

A woman in an advanced stage of pregnancy was found sprawled on the floor next to her bed, presumed dead. She seemed to have had a hard fall. The family were preparing to cremate the dead woman. Abida arrived on the scene and detected a very faint beat. She told the family that they would together rush her to the hospital. She was shocked that the woman's husband and in-laws insisted that the woman was dead ('you are no doctor'). Abida shouted, 'Right now, I am going to call the ambulance or the police. If the police come, they will arrest you all, because what you are doing is a criminal offence.' The woman was rushed to the facility and revived. She gave birth to a baby boy a few hours later and she went home two days later with her baby, both safe and healthy.

Two years later, Abida was standing in a queue. It was very hot, with no shade, and no option but to stand in a slow-moving line. She heard a voice: 'Namaste Abida ji, turned and saw a woman with a small child. When Abida could not recognize them. The woman said, 'I will tell you, but first let me go and get you some cold water.' She came back with the water and said, 'I am the woman who everyone said was dead and you saved. I wanted to thank you afterwards but had to leave for home, because I am not from here. I am coming back after two years and I have been searching for you. My son and I are standing here, alive, because of you.' She bent down to touch Abida's feet, crying and saying repeatedly, '*Aap kahin bhi ho, ishwar aapko aur aapke bachchon ke saath hamesha rahe, main roz yahi prarthana karti hoon* [Wherever you are, may God safeguard you and your children, always, I pray these words every day].'

~

Rainclouds had gathered and it was time for us to leave. "My parents died in 2016 and 2018—they were always poor but overcame their difficulties. My children are in good jobs: one is a working with a TV channel in Bhopal, the other works in electricals in Barwani. My sisters are all alive and safe and healthy. I am fortunate in this way.'

Kritika asked what became of her husband. Abida responded, 'Once, when they were a little older, my two boys turned on their father and said he had no right to treat me in such a way. They were very angry. I told them that they should not talk to him in this way. After all, he was their father. He died in hospital five years ago. I nursed him till the end. No matter what he did, he was still the head of our family.'

Abida said to us, 'My whole life changed after I became an AWW. I have been an AWW here in this village for the last thirty-seven years. People from many villages come to me for advice before they get any kind of medical treatment. Last year, I was sent to Mumbai for a big conference. I was asked to represent the AWW community.'

She laughed at this thought and added, 'Now I am known in so many villages and people consult me on so many things besides health. A man came to me recently saying that his daughter wants to be an ASHA worker.'

I asked, delicately, 'Has it never come in the way that you are a Muslim?'

Abida responded, 'Never. *Sabki insaniyat ek hi hai* [Our humanity is all the same].'

'What do you want to do after you retire?'

'I will retire after five years and start getting my pension'. I will be able to take care of myself. After that, I want to do some kind of social service.'

'After all that happened to you as a child, you could have been bitter—do you have some deep faith in God?'

'When I wanted help, there was nobody there to help me— now I don't want anyone else to be in my position. It is not about God that way. Every time I see someone I can help, I feel I am getting that person's *dua*.* So, I get many blessings from many people every day. That is enough.'

With these words ringing in our ears and Abida's story making our hearts full, we drove back to Barwani, speechless, still trying to understand.

* Blessing

25

Return to Barwani

A tiny face peers at me through the folds of her mother's ragged sari. Her dark eyes search my face. She cannot understand why she suffers, why no one looks her way, why even her mother cannot save her. I imagine that she is trying to say something, pleading silently. But I stand rooted, unable to move. I cannot look at her and I cannot look away.

That was the scene I described in the opening chapter, of a small baby girl and her mother in a remote hamlet of a tribal district called Barwani in Madhya Pradesh. The image of that tiny forlorn face comes back to me time and again, and each time, it gives me fresh resolve.

~

Barwani, with a population of 1.6 million, is one of a cluster of very poor tribal districts in the southwest of Madhya Pradesh. In 2018, the government included Barwani in a list of 112 districts from across the country that would receive special support under the Aspirational Districts Programme (ADP). This is a scheme to demonstrate how even the worst-off districts can be put on the path to recovery through a holistic approach that includes health, education and infrastructure.

In early 2022, Barwani became our sixth programme district. We chose Barwani, wanting to understand the unique health challenges in a highly impoverished region, and consequently, which changes might be called for in our approach. Our team in Barwani was made up mainly of an enthusiastic group of new recruits. They had already completed reconnaissance trips and initiated work in a few blocks.

My young colleague Shreya Ravichandran and I visited Barwani during the monsoon season, three months after the start of our programme there. I kept thinking of that baby and her mother, wondering where they might be today. Was she alive, was she healthy? She would be twelve or so—was she going to school? Did she run and play, have friends? But I had kept no record of the name and location of that village. I remembered only that I had visited the two poorest blocks in Barwani: Pati and Sendhwa. It would be almost impossible to find that same village and family, but I felt a pull to go to those blocks to see what might have changed, overall.

We were heading for Pati, the eponymous capital of a block that had 160 villages. The first sign of development we saw in Pati was the busy market area. There were stores selling hardware, low-cost textiles and cheap shoes—there were many fruit and vegetable vendors. We were keen to see if this level of development had reached the villages. We drove through the market and took the road into the hills and our destination, a village called Shidapur.[1] The programme officer responsible for Pati block, Nagesh Chaura, was in the lead. He was knowledgeable, with a good understanding of local customs.

Pati is almost entirely hills, with 106 villages and thousands of individual houses scattered across those hills. Many villages are isolated, with no access road—some are up to 3 kilometres away from the main road. A key reason for this dispersion is a tradition known as *falia,* where clans live together on large tracts of their ancestral land. Men inherit their individual plots but tradition requires that they maintain a considerable distance from their neighbouring relatives.

The hill road was new and in excellent condition, and our vehicle climbed smoothly uphill. We stopped at a scenic spot with a panoramic view. The monsoon sight of lush green hills and valleys as far as the eye could see was enchanting. There was a house with a red-brown tiled roof some distance away in the valley—a steep path led down to it from the main road. We spotted another house, still farther away.

This glance at the landscape was enough to tell us that the health situation in Pati block must be dire. How would an ASHA or ANM reach such distant dwellings? What would happen in an emergency? How could pre-schoolers walk long distances on such hilly terrain to reach an AWC? Our normal AAA model would have little impact here. Perhaps the most effective solution was to create small local health centres and NRCs—perhaps the government was thinking of something like this already under the ADP.

We got back to our vehicle. A half-hour later, we arrived at a point where the rocky hillside had been blasted away to create a passageway. The good road and the fresh corridor suggested there would have been a longer country road before this, approaching Shidapur village from another route. A light drizzle had started and the rock walls on either side were a wet black. Nagesh, pointing to the rubble on the road, said that rockfalls are common when it rains and we should return before the rain came down hard.

Coming out of the rocky passageway, we saw a cluster of small buildings at a distance. These were Surajpur's AWC and primary school, solidly constructed buildings plastered with white choona. Anyone arriving at this point, having traversed a splendid road surrounded by rolling green hills, now looking at white plastered pukka houses, would say that the ADP was doing great work. Next to the white buildings, even from this distance, we could see the kiosk selling junk foods in shiny mini packs. That kind of junk food-purveying kiosk has become almost ubiquitous in rural India—here, it was a sad signal that Surajpur village was now linked to the modern world.

We reached the village and stepped into the AWC. The ASHA and AWW were waiting for us. They confirmed that with such difficult terrain, and virtually no public transport, it was very difficult for them to do their work. They had managed to assemble five gaunt village women to meet us. The women were disinterested, staring into the distance and speaking in monosyllables. The ASHA, gamely trying to bring some life into the proceedings, pointed to a stoic old woman sitting on her haunches just behind us. She introduced her as the village dai.

The dai was taciturn, not unfriendly, and we were able to draw her out a little. She had been the village dai all her life. Home deliveries were still the norm, and it was difficult for her to get from one house to another. Distances were long and she was growing old—she did this job as a social service. If it was an emergency case, the woman would be carried to the main road and taken to the town. It was not clear where that transport came from—perhaps it would be called from Pati town in advance.

~

At this point, a tall man with ebony skin stepped into the room. He went to the window at the far end and sat down on a chair that somebody quickly brought for him. Nagesh whispered that this was the village baba and he had come to meet us. That was an honour, for the baba rarely ventured out of his house: people always went to see him. We also met the village AWW, a remarkable woman.[2]

After some time, the skies darkened. The air was moist and we heard the rumble of distant thunder. Nagesh said that we should leave immediately—if the rain came down, the rock passage would be dangerous. I had spotted some grey thatched houses behind the white-plastered structures. A local confirmed that this was the main section of the hamlet. I wanted to spend a few minutes walking through that area, but the rain was coming down now in large drops. We decided that this was not the time for valour and left for Barwani immediately.

The next day we visited Sendhwa, the largest block in Barwani, with 156 villages and a population of 3,20,000. It was just as poor as Pati, according to Kamlesh Mandriya, our Sendhwa block programme officer. He had an intriguing background, starting with a degree in physiotherapy from Bhopal, followed by a master's in public health from Chennai. He then joined Jawaharlal Nehru University (JNU) to do a second postgraduate degree, this time in sociology. At JNU, he developed strong leftist sensibilities, which seems to be almost de rigueur in that great institution. In December 2021, Kamlesh got caught up in the student riots on the university campus, which pitted right and left-wing groups against each other. He took a big rock on his forehead and was rushed to emergency care. His parents and six sisters back home had been concerned about the growing tensions—they had been calling him every day and he had been reassuring him that he was far away from any danger at JNU. Then an uncle showed them online news reports that listed the names of those injured in the riots. They pulled him out of JNU forthwith.

Kamlesh then found his way to TAF. He was young and in search of a virtuous mission in life, slightly confused, but full of idealism.

That day, Dr Madhura Nirkhe joined the team, coming in from Delhi. She was a visitor from Seattle who had visited our programme some months previously, fallen in love with TAF and stayed on.

~

The panchayat elections across Madhya Pradesh were due in a few days. The vying political parties had recruited youngsters to go out into the streets and campaign for them.

This essentially meant that they should make a loud noise, moving in long motorcycle processions—the two-wheelers must have been provided by the political party. That must have been an attractive proposition for a youth, to get Rs 200, a motorcycle to ride, a good meal and the imagined prestige of being a political campaigner.

Astride each motorcycle were three and even four frantic youth. They waved colourful party flags and bounced up and down on their motorcycles' seats. One braveheart balanced himself standing on top of the back seat, even as the motorcycle bumped its way forward. There was an air of carnival and good humour, no drunk or disorderly behaviour. When we got stuck in the crowd, a volunteer cleared the way, saying, 'Sorry uncle, sorry uncle', which would normally have been annoying, but in these circumstances, was quite reassuring.

Everywhere, there were large billboards with pictures of the major candidate. One that appeared most often was of the main woman candidate on the right side of the poster. She looked both grim and a little surprised by the greatness being thrust upon her. On the left side of the poster there was a more prominent image of the local baba, who happened to be the candidate's husband. He too was grim, but looked self-assured, as befitted a respectable baba.

~

We were going to the NRC located in the Government Civil Hospital in Sendhwa town. Kamlesh was concerned about a twenty-two-month-old named Arpita whom he had seen at the NRC a few days previously. Arpita's eyes were swollen and sealed shut from an infection. The staff said that she could be treated if taken to a doctor right away—they feared that the baby might go blind otherwise. The baby's parents were present, and Kamlesh had asked the father, whose name was Gopal, to take the baby for treatment right away. The man was spindly and wore an uncertain look—he looked no more than eighteen. He said that he was leaving to campaign in the election and would be gone for a few days. Kamlesh spoke to Gopal for more than an hour and finally convinced him to take the baby to the doctor right away.

The NRC in Sendhwa then consisted of three small, drab rooms with ten beds between them. The facility was always running to full capacity, taking in twenty children every month on average. We entered one of the rooms and saw, as always, the sad sight of thin, hollow-eyed mothers and their emaciated babies, many hooked up to tubes. In some cases, the baby slept in a hammock hanging from the side of the bed, a makeshift arrangement fashioned from a ragged sari.

Stepping into the next room, we saw Kamlesh in a state of high agitation. He said baby Arpita had not been taken to the doctor as her father had promised. Instead, her parents had taken her home without allowing her to complete the course of treatment for severe malnutrition. It was a Leave Against Medical Advice (LAMA) case. Kamlesh was intent on going immediately to the baby's house—we followed in his wake.

We were going now to Langada Mohadi,[3] a large village with a population of 3900. Suddenly, heavy rain came thundering down and we made slow progress. We arrived at the village school. Our vehicle could not get close to the building because of the mud, and the driver stopped about 5 metres away. No one had an umbrella and we made a dash for the school entrance. Kamlesh, Shreya, Madhura and I crashed into the building, thoroughly drenched, even though our sprint had taken only a few seconds. School was out, but the classroom was full of tykes, stuck because of the thunderstorm like us.

The rain eventually slowed to a slight drizzle—the sun was coming up. We set out for Arpita's home. The house stood alone across the way through a small green and yellow field. It looked inviting, but as soon as we stepped in, we realized the mud in the field had become soft and loamy because of the rain. Such things can be upsetting in normal times but are often hilarious when you are on a field trip. So we proceeded, more than ankle-deep in fresh mud. Madhura had her sandals in her hand and was proceeding with dignity—Shreya, following some errant logic, stayed in her slippers and kept saying, 'They cost only Rs 150', which was hysterical. I was in expensive trekking shoes that I had bought some months ago. They were a fetching red before they disappeared into the mud, and of course that set Shreya off. Madhura only smiled—she is far too graceful to burst out laughing because colleagues are stuck in mud. Meanwhile, Kamlesh had moved quickly and had already reached Arpita's home.

The house had two rooms, and opposite it, a shed with one cow and two goats. Arpita's father Gopal was standing in the doorway of the cow shed with a weak smile on his face. Kamlesh demanded to know why Gopal had not taken Arpita to the doctor to treat her eyes as he had promised, and why he had brought the baby home before completing her treatment for malnourishment. Gopal kept smiling lamely, saying nothing—there was a dash of fear in his smile, but also an assurance that he was on his home turf, and safe.

After a lot of questioning, Gopal said one word, 'chunaav', meaning that he had been involved with the election campaign. This led to another round of frustrated questioning, bordering on pleading, by Kamlesh. All the while, Gopal maintained his lame smile.

It hit me suddenly that I was inside the very same scene that I had experienced ten years previously, featuring a baby, her mother, an uncaring family, somewhere else deep in Barwani. As it happened then, I could feel the anger and frustration rising inside me.

By this time, a small group had formed. That included the ASHA, who kept reiterating that she had pleaded with Gopal to take the child to the doctor—it wasn't clear if that was really the case or if she was just trying to exonerate herself.

Madhura asked Kamlesh if she could try and convince Gopal. Kamlesh, who was sweating profusely and seemed under great strain, stepped aside. Madhura is as soft-spoken as she is firm. With the sweetest of smiles on her face, she asked Gopal why he would not allow the child to be treated, that the child might go blind if he didn't. The teenaged father kept that infuriating smile on his face, saying nothing, but he had relaxed a bit for he was facing a kind and elderly woman and not a man who was over six feet tall and shouting.

Madhura stepped away, shaking her head. Kamlesh again took over and demanded that we see the baby. Gopal's smile faltered and he shook his head, looking down. Meanwhile, Shreya had gone into the hut. She saw a tiny baby whimpering continuously in her mother's arms. Kunia, the mother, had been standing near the doorway, trying to follow the goings-on outside. She too had an unwavering smile on her face, but it was a smile that appealed for help. Now, the ASHA stepped into the hut and Kamlesh looked in. Kunia covered her head with her pallu, and mother and baby stepped out into the bright sunlight.

Baby Arpita had cupped her hands over her eyes and buried her head on her mother's breast to try and shut out the light from her already sealed eyes. It struck me that it was the kind of self-protective gesture an adult would make, and not a twenty-two-month-old. Arpita was still whimpering as though she knew that crying aloud would not get her any help. She was weeping to herself, alone in a cruel world, wondering why no one would help her. The back of her dress was open and her tiny ribs were showing. I walked a few steps away, turning my back on the scene. I could not bear to look at the baby.

Seeing the baby's distress, someone told Kunia to take the baby back inside. The mother shushed the baby to sleep and came back and stood in the doorway. Gopal stepped away from the cowshed and stood at the door of his house with his wife just behind him. He still had that fixed smile on his face but it had wilted, and he had started saying a few words.

There were now more people at the scene—mainly concerned villagers, all women. The pleading and persuasion continued from Kamlesh. Gopal said he couldn't leave now as the time for seeding his land was near—it is an important occasion when prayers are offered. Kamlesh said surely his brother could do the ceremony for him—the brother, who was in the crowd, nodded. Gopal shook his head, eyes down. Then he said that he was committed to go and campaign in the election and couldn't take the child anywhere. At this, someone asked Kunia if she wanted the baby to be taken for treatment, and she nodded her head hesitantly. That person told Gopal, 'Look, even your wife wants to save your baby.' The crowd had started scolding Gopal, telling him to save the child. But none of it had any impact on him. An hour passed, and Gopal was yet to be persuaded. Madhura was disgusted and said quietly to me, 'It is a girl child and the father doesn't give a damn if the baby dies—he has no intention of doing anything.'

I had an idea. I happened to be wearing my bright orange-red field shirt that day. I told Kamlesh to point at my shirt and tell Gopal that I was a policeman and had been watching all this, and that I felt that what Gopal was doing was against the law. I told Kamlesh to tell him that I was about to call several policemen— they would first knock him down, then knock down his house and then take the baby to the doctor. It was a bluff, of course, and I felt bad threatening Gopal with the promise of violence, despicable though he was.

The smile now disappeared from Gopal's face. Kamlesh saw the opening and said, 'Let's do this—I will come tomorrow morning in my own car and take the baby and the mother to the doctor.' Gopal said that he could not allow that, citing election duties again, but now he was looking anxious. Kamlesh said, 'All right, let's wait the three days till the election are over. By then you would have finished your campaigning and would have sown the seeds. You must promise to do this in front of all these people, or we will call the police right now.' Gopal finally agreed—the threat seemed to have worked and his wife smiled behind him.

It meant Arpita would suffer for a few more days but we left, optimistic. We emerged from the field and found a nearby handpump. We watched big chunks of mud fall away, laughing all the time. I called Kamlesh from Delhi three days later to find out if Gopal had fulfilled his promise. There was good news: Kamlesh had informed the government's local Medical Supervisor of the case. The Supervisor had taken ownership of Arpita's case. He had shown up at Arpita's house, and the baby was taken first to the doctor to get her eyes treated and then to be readmitted to the NRC.

Kamlesh sent me pictures of Arpita. In these, she has her eyes wide open and is staring straight into the camera, frowning. She still looks severely malnourished, but reports were that she is recovering well and would be ready to come back home in a couple of weeks. Arpita is in her mother's arms in the photo, and Kunia smiles proudly. And, on the other side of the baby, smiling broadly, seemingly happy, stands Gopal.

~

The episode of baby Arpita is essentially the same as those I have narrated involving Priya[4] and Dhara[5] earlier. There are always three characters in this tragedy: one has the power, the other has no power, the third is the victim.

We make a cameo appearance, neutralizing the brute. We feel good for a while but experience a deeper sadness that stays. Who is to say those babies will never become victims again? And what of the hundreds of thousands of Arpitas, Dharas and Priyas who are out there?

Lasting change requires that the powerful man give up his power at the family level. This is highly unlikely, for the family is his only place of authority.

A victim cannot stop being a victim by herself—someone else must effect that for her.

So the only lasting solution is that the one in the middle—the powerless woman—finds that power in her family and her social setting. There is enough evidence, and it is my personal experience, that this is possible.

Only then will mothers and children be safe, not just at home, but in society.

26

The Beginning

Chess—at once art, science and sport—has been my lifelong passion. The game, in essence, is a quest for truth, and on that journey, you pick up many lessons that apply equally to life. One is the importance of a *sense of danger*.

It happens when everything is going well over the board. You have worked hard and built a winning position. Then you start feeling the game is already won. Your concentration wavers, you glance at your opponent, you lose the moment. Imperceptibly, your position starts to drift—you discover, all too late, that it is crumbling. I wince even now when I recall such debacles.

You must have a sense for the danger that is embedded in many seemingly perfect positions. Without that, all your hard work and best laid plans may amount to nothing.

~

So far, our work had largely been supply-side-led. That made sense as a general programme design: lead with supply, and later, work on the demand side*—you cannot make promises to the community if health delivery is inadequate. The AAA platform was our flagship supply-side intervention. The process through which the three frontline workers teamed up to focus on the riskiest cases was having impact. By August 2021, with funds coming in, we were making plans to expand, with essentially the same supply-side approach. We planned to go from three districts to six, then eight, then twelve!

It looked like as though we were in a very strong position. But something was making me uneasy; perhaps it was seeing the situation with fresh eyes, after a long time away from the field because of the COVID lockdown.

I felt we were missing something. Our work was mainly in tribal areas, and yet, our expansion plans barely factored in the unique needs and challenges of tribal populations. We worked with community health workers, but not directly with the mothers. I knew from prior experience that lasting change happens only when grassroots communities take ownership. I sensed a whiff of danger, and was convinced we had to re-examine our predominantly supply-side approach before we went in for more geographic expansion.

There was only one way to understand the needs of the communities. A small team of us, including the programme officers responsible for each block, travelled to the most challenging villages and tiny hamlets in Chhindwara and Betul districts.

We talked to pregnant women, young mothers and their families. Over the course of many conversations through the months of July and August 2021, we saw how there were several invisible barriers to good health at the community level.

Abject unawareness: Earlier, in Dhana Chariya we saw how a woman named Salwa had not realized that she was pregnant

---

* The term 'supply-side' refers to delivery of services. 'Demand-side' refers to mobilization of communities to ensure that they get good quality health services.

with twins—and both babies had died. Often women did not even know that a nurse came to the village every month. Many were ignorant about how they should take care of themselves and their new-borns.

Extreme shyness: We saw how the women of Jad would not talk, or make eye contact, with anyone from the outside. In other interior villages, people ran away as soon as we entered the village. How could they be treated if they shunned the AAA health workers?

Isolation: Many villages were inaccesible because of difficult access roads. Therefore, otherwise manageable health situations became calamities.

Dangerous social norms: We saw how a mother in Barwani named Champa was totally subservient to her in-laws. Elsewhere, teenage pregnancies were abundant because underage sex had social sanction.

Perilous rituals and beliefs: Communities have many wonderful cultural norms and traditions. However, there are also any number of rituals and beliefs that are dangerous. For example, communities where jadi-booti paste was applied on the umbilical stump; 'auspicious' branding of newborns took place; the pregnant woman's diet was reduced after the sixth month and there was blind faith in babas.

Pernicious dependence on babas: Some of these faith healers are harmless. However, there are many who prescribe dangerous remedies that can even prove fatal.

Widely scattered habitations: We came across villages where houses were dispersed across many hills. Sometimes that was because of a system called *falia* where clans lived together in villages;

sometimes that meant that brothers were required to live a good distance away from each other's land.

Large-scale migration: In some border villages, as much as two-thirds of the population, entire families, would be away at any point. The problem was in reaching these moving populations with health services.

Poor health infrastructure: We saw many villages like Khoripaar, where the anganwadi centres had broken weighing scales and unstocked kitchens. Sometimes there was no AWC at all! And at the AWC, the problem went beyond the village, with wholly inadequate facilities in primary and community health centres. To make things worse, people talked of being treated callously in these facilities, leading to a fundamental distrust of the public health system.

Wayward health workers: Our team, at most times, has worked with outstanding AAA workers. But there are also villages where there is absenteeism or indifference. In many places government sanctioned health worker positions had not been filled by the government.

Sometimes you get up from the chess board when it is your opponent's move. You stroll about, keeping your mind empty. Then when you come back to the board you see, in a flash, a game-changing move that you had missed earlier.

And so it was, after my enforced break for COVID. We had encountered all these barriers and more in previous visits to the field. But over the course of these few weeks, it all came together in my mind —the realization that there are many barriers that the supply-side cannot resolve; and there are some where the supply side itself is the problem. And it came to me, that *these kinds of challenges can only be solved by the women who live with the problems every day.*

My pulse was racing as I imagined the possibilities. But I told myself that this was a tiny sample of villages, and that I needed more evidence.

~

These barriers were most obvious in Chhindwara district, where we had been working the longest. At that time, the TAF team in Chhindwara consisted of eight people. They were young, but already seasoned in field operations.

Typically, by 6 p.m., the Chhindwara team would return to their modest office, exhausted, to write up the notes from the day's work. On one such evening, I asked everyone to stay back to do a rough, rapid assessment of the extent of barriers in Chhindwara district.

Chhindwara has eleven blocks, 377 sub-centres[*] and about 2700 villages. Most programme officers would know every sub-centre; an experienced officer would know almost every village. I estimated that the exercise I had suggested at the end of the day's work would provide data points on at least 200 villages, many times more than the handful of villages that I had covered.

On the whiteboard, we listed the names of the five 'TAF blocks': Chaurai, Mokhed, Sausar, Bicchua and Tamia. Below each, we noted the names of the sub-centres in the block. On the horizontal axis, we set down columns for just five barriers: access, babas, awareness, anganwadi adequacy, AAA availability and attitude.[1] The programme officers were asked to rate the sub-centres against each barrier, with a five signifying a major barrier and a zero, no barrier.

_____

[*] A sub-centre is a cluster of, typically, five villages.

They threw themselves into the exercise—discussing, debating, arriving at a consensus about the extent of barriers in 156 sub-centres in the four blocks. The result: 37 per cent of villages had no barriers, 44 per cent had one or two barriers, and 19 per cent had three to four barriers.[2] The results broadly confirmed what we had seen on the ground: barriers were pervasive and a big issue. I could feel my pulse racing again.

There was a long silence in the room. I gently asked the group if the AAA platform would deliver results if a village had these kinds of barriers. It was a sensitive topic and the silence lingered. Then someone said '*mushkil hai* [It is difficult]', and there was a nodding of heads. I didn't push it any further.

It could have been said that this exercise was too quick and dirty to draw reliable conclusions. Yes, we were gathering information at sub-centre level—but it was only an impression, generalizing across five to six villages in that cluster. It was, after all, just the judgement of a single programme officer who oversaw that block, and that person might be biased. We would have to dig deeper, get even more detailed data.

In the weeks that followed, I sensed a vein of resistance to this research, and the emerging conclusions. I was challenging the effectiveness of TAF's pure core supply-side model—it was easy to take that personally. But I knew our managers would be convinced after they had seen more evidence.

So, we set out to get more granular data with a bigger sample. We had done the rough exercise on 12 August 2021. Three weeks later, I convened an all-staff meeting. In the first exercise, we had asked programme officers, mainly from one district, Chhindwara,[3] to provide their assessment of barriers at the sub-centre level. This time, we added the two adjacent districts—Seoni and Betul—and asked the programme officers from those districts to extend their estimation down to the village level wherever they could.[4] We also had some data of health statistics at the village level as reference points.

The teams broke out into discussion groups. The more experienced programme officers knew each one of the 150–200 villages under their charge. Visiting those villages time and again, seeing the tragedy that was being lived out, had formed graphic images in their minds. They were painting vivid pictures of access roads, scatter, migration, superstitions and levels of awareness.[5] The final tally bore out the findings from the previous analysis. There were multiple barriers to health delivery at the village level. The figures were almost the same.

So far, we had established that there was a problem—barriers at the village level. It was obvious now that a pure supply-side effort would have little impact. But what was the solution? All my experience in public health had taught me that the answers to some of the most complex public health problems can only come from the women who live with those problems every day. I was convinced that this problem could only be solved by village women, working together in groups.

We created a team of four to investigate this from the community solution side: Mihika Bapna, Punam Dhobale, Shreya Ravichandran and Aditi Revankar. The team addressed seven questions: Did the community see the problem and want a solution?[6] How difficult would it be to create women's groups? Is there scope for community change agents?* Would local government be supportive? How will this work relate to the supply side effort? What are the organization implications? In what time frame can results be expected?

~

* These are people from the larger community, willing and able to support the SHGs by spreading messages and mobilizing membership.

A few weeks later we were ready to present the findings to the leadership group of the organization. Then COVID-19 raised its ugly head again and the meeting was postponed till February 2022. We invited twenty-four members of the Avahan team to an offsite location—the leadership group of ten, and fourteen programme officers from TAF's six districts. I got straight into a description of what I saw as a huge problem and touched on the solution. We did that through a sequence of one-line messages that rolled slowly for five minutes, with no commentary. The messages were addressed directly to the frontline of our work—the programme officers.

An Integrated Supply Side+Community Programme is Essential for Us to Realise Our Mission

Our flagship supply-side programme is world class . . .

But it does not go far enough on its own . . .

That is because every village has multiple barriers to health access . . .

And the supply-side effort is not designed to address those . . .

But active, aware, local women coming together in groups can address those barriers by . . .

Creating awareness, providing safety, taking responsibility, advocating . . .

The communities we spoke with were keen, wanted help . . .

We met locals who could be powerful change agents . . .

This community effort must be integrated with our supply-side effort . . .

We can create that programme . . . that is not the biggest challenge . . .

Which is evolving our organization to take on this challenge . . .

It will call for new roles, and kills, more staff per block,

Evolving our values and culture . . .

Most importantly, it will mean much more freedom, with responsibility, for our programme officers . . .

Because integration happens at block and village levels . . .

That is why you, the programme officers, are the most important people in the room today, and in TAF of the future.

~

We spent the next two days examining each statement in the light of data and analyses. The session that generated the most debate was the one on organization. In August 2021, when we started this exercise, we had a team of forty-five—now, six months later, we would need at least twice that number. We had always worked with one programme officer per block,[7] managing a largely supply-side effort. Now we needed a team of three to four staff in a block because they would be covering both demand and supply, and the integration of these two aspects of health delivery.

We would need programme officers with a different set of skills to complement our existing staff, who were consummate operators. The combined team would have that plus more strategic thinking and comfort with data—in effect, a group of people who were creative and able to take charge rather than 'be told'.

That in turn required more managers—and all managers would need to adopt a different style from what had been the norm till now. Our managers are exceptional, capable of implementing a complex delivery plan flawlessly. But so far, they had told their teams what needed to be done. Now it would be the frontline staff who would get the first read of situations. The managers would, in a sense, be dependent on them, and their job would be to listen and enable, more than tell.

All this amounted to a massive change in the culture of the organization. And that had to be done without compromising on our values.

I am sure many people left that milestone meeting with a lot of questions, uncertainty and some trepidation. That was good because the idea was to shake things up a bit. Some soul-searching and inevitable turmoil were only to be expected when change of this magnitude is launched in an organization that had begun work only five years ago. But I could sense a new excitement and the energy in a team that has boldly stepped into a new adventure.

Article in a leading national journal, 2025:

A quiet revolution has been spreading since 2022 in thousands of villages in the districts of Chhindwara, Betul and Seoni. The movement is driven by women's groups. It all began when a cluster of women, working in partnership with The Antara Foundation (TAF), came together to improve maternal and child health in the state.

The health goal was to transform hitherto disempowered women, barely aware of their health needs, into active consumers of maternal and child health service. This happened in three stages.

In the first phase, the emphasis was on awareness. Adolescents learnt about their bodies. Women learnt about how to take care of their health, especially in the antenatal period. They were told about the importance of institutional delivery and newborn care. They learnt about government health services and how to access these. The sessions were co-led by the ASHA worker, together with a woman from the group.

In the second phase, the women became active and aware consumers. They knew what good health meant, for themselves and for their children, and availed of health services regularly. The AAA workers responded positively, for they felt acknowledged and respected for the job they did. As women's health-seeking behaviour improved, so did the health record of the village.

In the third phase, they became agents for change. Their villages had many barriers to good health. Now they started advocating for change—for example, better access roads—in groups with the government, sometimes the Collectorate in district headquarters and even with the authorities in Bhopal. They ensured that the three community health workers were doing their jobs, demanding a change if one of them was slack. Community audits of health services provision at the village level became routine. They respectfully cautioned women in meetings to not go to babas for health matters. They even took on the thorny issue of endemic alcoholism. Some women were trained to speak to the media, and the voice of the community became increasingly important, and respected by the public and government, alike.

The movement gathered momentum, spreading organically from village to village. A voluntary cadre of women who were willing and able to go to other villages to spread awareness and start self-help groups focused on wellness.

There are vibrant examples of women's groups in public health and in the broader social sector. The striking feature of the programme that is spreading in Madhya Pradesh, is the extent to which women get involved in both demand and supply sides of health services—ensuring that there is effective health delivery and serving as responsible and empowered consumers.

I read this imagined article, and each time I feel exhilarated, and confident that it will happen.

～

And so, we approach the close of this story, even as the adventure continues. TAF would not have reached where it is today, without the support of many people. But among these, one person has played a very different role.

27

Bill

Kamla, the sex-worker, got up to make her big announcement. A sizable crowd of her peers had gathered in their small office. They sat on the floor, on a tattered dari that had been found for the event—some women stood against the walls. They had been told that a very important person was visiting and there would be filter coffee, bondas and murukku.

Despite our protests, the women insisted that we sit on chairs, facing the crowd, because that was the custom. Now Kamla turned towards us, leaning forward with her hands folded in namaste. Each of us received a shawl—the traditional Tamilian welcome.

Then she stepped forward to face the crowd, paused for effect and shouted: 'Today we have a very important guest—MR BILL GATES!!'

To my horror, I realized that she was pointing at me. Even as I jumped up to clarify that I was not Bill Gates, the room exploded in a noise of frenzied flat-palm clapping, piercing whistles and raucous shouting—the sex workers wanted to give a befitting welcome to the important visitor and his team. But one woman, never one to be impressed easily, called out: 'But who is Bill Gates?'

Kamla shot an embarrassed look at me. Then she said, with a sharp glance at the woman who had asked the question: 'He is the one who pays for this centre, clinic, medicines and all, not only here, but in every town in this district' And then, triumphantly, '. . . and they say not only this district, but the next one also!'. The questioner, chastened, said: 'If he is helping so many sisters, he must be a good person.'

At this the crowd went wild. I jumped up again and tried to say that I was not Bill Gates, but no one was interested; in some sections dancing had begun. We joined in the celebrations and I enjoyed a few moments of unearned adoration.

The women didn't know or care who Bill Gates was—their world was too far removed. What they cherished was the *concept* of Bill—an invisible force, that would take care of them unconditionally. For those who receive little love, that is a miracle.

~

I first met Bill in the fall of 2002, at the BMGF's old office in Seattle. Over the next ten years we travelled together to some unlikely places. It began with field trips to Avahan sites and locales in five states. The communities most affected by HIV, primarily sex workers, were stigmatized and difficult to access. It was crucial to learn how they saw the problem and what they thought were the solutions. So, we went out and talked to sex workers, transgenders and MSMs*, in their own milieus. Sometimes it was in their community centres, like the one just described. We also visited large brothels that housed several thousand women as well

---

* The acronym for 'men who have sex with men'. It is the appropriate term, connoting much more than what is loosely referred to as the 'gay' community.

as small houses, with a motherly madam and four to six young women, living like family.

At McKinsey, I was paid a lot of money to solve other people's problems. It is a heady feeling and there is a certain persona that goes with it—restrained, confident and nicely arrogant. But at some point, I started feeling like I was losing touch with myself.

Avahan, the offer that could not be refused, was the start of a continuing adventure and my rebirth. And part of that revival, without my realizing it, was observing Bill's ways.

~

It has been said that Bill Gates is one of the most intelligent people on this planet. I think that statement is absurd. Because it is a big planet and it all depends. Who is to say that the monk who has fathomed the secrets of the universe is not the most intelligent? Or Tendulkar, with his perfect timing when he plays that cover drive, who has the most exquisite stroke that only God can better?

From what I have seen, the greatest manifestation of intelligence is curiosity. It is the way of the child, to whom everything is wonder, only waiting to be understood. It is in the discovery of things too ordinary to be found. It is in the ability to connect just a few of those seemingly unrelated dots and thereby accomplish what looks like a great leap of insight. Alas, the natural curiosity of the child is so often squeezed out early in life or later evaporates in the heat of everyday living.

Seen this way, Bill is a very intelligent person, because he has a veritable thirst for learning and can connect two and two to arrive at an unusual number—I have seen this many times.

On one occasion, we were discussing Indian authors when Bill said he preferred Rohinton Mistry to Amitav Ghosh and that he loved *Such a Long Journey*. It was a statement, but he was really asking what I thought. And I had to confess that I had read Ghosh but not Mistry. He moved on without making me feel small, for Bill never disrespects anyone's lack of knowledge.

Another time, he asked me out of the blue if the government's appeal to people to voluntarily give up their subsidy on cooking gas, had substantially increased consumption. I had barely thought of the subsidy, or cooking gas, and said 'Bill, I don't know the answer to that.' He moved on, because 'I don't know' is a very acceptable answer for him.

There may have been some other occasions when I did not know the answers to Bill's innocuous questions. But, in my defence, I have known many answers and may even have asked him a few questions that made him think hard.

Anyway, I did some reading and I now know why Mistry is so good, and the impact of the subsidy on cooking gas.

~

It seems to me that humility flows out of curiosity. For curiosity is to keep yourself open, because so often, the answer is with someone else—humility is acknowledging that. It takes a self-assured person to ask about the way forward.

In our work in TAF, we describe how the datasets of the three frontline workers often do not match and how crucial it is to achieve one version of the truth. Many will ask a terse 'why' and say a quick 'of course' even before the other person has answered fully and they will change the topic. The curious-humble one will ask many more questions.

I was on a trip with Bill to a remote village somewhere deep in Bihar. We had to park the van and trudge to a small and muddy river. The way across the creek was by a boat, with the boatman standing and pulling on an aerial rope. Strangely, we were also required to stand throughout.

Reaching the other side, we set out for a small village across flat and scrubby land. It was blazing hot, easily over 45° C. We reached the village's modest AWC. The three frontline workers looked disinterested—few of them had heard of Bill in these remote rural areas. After introductions, Bill asked to see the many enormous registers that they were required to maintain. He spread out the registers, side by side. His forefinger moved from record to record, trying to reconcile numbers.

A long and animated discussion ensued. Instead of pressing the women about the obvious discrepancies, his tone was respectful, trying to get to the root causes. The women were animated now, explaining, for example, that the registers were heavy and tough to carry from house to house. So, they would jot the numbers down on scraps of paper and transcribe them to the registers, sometimes only days later. They were happy and excited that someone was so interested in their work.

It was very hot inside the tiny room. The team and I were unprepared for such a long meeting. We were drenched in sweat, dreading the long walk back. Someone muttered 'Bill is asking them to explain everything we told him yesterday', entirely missing the point. I saw that Bill's shirt was dry and he looked cool, and that puzzles me to this day.

This curiosity-humility-respect cycle sometimes plays out in my meetings with Bill. I go prepared to talk about certain topics. Somewhere, Bill asks an unrelated question. I explain, and he asks another question, and another. All the while, he is scribbling on his yellow A4 pad, with a BIC pen.

After the meeting, I always talk to my team back in India. They are keen to know what Bill has told me and was there any advice for TAF? I tell them he asked a lot of questions throughout and took notes. They say little after that, disappointed that their leader has squandered a great opportunity.

~

It occurs to me that the notion of conviction is highly overrated. It is usually taken as a marker of leadership ('the courage of his convictions'), forgetting that some of the greatest tyrants in history were driven by their convictions. The important thing is really whether you are open to changing those convictions.

A year after we started Avahan, I came to the foundation in Seattle for a senior staff meeting. It seemed to me there was a palpable nervousness in the air during such meetings with Bill. If he had a strong view, there wasn't a lot of challenge.

Somewhere during the meeting Bill said something that greatly upset me. I remember the words exactly: 'The Avahan team is doing some amazing work in India. But we are not into delivering products and services—that is government's job. Ours is to make sure we support developing the right products. Avahan is great but it is an aberration, and we will never do something like that again.' I ventured to say that in India some products are well established, but they don't reach the people who need them. I even cited the measles vaccine. I said, heart in mouth, that delivery also needed to be seen as a technology. Bill listened—he showed no expression and said nothing.

Afterwards, someone explained to me that staying away from delivery and focusing on the product was something Bill believed in strongly, and was an axiom at the foundation. I should accept that and not get too dejected.

Aberration, aberration, aberration.

That word rang in my head all the way back to India. My team was distraught because we were convinced that helping achieve delivery at scale was often the right, and the only way, forward. The idea that it was not appreciated by Bill was tough to swallow. I told the team that the best thing we could do was to keep our heads down and focus on the work for the next few years.

Bill's next visit to India was two years later. By that time our programme was in full swing. I had sent reports to the foundation and made a couple of trips. But it is the nature of grassroots work that you must engage with the field to truly understand it. I was determined to try and convey all that we are doing to Bill on this trip. The problem was that we had less than two days with him.

The morning of the visit, we were in Chennai, and the plan was to take Bill and Melinda to a sex workers' meeting. We arranged for a meeting hall and asked the sex workers we were working with to describe their experience with Avahan. Many questions were asked, and there was a good give and take, but there was also a lot of digressing and important aspects were lost in translation. I wasn't quite sure how Bill would have felt.

After this we had a smaller meeting with some of our programme partners. Just before it, Bill and I had a few moments together. He said: 'I am amazed to see what you guys are doing here with Avahan. You are changing the lives of so many women. Even if you don't avert a single infection, I would say Avahan is a huge success.' This was after he had spent just a few hours with our programme, talking directly with the community.

Seven years later, I led an effort with colleagues from the foundation in Seattle, to open ambitious new programmes in maternal and child health in two important states—Bihar and Uttar Pradesh. These programs were modelled on the core learnings from Avahan. So, as Avahan wound down, two vibrant sister programs were born. Today, these are exemplars of high-impact service delivery.

Bill and Melinda were present at the inauguration of one
of these programmes. It was a major shift in the foundation's
thinking on getting involved directly in service delivery.

~

My TAF teammates in the field often encounter the worst forms
of human suffering—we have seen some examples in these pages.
The team is very young, mostly women, and for many it is their
first job. In the evenings, back at home base, they share their
experiences. Sometimes I hear it said, 'I almost cried, right then
and there.' And I ask, 'Why didn't you cry?'

They look surprised, as though crying in public is wrong. It
might upset the victim, some say; they had to be strong. I tell
them sometimes of an incident that happened many years ago.

On a hot steamy day, ten sex workers were talking about their
life experiences, sitting in a circle on the floor. Bill and I sat at the
edge of the circle.[1] A woman narrated how she had hidden the fact
that she was a sex worker from her daughter, aged fifteen. It was the
only way she could keep her child in school. The girl's classmates
found out and teased her relentlessly; she was ostracized. One day
the sex worker came home and found her daughter hanging from
the ceiling fan. The girl had left a note for her mother that said
she could not take it anymore. As sex workers often do when they
speak of personal suffering, the woman had kept a smile on her
face throughout.

To my left, Bill's hands were folded over his raised knees,
his head facing down. No one noticed, but I could hear him
sobbing quietly.

An old-timer told me when I started out: 'Never forget we are
in public health. You cannot stop for each individual tragedy—we
must move on.' I thought that was wisdom then; now I know that

these situations are not black and white. I tell the young people to never feel ashamed about shedding tears in public. We are only experiencing a tiny fraction of the other person's suffering. *There is always room for compassion.*

~

TAF would not be what it is today, without Bill.

People ask: 'So, what is Bill Gates really like?' And I tell them: 'I hardly know Bill.' They move away, disappointed, maybe thinking 'He could at least have had the decency to make something up'.

I can't say that I know Bill as his close associates and friends might know him. But over the years, I have certainly developed a concept. It is an amalgam of some essential attitudes that I have seen in Bill—curiosity, humility, respect, compassion and openness. It adds up to a simple precept: *being authentic.* It has been a series of small affirmations and these have been instrumental in shaping TAF. Observing Bill at various times has given me the courage and conviction to keep Antara going.

The interesting aspect is that I cannot remember a single occasion when Bill strongly advised me to do something or cautioned me not to follow a certain path. It is as though he has always understood that we are intent on something good and respected that quest enough to leave it alone.

TAF, to us, is something unalloyed. We don't compromise. We won't get diverted. There is no pretence.

We too, are trying our best to be authentic.

Epilogue

Our programme in Rajasthan was TAF's early childhood. First the toddler, exploring her new environment—everything was discovery. Then the child, finding the building blocks. Soon, growing into adolescence, experiencing the joy and the pain of creating and becoming.

Then, TAF moved on to Madhya Pradesh. She saw new places, met different people—she learnt and built upon her childhood experiences. Today, she finds herself atop a hill, marvelling at the great vistas ahead and the faraway mountains.

TAF has grown quickly from newborn to adult, even as I hurtle back to early childhood. Twenty years ago, I was in a familiar place—comfortable, been there and done all that. With that attitude comes the dimming of curiosity. And that is when we start growing old—it could happen at any stage or age in life.

Perhaps it was prescience or just an inner restlessness that made me step out. Immediately, I found myself in another world, a place I could never have imagined—I have told that story before. One more time in life, I was the toddler, then the finder and then the shaper. The incipient exuberance and unrepressed joy of a baby evaporates as the child grows. At some point later in life, if a person feels as though he is losing that spirit, he must learn ways to go back and find it.

In these pages, and in my previous book, I tried to describe the extraordinary adventure that followed my stepping out. In this adventure, I see the best and worst aspects of human nature. I meet the protectors and the destroyers, the humble and those drunk on power, the optimists and the cynics, those who toil and those who ride on others' backs. These experiences have helped me find myself and accept that I too have different sides. A series of contradictions is part of the voyage—they offer a trove of learnings.

TAF has emerged out of distant dreams. Now many have joined her on the journey and a caravan is forming. A new adventure is taking shape. Soon, it will be time for me to step back, perhaps away and see the team move ahead, for that is the natural order of things. The journey will be arduous and long, but it is certain that it will reach the right destination, because we all made a choice to help right a wrong and we would have given it our all.

Acknowledgements

Many people have played a role in building TAF and in telling the story of *How the Light Gets In.* I would like to express my deep gratitude to them.

Firstly, I am grateful to the communities of women and children, who we are privileged to serve. These valiant women carry a full load—working in the fields, taking care of home and family. Often, they have little say about their personal needs. They have welcomed us into their homes and shared their life stories.

We have engaged, directly and indirectly, with several thousand frontline workers, the ANMs, AWWs and ASHAs. We are grateful to them and their supervisors, for allowing us to work with them closely in a spirit of partnership.

I would like to thank the governments of Chhattisgarh, Rajasthan and Madhya Pradesh for their support. We are grateful to the collectors in more than forty districts where we have engaged so far and the senior leadership in Raipur, Jaipur and Bhopal.

Words are not enough to express how grateful I will always be to Chief Minister Vasundhara Raje in Rajasthan. She had faith that TAF would deliver. She supported our work at every stage magnanimously, and visibly, sending out a strong message.

We are indebted to RNT. He was the first person to show belief in TAF and support our work generously, through the Tata Trusts. This was the Trusts' first major foray into maternal and child health, including nutrition. From that perspective, I am particularly grateful for Mr Tata's support and encouragement.

Thank you to our donors and sponsors—in particular, the support of Dilip Wagle, Jaideep Khanna, Tom Kagerer of LGT and Sapphira Goradia, has been and continues to be, a great boost. Thank you also to the colleagues from McKinsey who generously supported us in Madhya Pradesh, when we needed funding urgently. Thanks especially to Ramesh Mangaleswaran and Ajay Dhankhar, who got that process rolling.

Our programme was initially funded by three sponsors who came forward when TAF was but an idea—Dr Cyrus Poonawalla, Arjun Malhotra and Shiv Nadar. I am very grateful to them

There are many TAF team members, past and present, who have played important roles in building our venture. Piyush Mehra played a crucial role, leading the team during our most critical years. Neerja Jham, Paras Nath Sidh and Piyush Bhatt have been with TAF from the start of our first programme and kept the flag flying high. Two people—Madhura Nirkhe and Srividya Prakash, have made immense contributions to TAF, from the outside.

Above all, I want to thank my friend and colleague Reenu Uppal. Reenu has stood tall and been a pillar of strength throughout TAF.

I am grateful to a few people who helped me put this story together. Arnaz Shaikh has made a tremendous effort with research, while ensuring that all footnotes, and citations are flawless. Aditi Revankar and Arpita Das carefully studied the manuscript even as it was developing and made many useful suggestions. Krupa Verghese was of great help with the Appendices. Thank you, Shreya Ravichandran for your all-round support.

I never forget that TAF has been built on the shoulders of many alumni. It is too long a list to write down but I want to say thank you to each and every one of you.

Rural Madhya Pradesh is beautiful, with trees that have great character. I have been able to introduce some of those trees in these pages, with the guidance of that doyen of Indian naturalists, Pradeep Krishen.

I want to thank Mark Suzman, president of the BMGF, who was kind enough to vet sections of the document. He brought not only his knowledge of the foundation, but also his experience as an author.

Thank you to Penguin Random House India, especially publisher Milee Ashwarya. Penguin has a wonderful team, and I especially want to thank copy editor Aparna Abhijit and creative head Gunjan Ahlawat.

Thanks to our children Aman and Ashwin, and their partners Sandy and Alison, for your encouragement from the other side of the world.

I am indebted to my partner Anjali for her support, ideas and encouragement. She has helped me shape TAF from its conception and through its development, with sage advice at crucial stages.

This is a long list and it is possible I may have missed some names inadvertently. To each of them, I offer sincere apologies.

Appendix 1: India's Public Health and Nutrition System

India's public health system is designed to reach every village of this vast country. It encompasses health infrastructure and a system for providing preventive and curative services from tertiary to community levels. There is a sound policy framework.

The design of the public health system cannot be faulted—the challenge has been in consistent implementation. There have been notable gains, but also many areas of shortfall. The record is uneven. For example, Kerala and Tamil Nadu have world-class outcomes in maternal and child health, including nutrition. Several northern states, including Madhya Pradesh, fall far behind.

Why this situation exists has been analysed thoroughly by experts. It is not within the ambit of this short note to get into the debate about why the state of India's public health is where it is. Instead, this section focuses on a description, not a dissection, of the public health system.

The Rural Health System

The ministry of health and family welfare is the authority on health-related matters in the country. Health is a state subject and state-wise variations exist in the implementation of national guidelines to account for local realities.

Broadly, India has a three-tier rural public health system based on the following population norms:[1]

Centre	Plain Area	Hilly/Tribal/ Difficult Area
Sub Health Centre	5000	3000
Primary Health Centre	30,000	20,000
Community Health Centre	1,20,000	80,000

At the district level, there are sub-divisional/sub-district hospitals and district hospitals that have specialists. This is the highest level of referral in the rural health pyramid.

The Sub Health Centre or SHC is the first point of care for rural populations. Its purpose is primarily preventive and promotive health, but it also provides basic curative care.

The services provided through the SHC include maternal healthcare, full immunization, counselling on family planning and provision of contraceptives, treatment for minor ailments, adolescent healthcare, school health services and outreach services at the village. All this is to be coordinated service delivery with the ASHA, AWW,[2] Village Health Sanitation and Nutrition Committee (VHSNC) and other platforms.

As per the Rural Health Statistics 2021–22, there are about 1,60,000 SHCs in rural areas.[3]

The Primary Health Centre or PHC is the first level of referral from the SHC and the first point of contact between a village and a medical officer. The services at the PHC are focused on curative health with some preventive, promotive and family welfare services. The PHC is required to be managed by a medical officer, supported by paramedical and other staff. There are about 25,000 PHCs in rural India.[4]

The Community Health Centre or CHC provides the tertiary level of care at a block level. A CHC is required to have four medical specialists—surgeon, physician, obstetrician/gynaecologist and paediatrician—supported by paramedical and other staff. It is required to have thirty indoor beds with one operation theatre, X-ray, labour room and laboratory facilities. It serves as a referral unit for four PHCs and is meant to have adequate facilities for obstetric care and specialist consultations. There are about 5500 rural CHCs in the country.[5]

The National Health Policy, 2017, recommended strengthening the delivery of primary healthcare through the establishment of Health and Wellness Centres (HWCs) for comprehensive primary care. In February 2018, the government announced that 1,50,000 HWCs would be set up by converting existing SHCs and PHCs into HWCs.[6]

As HWCs, both SHCs and PHCs would provide an expanded range of services, comprising a package of twelve essential services covering maternal, neonatal and child health services, adolescent care, family planning.

Nutrition services

While India's health system caters to the needs for preventive, promotive and curative health, addressing challenges of malnourishment lies within the jurisdiction of the ministry of Women and Child Development.[7] In 1975, the ministry launched the world's largest programme for early childhood care and development—the Integrated Child Development Services (ICDS) scheme. Pregnant women, lactating mothers and children in the age group of zero to six years are meant to be the beneficiaries of this national scheme. The ICDS scheme provides a package of six services:

1. Supplementary nutrition
2. Pre-school non-formal education
3. Nutrition and health education
4. Immunization
5. Health check-up
6. Referral services

While the first two services are provided by AWWs at AWCs run under the ICDS scheme, the remaining services are provided by the Ministry/Department of Health. Close convergence is therefore required with the health system for effective delivery of all the services. This convergence is facilitated by having an AWC as the focal point of service delivery. An anganwadi is managed by an AWW and an anganwadi helper (AWH). The ICDS team in a district comprises.

The provision of comprehensive health and nutrition services to all beneficiaries in a village depends on the convergence between the health system and the ICDS system.

Appendix 2: Profile of Madhya Pradesh: Tribes and Health Status

Geography

Madhya Pradesh (MP) is the second largest state in India in terms of size. It has fifty-two districts and a rural population of 72 million.[1] The state has the largest forest cover in India, spread over a quarter of the land area.[2] Nine of India's twelve national forests and parks are in Madhya Pradesh.

With plateaus, plains and mountain ranges, the state's topography is defined by the Narmada Sone Valley. This region has poor alluvial soil, unsuitable for agricultural activities. To the north lie the Central Highlands, to the south the Satpura-Maikal ranges, and to the south-east, the eastern plateau. Four of the districts in which TAF works—Chhindwara, Betul, Seoni and Khargone—lie in the Satpura–Maikal ranges.

Tribal populations

MP has the highest tribal population among Indian states, with over 15 million people (20 per cent of state population and 15 per cent of the nation's tribal population). There are forty-six tribes, including Gond, Bhil, Baiga, Korku, Bharia, Halba, Kol, Mariya and Sahariya. Of these, Baiga, Bharia and Sahariya are classified as PVTGs[3]—a government sub-classification for groups that are considered more vulnerable. The districts in which TAF operates have multiple tribes (37 per cent of population). In some districts where we work, the tribal percentage is large, such as Betul (50 per cent ST population) and Barwani (78 per cent ST population).[4]

State health status

While the state has made significant strides in improving health and nutrition outcomes, it continues to have the highest infant mortality rate (43 deaths per thousand live births)[5] and the second highest maternal mortality ratio (173 deaths per 1,00,000 live births).[6] MP is one of the eight Empowered Action Group (EAG) states, comprised of states that perform poorly on health and nutrition indicators and are earmarked for focused attention. Among the EAG states, MP has the highest rates of anaemia among children (73 per cent). Close to 60 per cent of women in the state are anaemic. While MP has made a reduction in malnutrition prevalence, about 20 per cent children continue to be wasted and almost 40 per cent stunted.[7]

Tribal health

Across India, tribals have poorer health outcomes than non-tribal populations. Teenage pregnancy is highest among the STs and institutional delivery is low. A child born to an ST family has 19 per cent higher risk of dying in the neonatal period and 45 per cent greater risk of dying in the post-neonatal period compared with other social classes.[8]

The state of MP's health and nutrition indicators are of particular concern given its high share of vulnerable populations. These tribal populations are characterized by lack of access, poor quality of care and social norms and practices detrimental to the health of women and children. More than half of the rural tribal population lives below the poverty line.[9] They primarily reside in rural and remote areas where access to health facilities and trained medical staff is limited. Rates of teenage pregnancy among tribals in MP are twice that of other social groups. Similarly, tribal child mortality rates are close to 14 per cent, compared to about 5 per cent among other groups. Tribals are worse off in institutional delivery (82 per cent among tribals versus 96 per cent among others) and stunting (40 per cent among tribals vs 27 per cent among others). Scheduled tribes have the lowest percentage of women using a hygienic method for menstrual protection—41 per cent—and the highest percentage of women who experienced violence during a pregnancy—3.3 per cent.[10] Tribals in MP have also been found to be particularly vulnerable to genetic conditions like sickle cell anaemia, with the state estimated to have the highest load of sickle cell carriers.[11]

Certain tribes are uniquely challenged. For example, there is a particularly high incidence of pulmonary tuberculosis among the Sahariya tribal community because of poor living conditions, malnourishment and higher tobacco consumption.[12] Studies among the Gonds have shown that tobacco use begins at the age of six and increases with age, putting them at high risk of oral cancer.[13] Korkus and Gonds have also been shown to be at high risk of sickle cell anaemia.[14]

Though they are at higher risk of poor health, tribal communities in MP do not receive sufficient quality health services. A study of Sahariya tribal women showed that more than 50 per cent women did not receive a single dose of the tetanus toxoid vaccine during their pregnancy and only 25 per cent were given iron and folic acid tablets. About 11 per cent of these women reported that antenatal care services were too far from their homes, or too inconvenient to visit.[15] In another study conducted among Korku women, it was seen that less than 20 per cent pregnant women in the community received advice on proper diet, signs of danger, delivery care and care of newborns.[16]

The high burden on tribal populations in MP demands focused attention on improving their health and nutrition status.

Appendix 3: The Antara Foundation Model

Vision

The Antara Foundation's vision is for every mother and each child to have an equal start to a healthy life.

The TAF approach

Over the last few years, India has made huge strides in maternal and child health outcomes, but there is still a long way to go. A leading indicator is that twenty-eight[1] infants die out of every 1000 live births in the country, one of the highest in the world.

On the face of it, mortality and morbidity, especially among the poorest rural mothers and children, is largely preventable. Remedies are simple and well-known. For example, regular consumption of iron tablets can ensure safe pregnancy, and proper breastfeeding after delivery can ensure good health for the child.

The solutions are much more complex. This brief note describes the TAF approach.

Scale—the central tenet

Scale is the fulcrum of everything we do at TAF. All our interventions are designed for scale. 'Scale' is often used interchangeably with coverage. It is, however, much more than that. It involves a complex relationship between coverage, speed and quality, belief in the power of community and effective partnerships with the government. At TAF, we work with the fundamental principle that women living closest to the problem know the best solutions. Adequately supported, they can play a leading role in the design and delivery of programmes. The crux of our scaling model is that we work in partnership with the government, leveraging its system and resources. This approach helps us achieve massive scale and be sustainable.

The operating model

There are two aspects to TAF's operating model—supply and demand—which come together in an integrated manner:

1. *Supply side* refers to interventions aimed at improving the efficiency and effectiveness of service delivery by the health system. TAF's supply side interventions work in tandem with the government and covers the entire spectrum of service delivery, from village-level services delivered by frontline health workers to facility-level care provided by staff nurses. By partnering with the government, we strengthen the existing health system without creating redundancies and duplication of effort. TAF's supply-side interventions include the following:

    a. *The AAA platform:* The AAA platform includes the government's frontline community health workers—the

ANM, the ASHA and the AWW—working with the guidance of supervisors and the newly appointed technical cadre of CHO. This intervention brings together the three frontline workers and enables them to share and use data to plan last-mile service delivery collaboratively. By improving grassroots-level data use, this intervention helps workers identify high-risk beneficiaries and prioritize their services.

b. *Technical capacity building of community health workers and supervisors:* This intervention focuses on capacity building of community health workers and their supervisors on key maternal, neonatal and child health and nutrition (MNCHN) concepts. This knowledge development is provided through classroom training, on-field hand-holding, refresher training and focused hand-holding of weaker performing frontline workers. The capacity building aims to ensure that improvements in knowledge levels lead to better skills and eventually, improvements in the quality of services delivered to beneficiaries.

c. *Supportive supervision training to supervisory cadre:* Capacity building of the supervisory cadre helps to improve their data use and supervisory skills. Supervisors are equipped with tools to conduct agenda-driven meetings, data-based reviews and are taught how to be supportive leaders to frontline workers. This intervention also facilitates supervisors of different departments to work collaboratively, ensuring that frontline workers under their supervision also work together and beneficiaries receive comprehensive services. This intervention also ensures the sustainability of TAF's interventions, with supervisors being trained to perform the role of TAF's programme officers once TAF exists the state.

d. *Nurse mentoring and facility enhancement:* This intervention involves coaching and mentoring of nurses at high-burden delivery points. Through focused mentoring by our cadre of nurse mentors, we aim to enhance the quality of service at these facilities and ensure safe deliveries (through better organization of facility, complication management, infection prevention practices, record-keeping and managing supplies).

e. *Rationalization of records:* Revising record-keeping tools of frontline workers improves the quality of beneficiary data being collected and used in planning. TAF rationalized the ASHA Diary to ensure that comprehensive beneficiary data is available in one place, and ASHAs no longer maintain multiple records for different services they provide. The revised ASHA Diary helps to ensure efficient, data-driven planning and follow-up of services.

2. *Demand side* initiatives refer to measures taken to create more active and aware consumers who can use their individual and collective agency to demand their health entitlements. They are empowered to understand and address barriers to their health services and contribute to creating a stronger health supply system. The crux of TAF's demand side initiative is women's groups who can act as agents of transformation in the community. The progression of change in the community occurs in three stages—from basic awareness to health-seeking behaviour, to active, aware consumers and agents for change.

Supply and demand-side interventions in isolation would be insufficient to adequately bring about structural changes in the health systems and improve women's uptake of health services. An integrated programme, where supply and demand come together, is needed to ensure public health system improvement at scale. In an integrated model, beneficiaries strengthen health systems by participating in decision-making platforms along with supply-side actors, and frontline workers work to educate beneficiaries on breaking barriers so that they are empowered to make their own health decisions. Through the integrated model, TAF covers the entire ecosystem of healthcare, from beneficiaries to frontline workers to facility staff and supervisors, across the health system and brings them together for impact.

Managing knowledge and organization

We have a growing bank of knowledge that emanates from grassroots implementation. This spans tools, methods and frameworks for scaling up, managing complex programs and organization building, especially in a public health start-up context.

There is rigorous programme monitoring and evaluation processes that will provide a rich lore of information.

Our aim in knowledge management is twofold: to inform our own programme effectiveness and to share knowledge with other practioners in India and abroad.

The team that implements this model is young, dynamic and passionate about working for India's marginalized women and children. With an average age of thirty, the TAF team is comprised of some of the brightest minds across the country. Over 50 per cent of programme officers and fellows are from non-public health backgrounds. They are data-savvy, astute implementors and creative problem solvers, and come from some of India's premier universities. At the time of writing, the team is 112 people-strong, across eight locations in MP, and a headquarters in Delhi.

To enable the field team to have maximum impact, we have a strong back-end support system. A robust monitoring and evaluation system and team tracks data from the field and progress on a real-time basis and helps improve programme implementation. A creative communications team helps us communicate effectively with the beneficiaries as well as the outside world, to garner support. We are setting up a 'Knowledge Centre' to document and widely share the fountain of knowledge emerging from our work and inform national and global health policies. Most importantly, we strive to maintain a culture of freedom with responsibility and humility, ensuring that everyone brings the best version of themselves to work.

Notes

Introduction

1. The first is the subject of my book *A Stranger Truth* (New Delhi: Juggernaut, 2018) and the second, of this book.

Chapter 1: Faded Blossoms

1. This and all other names in this chapter are disguised.
2. Name disguised.
3. Name disguised.

Chapter 2: Antara Foundation

1. I describe the shock of this discovery and the aftermath, in my book *A Stranger Truth*.
2. 'Avahan—The India AIDS Initiative: The business of HIV prevention at scale', Bill & Melinda Gates Foundation, New Delhi, 2008, p. 10; Data on numbers of sex workers and condoms distributed is from Avahan internal monitoring data.
3. The figures are for 2006, when I had this conversation. More detail on maternal and child deaths can be found in Appendix 1; *The State of the world's children 2008: Child survival*, UNICEF, 2007, p. 115, https://www.unicef.org/media/84861/file/SOWC-2008.pdf.

4. This is the period of great angst I describe in more detail in *A Stranger Truth*.

Chapter 3: Nation-Building, Almost

1. Michael Pickles, Marie-Claude Boily, Peter Vickerman, Catherine M. Lowndes, Stephen Moses, James F. Blanchard, Kathleen N. Deering, et al., 'Assessment of the Population-Level Effectiveness of the Avahan HIV-Prevention Programme in South India: A Preplanned, Causal-Pathway-Based Modelling Analysis', *The Lancet Global Health* 1, no. 5, 1 November 2013, pp. 289–99, https://doi.org/10.1016/s2214-109x(13)70083-4, citing evidence that suggests Avahan averted an estimated 6,06,000 deaths from HIV over ten years.
2. I have disguised the exact terms of reference, though this is directionally correct.
3. This data on spending was never available, but it was easy to do a very rough estimate by asking the number of staff in the field, applying a notional salary cost, doubling that for travel and adding something for overheads. Salaries are usually the biggest item in field-based NGOs. A crude arithmetic, but at least indicative of the scale of generosity.

Chapter 4: Shoebox Solace

1. Three titans of American business were born within five years of Jamshetji's birth in 1839. They were Andrew Carnegie, J.P. Morgan and John D. Rockefeller. All four independently developed the conviction that it is the obligation of the rich to give their wealth back to society. As Carnegie put it in *The Gospel of Wealth* in 1889, 'A man who dies thus rich, dies disgraced.'
2. Amrit Raj and Siddharth Philip, 'Ratan Tata Reveals His Post-Retirement Plans', *Mint*, 10 July 2012, https://www.livemint.com/Companies/H0VkO5iCkTMeSNfCBOHN1M/Ratan-Tata-reveals-his-postretirement-plans.html.; 'Charlie Rose Season 1: Innovation Forum', *Charlie Rose* 27:18–27:39, 5 July 2012, https://charlierose.com/videos/22136.

3. I address most people by their first name, sometimes adding 'ji' at the end. That practice seemed much too familiar here. I always used 'Mr Tata', though he called me Ashok. In this narrative, I refer to him as RNT, as do many people.

4. The terminology used in this section is explained in Appendix 3.

5. Avahan's programme board consisted of more than twenty leaders from the government, business, media, sports and the social sector—everyone from Ratan Tata to Rahul Dravid. I had told the board members that while their counsel would always be welcome, I expected their real utility to show between board meetings— to use their voice to reduce stigma, win support for the cause of HIV prevention and open doors. Before they could do this, it was essential to provide the board with a quick education in what HIV was about. I even had sex workers do the teaching, which is what RNT is alluding to here. I described one such meeting, a disaster, in *A Stranger Truth,* Chapter 9.

6. Name and specialization disguised.

7. I always addressed Vasundhara Raje as 'ma'am'. In this narrative, I refer to her by her first name for convenience.

Chapter 5: Akshada

1. Indian companies are required to give 2 per cent of their profit before tax to charitable causes as part of their CSR.

2. Tata Motors did not have a head at that time. The company was one of several that came under Cyrus Mistry. As everyone knows, the storm broke between Tata and Mistry two years later. Mistry died in a tragic car accident in November 2022.

3. Name disguised.

4. I have described two of those offers in this chapter; the third I prefer not to, even with the name disguised. A fourth offer was to come later, but from the same person who had made the second offer, through another channel.

Chapter 6: Not a Shadow

1. How this played out is described in detail later.

Chapter 7: River of Cows

1. Our agreement with the government was that we would work intensively in two 'focus districts'. These were Jhalawar and the adjacent district of Baran (Udaipur had initially been selected). We would develop solutions in these places. If the government was convinced about these solutions, they would roll them out across the entire state.

2. 'Census 2011: A-01: Number of villages, towns, households, population and area (India, states/UTs, districts and Sub-districts)', Office of Registrar General & Census Commissioner, Ministry of Home Affairs, Government of India, March 2011, https://censusindia.gov.in/nada/index.php/catalog/42526.

3. These health workers are profiled more fully in the chapter to follow.

Chapter 8: Sisters of Mercy

1. Name of this village has been disguised; everything else about the village—data and descriptions—is real.

2. The way the three health workers team up varies to some extent from state to state. In this chapter, we are describing the 'standard' model as we saw it in Rajasthan when we worked there.

3. All names in this chapter have been disguised.

4. We had done something analogous to this in the Avahan programme. There, we had worked with maps that the sex workers had made of the local areas in which they plied their trade. Together, they understood exactly where the sex workers most at risk were located (described in *A Stranger Truth,* Chapter 5). That Avahan experience gave me the confidence that we were on the right track.

5. To ensure privacy, the households are not named. The household number on the map may also be different, as it follows the numbering system of the women and child welfare department, which may be different from the number on the house.

6. From this exercise, I got the impression that Vasundhara Raje was familiar with every gram panchayat and possibly most of the

villages in these two districts. They had been her parliamentary constituencies for a long time, but it was still impressive.

7.   Nowhere near as elaborate a system as we have in our MP programme today, but still convincing.

Chapter 9: Mandarins

1.   This, and all other names of government officials in this chapter, are disguised.
2.   Name disguised
3.   'Performance of Key Health Management Information System (HMIS) Indicators for Rajasthan 2013–14', HMIS Ministry of Health and Family Welfare, Government of India, 2014.
4.   The Biblical allusion to the three aspects of God. Most names in this section—of people, places and institutions—are disguised. Some minor details have been altered.
5.   Fictitious name.
6.   A year later, the simplified ANM register developed by TAF was introduced across the state. It had been validated by senior ANMs and benchmarked against the exiting registers.
7.   Name disguised.

Chapter 10: Where Rabbits Weep

1.   Name disguised.
2.   Village name disguised.
3.   Name disguised.
4.   Name disguised.
5.   That translated into a weight-for-height that was 'severely wasted'. She was more than five standard deviations from the norm for SAM, which is three standard deviations.

Chapter 11: Push and Pull

1.   With Avahan, by and large, we had no problems with government. It was a build-operate-transfer model and we posed no threat to any bureaucrat or politician.

2.   Chapter 8.
3.   Chapter 8 introduced the three female health workers: ANM, ASHA and AWW. We called them, collectively, the AAA ('Triple A') workers. The AAA platform was the innovation that allowed the AAA workers to team up over a village map, sharing data to identify the women and children most at risk to illness, in the village. This is described in more detail in the annexures.
4.   Chapter 9.
5.   Name disguised.
6.   Name disguised.
7.   Name disguised.
8.   The app, however, is stuck in bureaucratic quicksand. We have offered several times to hand it over, or transfer whatever we have learnt, to the government. Word is that the government is making a coordinated effort to develop its own product.
9.   Later in this narrative, it will become apparent that we were banking on an extension of our work for another two years so as to be able to provide this support.
10. '12th Common Review Mission (CRM) Report 2018', National Health Mission 2018, pp. 30, 180, 187, https://nhm.gov.in/ New_Updates_2018/Monitoring/CRM/12th/12th-CRM_Report. pdf; Progress Report 2018–19, Ministry of Health and Family Welfare & National Health Mission, Government of India, 2019, pp. 82–3, https://rajswasthya.nic.in/PDF/Final%20Pragati%20 Prativedan%202018-19%20in%20multicolour.pdf.
11. In a 2023 study of our current programme, Akshita in Madhya Pradesh, 98 per cent of Community Health Workers (CHWs) stated that their way of providing care has improved because of the AAA platform. [Independent evaluation commissioned by The Antara Foundation; sponsored by our donor, Liechtenstein Global Trust (LGT) Venture Philanthropy and conducted by 60 Decibels, a global impact evaluation company.]

Chapter 12: The Band Played On

1.   Of course, we could take no funding from the Gates Foundation because we still did not have the FCRA permission.
2.   See Chapter 3 for more details on this.

3. See Chapter 9.
4. Name disguised.
5. Chapters 2 and 3.
6. In English on YouTube, in Hindi on Hotstar.

Chapter 13: Beyond Havelock

1. Swami Paramhansa's lucid commentary, Chapter II, Verse 47.
2. Jaideep's aunt had been associated with the long-established NGO, Mobile Creches, for a long time. Anjali had been involved for many years with the NGO.
3. Rupert Neate, 'Amazon's Jeff Bezos Pays out $38bn in Divorce Settlement', *Guardian*, 30 June 2019, https://www.theguardian.com/technology/2019/jun/30/amazon-jeff-bezos-ex-wife-mackenzie-handed-38bn-in-divorce-settlement.
4. MacKenzie Scott, 'Seeding by Ceding', Medium, 15 June 2021, https://mackenzie-scott.medium.com/seeding-by-ceding-ea6de642bf.
5. MacKenzie Scott, '116 Organizations Driving Change', Medium, 28 July 2020, https://mackenzie-scott.medium.com/116-organizations-driving-change-67354c6d733d.
6. MacKenzie Scott, 'No Dollar Signs This Time', Medium, 9 December 2021, https://mackenzie-scott.medium.com/no-dollar-signs-this-time-ec7ab2a87261; MacKenzie Scott, '384 Ways to Help', Medium, 15 December 2020, https://mackenzie-scott.medium.com/384-ways-to-help-45d0b9ac6ad8.
7. Maggie McGrath, 'Why MacKenzie Scott Is The World's Most Powerful Woman', *Forbes*, 7 December 2021, https://www.forbes.com/sites/maggiemcgrath/2021/12/07/why-mackenzie-scott-is-the-worlds-most-powerful-woman/?sh=6b26b43c1574.
8. MacKenzie Scott, 'Seeding by Ceding', Medium, 15 June 2021, https://mackenzie-scott.medium.com/seeding-by-ceding-ea6de642bf.

Chapter 15: Khoripaar

1. Village name disguised; all other details accurate.
2. 'Panna's Poaching Nexus Exposed', 31 October 2011, https://www.downtoearth.org.in/coverage/pannas-poaching-nexus-exposed-34239.

356

Notes

3. The 108 emergency ambulance system was first pioneered by a private sector company across rural areas in the former state of Andhra Pradesh. Today it operates in fifteen states. An ambulance can be expected to arrive within an hour, sometimes faster, in response to an emergency call from any village. That can be too late, as in the case of Dhulari's baby. But overall, it is an excellent government service that works despite the constraints of bad roads and difficult weather conditions.

4. Under the government's Janani Suraksha Yojana (JSY) programme, a woman who has her baby delivered in a government facility gets an incentive of Rs 1400. The ASHA who brings her there gets Rs 300. The JSY has led to a much higher rate of institutional deliveries. However, infant mortality has not come down by as much because women often leave the facility too soon after delivery.

Chapter 16: Jad

1. More details about the tribes of Madhya Pradesh can be found in Appendix.

2. Census 2011: A-01: Number of villages, towns, households, population and area (India, states/UTs, districts and Sub-districts), Office of Registrar General & Census Commissioner, Ministry of Home Affairs, Government of India, March 2011, https://censusindia.gov.in/nada/index.php/catalog/42526; 'Census 2011: A-11 Appendix: District wise scheduled tribe population (Appendix), Madhya Pradesh', Office of Registrar General & Census Commissioner, Ministry of Home Affairs, Government of India, March 2011, https://censusindia.gov.in/nada/index.php/catalog/43022; 'Tribal Health in Madhya Pradesh: A Roadmap', Atal Bihari Vajpayee Institute of Good Governance and Policy Analysis, 2021, p. 3, http://aiggpa.mp.gov.in/uploads/project/tribal_health.pdf.

3. There is no better source than Pradip Krishen's magnificent book *Jungle Trees of Central India* (Gurgaon: PRHI, 2014).

4. I am no expert, so this was written by referring to Pradip Krishen's book. I may well have got it wrong.

5. I found out later that many Bharia villages had 'doctors' who treated ailments in this way. His sense was that more people were now going to their competitors, the *phook* (black magic) healers.

Chapter 17: Dai

1. Village name disguised.
2. It is of course risky to generalize about the social status of tribes. For example, in Chapter 15, we described our visit to two small Mawasi villages—Khoripaar and Majirapaar—located just a few kilometres from each other within the same forest. Khoripaar was backward in every way; Majirapaar was far ahead in development.
3. Indeed, the percentage of institutional deliveries is one public health statistic that has improved greatly. in India's public health record, even in states with the poorest health record.
4. Per 1,00,000 live births; 'Trends in Maternal Mortality 2000 to 2017: Estimates by WHO, UNICEF, UNFPA, World Bank Group and the United Nations Population Division: Executive Summary', World Health Organization, 2019, https://apps.who.int/iris/handle/10665/327596.
5. In 2005, institutional deliveries in India accounted for only 41 per cent of total deliveries. By 2015, that number had increased to 79 per cent. India's MMR came down to 130 by 2014–16 and 103 in 2017–19. This figure is still well above the global Sustainable Development Goal of seventy. The same rates for tribal areas are significantly higher (see appendix); 'National Family Health Survey (NFHS-3), 2005–06: India', Ministry of Health and Family Welfare, Government of India, 2007, http://rchiips.org/nfhs/NFHS-3%20Data/VOL-1/India_volume_I_corrected_17oct08.pdf; 'National Family Health Survey (NFHS-4), 2015-16: India', Ministry of Health and Family Welfare, Government of India, 2017, http://rchiips.org/nfhs/nfhs-4Reports/India.pdf; Ministry of Women and Child Development, Government of India, December 2022, https://pib.gov.in/FeaturesDeatils.aspx?NoteId=151238&ModuleId%20=%202#:~:text=MMR%20in%20the%20country%20declined,MMR%20of%20211%20.
6. Name disguised.

Chapter 18: Baba

1. I describe this field trip later in Chapter 25.
2. Name adjusted.
3. Hazrat Khwaja Moinuddin Hasan Chisti was born in Iran. He was a great saint who moved to India and founded the 'Chisti Order of Sufis'. For the longest time, the Mughal Emperor, Akbar didn't have a male heir. Akbar visited Chisti's home in Ajmer and was soon after blessed with Salim, his first of three sons; 'Biography - Khwaja Moinuddin Chishti Rehmatullah Alaih', ShereKhudaHazratAli. com, 27 July 2020, https://www.sherekhudahazratali.com/2014/12/ biography-khwaja-moinuddin-chishti.html; 'Dargah-e-Sheikh Salim Chishti', Uttar Pradesh Tourism, https://www.uptourism.gov.in/en/ article/dargah-e-sheikh-salim-chishti.

Chapter 19: Down Below

1. All names—village and people (except for my colleagues in TAF, of course)—in this section are disguised.
2. The drivers who took us to Khoripaar on two journeys, described in Chapters 17 and 24, fell into the earlier two categories.
3. Such government boarding schools, reserved for girls from the Scheduled Tribes community, are not unusual in Madhya Pradesh. There are eight in Chhindwara district alone.

Chapter 20: Gwalior

1. From the Kachhapaghatas in the tenth century, Slave and Tughlaq dynasty, Tomars in the fourteenth century and the Scindias in the eighteenth century; 'Complete History of Gwalior Madhya Pradesh', Indian Holiday.com, https://www.indianholiday.com/ gwalior/history-of-gwalior.html.
2. 'The Gwalior Fort: A Layered History', Indian Culture, https:// indianculture.gov.in/forts-of-india/discovering-the-forts-of-india/ gwalior-fort-layered-history.
3. The government launched the National Smart Cities Mission in 2015. The idea is to push local development of a hundred designated cities across the country, primarily by harnessing technology.

4. 'OBC' is an umbrella government classification that includes many castes that are deemed educationally and socially backward. In 2006, the National Sample Survey estimated that 41 per cent of the Indian population fell in this category! Today, OBC includes groups who are politically powerful (Narendra Modi is from the community) and economically well off, as well as the poor and marginalized we met in this village.

5. For example, see Chapter 18, 'Dai'.

6. In April 1982, the dacoits (who called themselves '*baghis*'—rebels) of Chambal, more than 200 in number, laid down their arms in mass surrender, responding to the call of social activists Jayaprakash Narayan and Vinobha Bhave. It was exactly 50 years since dacoity had begun in the Chambal.

7. Name of village disguised.

8. Name disguised.

9. She never told us her name. Kamla is a made-up name.

10. For those not familiar, especially in northern India, having studied up till grades 8, 10 or 12 are considered important achievements, especially for a woman. It also implied that she came from a broad-minded family in that they let their daughter go that far with her studies.

Chapter 21: Return to Khoripaar

1. I describe that trip in Chapter 17, which the reader could skim through at this point.

Chapter 22: Ghansour

1. Name disguised.

Chapter 23: Beyond the Call

1. We decided not to use a collective group name, as I have done here, because their jobs are distinct and deserve individual recognition. Another reason for the shorthand is that our real titles are convoluted, and this would otherwise be a longer, possibly indecipherable chapter. Sorry, TAF team!

Chapter 24: Abida

1. Abida is a disguised name. The names of all places, except Rajpur, Barwani and Pati, have also been disguised.
2. Devni is in Pati block, which is the setting for the opening chapter (Faded Blossoms) of this book. The next chapter (Return to Barwani) describes other aspects of this visit to Devni in more detail.
3. Abida spoke to Kritika and I across three visits. It was along a conversation with many more twists and turns, places, people, and ups and down. This is an abridged version entirely faithful to the story that Abida told of her life.
4. Rajpur is large town (pop. 18,000) in the block of the same name, in Barwani district.
5. Several years later, three more children were born—two boys and a girl. Of these nine siblings, two died when they were children.
6. The reasons for this scatter are described in Chapter 25.

Chapter 25: Return to Barwani

1. Name disguised.
2. I describe these encounters in more detail in chapters 20 and 26 respectively.
3. Sendhwa has villages with unusual names. Besides Langada Mohadi, we were in the vicinity of Karwajhira and Kadhaipani villages.
4. Chapter 1.
5. Chapter 10.

Chapter 26: The Beginning

1. The group agreed that these were important barriers. There were many more barriers, but at that stage, I wanted to keep the exercise simple and kept the list to five.
2. The following week, Prerna Gopal and my chief of staff, Shreya Ravichandran, took the team in neighbouring Betul district through the same exercise. The results were almost the same.
3. Chhindwara was where we had started work in 2019, and so we had the maximum data related to conditions there.

4. We had given advance notice to the programme officers. Many had visited individual villages to have a close look at barriers.

5. This may seem improbable, but it is not. Former India cricket captain Rahul Dravid once told me that he remembered every one of his 150-odd dismissals. A chess grandmaster would remember all his major games, as well as many important ones going back in chess history for over a hundred years.

6. I had learnt from previous work that when the community sees a problem, it does not mean that they want an immediate solution. It depends on whether they have more pressing problems at hand that they want solved first.

7. An astonishing number, considering a person typically less than thirty years old, often in their first job, could manage a block of 150–200 villages, amounting to about 800 people. It speaks to our high government leverage model and the immense capability of our frontline staff.

Chapter 27: Bill

1. I related this story earlier in my book *A Stranger Truth*, pp. 160–161.

Appendix 1: India's Public Health and Nutrition System

1. 'Rural Health Statistics 2021-22; Statistics Division', Ministry of Health & Family Welfare, Government of India, 31 March 2022, pp. 13, 15, https://hmis.mohfw.gov.in/downloadfile?filepath=publications/Rural-Health-Statistics/RHS%202021-22.pdf.

2. The coordinated working of these AAA health workers, through our AAA platform is an important aspect of TAF's work, described in the book.

3. 'Rural Health Statistics 2021-22; Statistics Division', Ministry of Health & Family Welfare, Government of India, 31 March 2022, pp. 13, 15, https://hmis.mohfw.gov.in/downloadfile?filepath=publications/Rural-Health-Statistics/RHS%202021-22.pdf.

4. Ibid.

5. Ibid.
6. 'Ayushman Bharat: Comprehensive Primary Health Care through Health and Wellness Centres: Operational Guidelines', Ministry of Health & Family Welfare, Government of India, 2018, https://www.nhm.gov.in/New_Updates_2018/NHM_Components/Health_System_Stregthening/Comprehensive_primary_health_care/letter/Operational_Guidelines_For_CPHC.pdf.
7. Malnutrition covers three types of conditions:
    a. Wasting, which refers to low weight for height.
    b. Stunting, which refers to low weight for age.
    c. Underweight, which refers to low weight for age.
'Malnutrition', World Health Organization, 9 June 2021, https://www.who.int/news-room/fact-sheets/detail/malnutrition#:~:text=The%20term%20malnutrition%20addresses%203,low%20weight%2Dfor%2Dage)%3B.

Appendix 2: Profile of Madhya Pradesh: Tribes and Health Status

1. 'Census 2011: A-01: Number of villages, towns, households, population and area (India, states/UTs, districts and Sub-districts)', Office of Registrar General & Census Commissioner, India. Ministry of Home Affairs, Government of India, March 2011, https://censusindia.gov.in/census.website/data/census-tables.
2. '16th India State of Forest Report Volume 2', Ministry of Environment, Forest and Climate Change, 2019, p. 141, https://fsi.nic.in/isfr19/vol2/isfr-2019-vol-ii-madhya-pradesh.pdf.
3. 'Tribal Health in Madhya Pradesh: A Roadmap', Atal Bihari Vajpayee Institute of Good Governance and Policy Analysis, 2021, p. 3, http://aiggpa.mp.gov.in/uploads/project/tribal_health.pdf.
4. 'Census 2011: A-01: Number of villages, towns, households, population and area (India, states/UTs, districts and Sub-districts)', Office of Registrar General & Census Commissioner, India, Ministry of Home Affairs, Government of India, March 2011, https://censusindia.gov.in/census.website/data/census-tables; Census 2011: A-11 Appendix: District wise scheduled tribe population (Appendix), Madhya Pradesh, Office of Registrar General & Census Commissioner, Ministry of Home Affairs,

Government of India, March 2011, https://censusindia.gov.in/nada/index.php/catalog/43022.

5. 'India (ORGI), Sample Registration System Bulletin', Office of the Registrar General & Census Commissioner, May 2022, p. 3, https://censusindia.gov.in/nada/index.php/catalog/42687/download/46357/SRS_Bulletin_2020_Vol_55_No_1.pdf.

6. 'Sample Registration System Bulletin on Maternal Mortality', Office of the Registrar General & Census Commissioner, Ministry of Home Affairs, Government of India, 2018–20, p. 3, https://censusindia.gov.in/nada/index.php/catalog/44379/download/48052/SRS_MMR_Bulletin_2018_2020.pdf.

7. 'National Family Health Survey (NFHS-5): State Factsheet Madhya Pradesh, 2019-21', Ministry of Health and Family Welfare, Government of India, 2022, https://main.mohfw.gov.in/sites/default/files/NFHS-5_Phase-II_0.pdf.

8. Jai P. Narain, 'Health of Tribal Populations in India: How Long Can We Afford to Neglect?', *Indian Journal of Medical Research* 149, no. 3, 1 March 2019, p. 313, https://doi.org/10.4103/ijmr.ijmr_2079_18.

9. 'Madhya Pradesh: Social Inclusion', World Bank Group, May 2016, https://documents.worldbank.org/curated/en/440101468179096702/pdf/105860-BRI-P157572-ADD-SERIES-India-state-briefs-PUBLIC-MadhyaPradesh-Social.pdf.

10. 'National Family Health Survey (NFHS-5): Madhya Pradesh, 2019-21', Ministry of Health and Family Welfare, Government of India, 2021, http://rchiips.org/nfhs/NFHS-5Reports/Madhya_pradesh.pdf.

11. Roshan B. Colah, Malay B. Mukherjee, Snehal L. Martin and Kanjaksha Ghosh, 'Sickle Cell Disease in Tribal Populations in India', *PubMed* 141, no. 5, 1 May 2015, pp. 509–15, https://doi.org/10.4103/0971-5916.159492.

12. V. Ramgopal Rao, Jyothi Bhat, R.A. Yadav, R. Sharma and M. Muniyandi, 'Declining Tuberculosis Prevalence in Saharia, a Particularly Vulnerable Tribal Community in Central India: Evidences for Action', *BMC Infectious Diseases* 19, no. 1, 20 February 2019, https://doi.org/10.1186/s12879-019-3815-8.

13. Surendra Kumar and M. Muniyandi, 'Tobacco Use and Oral Leukoplakia: Cross-Sectional Study among the Gond Tribe in Madhya Pradesh', *Asian Pacific Journal of Cancer Prevention* 16, no. 4, 1 January 2015, pp. 1515–18, https://doi.org/10.7314/apjcp.2015.16.4.1515.
14. 'Tribal Health Bulletin: Vol. 22', National Institute of Research in Tribal Health (Indian Council of Medical Research), Jabalpur, 2015, https://www.nirth.res.in/publications/tribal_health_bulletin/thb22(1&2)_2015.pdf.
15. 'Tribal Health Bulletin: Vol. 23 No. 1', National Institute of Research in Tribal Health (Indian Council of Medical Research), Jabalpur, 2016, pp. 51–59, https://www.nirth.res.in/publications/tribal_health_bulletin/thb23(1)2016.pdf.
16. 'Tribal Health Bulletin: Vol. 23 No. 1', National Institute of Research in Tribal Health (Indian Council of Medical Research), Jabalpur, 2016, pp. 60–65, https://www.nirth.res.in/publications/tribal_health_bulletin/thb23(1)2016.pdf.

Appendix 3: The Antara Foundation Model

1. 'Sample Registration System Bulletin', Office of the Registrar General & Census Commissioner, Government of India, May 2022, p. 1, https://censusindia.gov.in/nada/index.php/catalog/42687/download/46357/SRS_Bulletin_2020_Vol_55_No_1.pdf.